INTRODUCTION

Welcome to the world of digital publishing ~ the book you now hold in your hand, while unchanged from the original **1967** edition, was printed using the latest state of the art digital technology. The advent of print-on-demand has forever changed the publishing process, never has information been so accessible and it is our hope that this book serves your informational needs for years to come. If this is your first exposure to digital publishing, we hope that you are pleased with the results. Many more titles of interest to the classic automobile and motorcycle enthusiast, collector and restorer are available via our website at **www.VelocePress.com.** We hope that you find this title as interesting as we do.

NOTE FROM THE PUBLISHER

The information presented is true and complete to the best of our knowledge. All recommendations are made without any guarantees on the part of the author or the publisher, who also disclaim all liability incurred with the use of this information.

TRADEMARKS

We recognize that some words, model names and designations, for example, mentioned herein are the property of the trademark holder. We use them for identification purposes only. This is not an official publication.

INFORMATION ON THE USE OF THIS PUBLICATION

This manual is an invaluable resource for the classic **HONDA** enthusiast and a "must have" for owners interested in performing their own maintenance. However, in today's information age we are constantly subject to changes in common practice, new technology, availability of improved materials and increased awareness of chemical toxicity. As such, it is advised that the user consult with an experienced professional prior to undertaking any procedure described herein. While every care has been taken to ensure correctness of information, it is obviously not possible to guarantee complete freedom from errors or omissions or to accept liability arising from such errors or omissions. Therefore, any individual that uses the information contained within, or elects to perform or participate in do-it-yourself repairs or modifications acknowledges that there is a risk factor involved and that the publisher or its associates cannot be held responsible for personal injury or property damage resulting from the use of the information or the outcome of such procedures.

It is important that the reader recognizes that any instructions may refer to either the right-hand or left-hand sides of the vehicle or the components and that the directions are followed carefully. One final word of advice, this publication is intended to be used as a reference guide, and when in doubt the reader should consult with a qualified technician.

www.VelocePress.com

SHOP MANUAL
MODEL C92·C95·CB92·CA95

ANNOUNCEMENT

We are happy to reproduce this Shop Manual and Owner's Handbook covering the 125cc and 150cc ranges of the extremely popular Honda motorcycle line. This book has been published in response to numerous and increasing demands from many customers; including motorcycle dealers, bookstore and newsstand managers, motorcycling enthusiasts, and — of course — Honda owners and prospective owners.

Two further books on Honda motorcycles have been made available by Floyd Clymer Publications. One covers Honda machines in the 50cc category, with special emphasis on the Super Cub (C 100) and Sport Cub (C 110) models. The other book covers the Honda large-capacity range: 250cc and 300cc machines.

These books were originally printed in Japan and translated in that country. There are some expressions that differ from our own but we have left the wording exactly as it appears in the original books.

Floyd Clymer

PREFACE

This Shop Manual contains general data and information, and procedures relative to vehicle maintenance, over-haul and repairs for the models covered by Honda 125 and Honda 150 equivalent to C92, CS92, CB92, C95, CA95.

Therefore, information in this manual will be suitable instruction for servicemen and mechanics of Honda to assist them to efficiently service and repair these machines.

The contents of this book are divided into nine chapters, including engine, chassis, electric-setting, and maintenance. These chapters include respectively paragraphs on disassembly, inspection and service, and re-assembly. Except those which need special advices, no explanation is given for those which can be re-assembled if worked conversely to disassembling.

A service memo column is attached to the end of the respective paragraphs so that you may make notes of necessary items in our service bulletins. We hope this will be of some use to you.

Special tools referred in this manual are shown on the Spare Parts List for the convenience of ordering them. Their respective usages illustrated in the texts of this manual.

The specifications shown in the texts of various chapters indicate the allowable maximum limits between the standard values held when newly assembled, and wear limit. They are respectively shown in the list attached to the end of this book.

This manual will be revised without notice.

HONDA MOTOR CO., LTD.
EXPORT DEPARTMENT
#5-5, YAESU-CHO
CHUO-KU, TOKYO
JAPAN

CONTENTS

ENGINE AND FRAME SERIAL NUMBER 1

I. ENGINE 2
- I-1 Engine replacement 3
- I-2 Cylinder head and cam chain 9
- I-3 Cylinder, piston and piston ring 25
- I-4 Crank shaft and connecting rod 33
- I-5 Clutch 41
- I-6 Transmission and kick starter 47
- I-7 Lubrication and breather 57
- I-8 Carburettor 64

II. CHASSIS
- II-1 Handle and verious controls 70
- II-2 Front fork 72
- II-3 Front cushions 76
- II-4 Rear fork and rear cushion 78
- II-5 Rear wheel and rear brake 81
- II-6 Front wheel and braek 85
- II-7 Drive chain and flange 87
- II-8 Fuel tank and fuel cock 89
- II-9 Air intake 92
- II-10 Exhausts 93
- II-11 Step bar, main stand and brake pedal 94
- II-12 Frame 96
- II-13 Seat 98
- II-14 Speedometer, handle lock and auxiliary tool kit 98

III. ELECTRICAL EQUIPMENT
- III-1 Battery 100
- III-2 Charging system 103
- III-3 Ignition system 105
- III-4 Electric starter 111
- III-5 Miscellancous equipment 115
- III-6 Switch 119
- III-7 Service tester 122

WIRING DIAGRAM 124, 125

IV. ADJUSTMENT AND SERVICE

    IV-1   Ignition timing 126
    IV-2   Valve tappet clearance adjustment 127
    IV-3   Carburettor adjustment 129
    IV-4   Clutch adjustment 129
    IV-5   Drive chain adjustment 130
    IV-6   Cam chain adjustment 131
    IV-7   Brake adjustment 132
    IV-8   Cleaning air cleaner 135
    IV-9   Cleaning oil filter 135
    IV-10 Cleaning fuel strainer 136
    IV-11 Throttle cable and grip adjustment 136
    IV-12 Adjustment of change pedal 137
    IV-13 Battery service 138
    IV-14 Spark plug service 138
    IV-15 Adjustment of head lamp and stop light timing 138
    IV-16 Lubrication 139

V. PERIODICAL MAINTENANCE 141

VI. RACING KIT FOR CB92 142

    VI-1   Relevant parts for engine 142
    VI-2   Relevant parts for frame 144

VII. SERVICE TOOL 148

VIII. TECHNICAL DATA

    VIII-1 General data 152
    VIII-2 Dimension and limits 155
    VIII-3 Torque specification 161

IX. TROUBLE SHOOTING 164

ENGINE AND FRAME SERIAL NUMBERS

The locations of the engine and frame serial numbers on Benly and Honda motorcycles are shown in Fig. 1 and Fig. 2.

Representation of typical numbers are shown as follows.

	(Model)	(Year)	(Serial No.)
Engine serial number	C92E —	0	2357
Frame `"`	C92 —	60 —	3571

Mistake and confusion can be avoided if the correct engine number and/or frame number is referred to the Parts List or Service Bulletin when ordering necessary replacement parts and is furnished in correspondence.

The warranty claims will not be approved in cases where the correct information of them is not furnished in applications.

This information is also used for car registration and for identification of motorcycles.

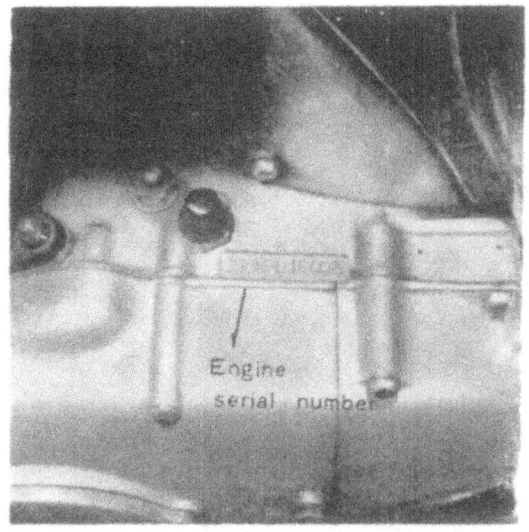

Fig. 1. Engine No.

Fig. 2. Frame No.

1. ENGINE

The engine used in Benly and Honda motorcycles is made with twin cylinder over head cam shaft driven by cam chain attached on the left hand side of cylinder and converted from the crank shaft.

The **crank shaft** of standard C92 and C95 is supported by two main ball bearings, and for CB92 and CA95 is supported by one intermediate roller bearing and two outer ball bearings. The crank pin is perfectly fitted by pressing machine into crank shafts and balancer weight. **Over-square type** of piston and stroke exhibit high RPM, and the shape of the port and combustion chamber result in an efficient and also economical performance of engine.

Lubricant collected in the sump under crank case is force fed to the crank shaft main bearings, connecting rods, cylinder and piston, cam shaft and valves, by the operation of a plunger pump located on the right side of crank case and driven from crank shaft.

On the right end of the crank shaft, a centrifugal type **oil filter** is provided in order to be of use seperating sediment in the lubricant.

A single **carburetter** which is of special design is attached on the cylinder head through the medium of a heat insulator.

The **transmission** gears and gear changing devices are enclosed in the gear case which is compactly combined with the crank case. The multiplate clutch is provided on the gear box and immersed in the oil bath inside of the right side cover.

SERVICE

Servicing of the engine may be done partially as described in the following items, according to the location of trouble decided by diagnosis.

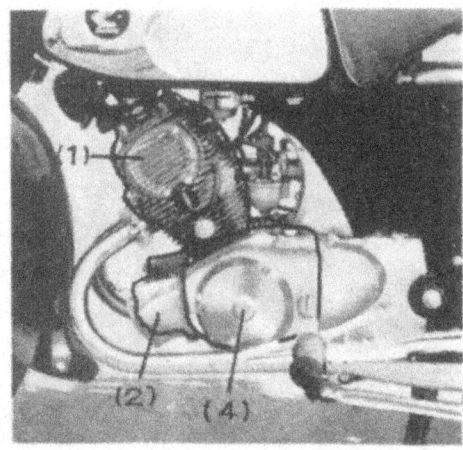

Fig. 3. Portions connected with servicing

Fig. 4. Portions connected with servicing

(1) In cases where trouble exists in portion of the cylinder head and/or the cylinder and pistons:
Dismount the engine from the frame, remove the left crank case cover and disconnect the cam chain. (Fig. 3)

(2) In cases of troubles existing in the starting motor, dismount and disassemble it. (Fig. 3)

(3) In cases of troubles existing in the clutch system, remove right crank case cover and disassemble the clutch. (Fig. 3)

(4) In cases of troubles existing in the A. C. dynamo and/or starting clutch, remove left side cover and disassemble. (Fig. 4)

(5) For troubles occuring in the transmission, dismount the engine from the frame and open up the under-crank case after seperating both side covers. (Fig. 4)

1 - 1. ENGINE REPLACEMENT

I. Engine Removal

Engine removal from the frame would follow the following procedures.

(1) Remove the step bar fixed on the under crank case, for standard engine (Fig. 5)

(2') Remove the left side change pedal link from the engine and the left step plate (Fig. 6) and disconnect the left step-plate, for CB92, CA95 engines (Fig. 7)

Fig. 5. Step bar removal

Fig. 6. Removing change pedal (CB92)

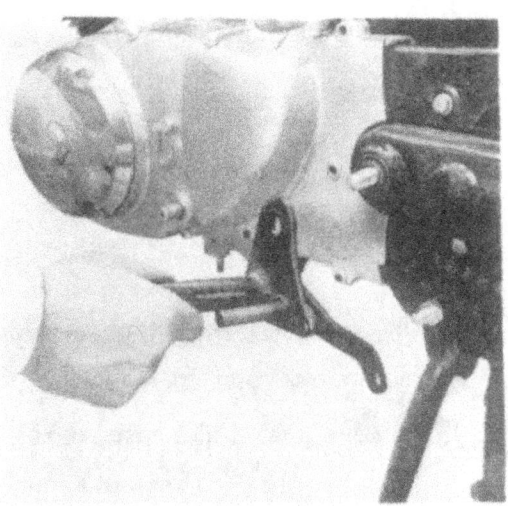

Fig. 7. Removing left step plate (CB92)

(2) Remove the exhaust pipes with mufflers on both side of the engine at the exhaust ports and muffler brackets. (Fig. 8)

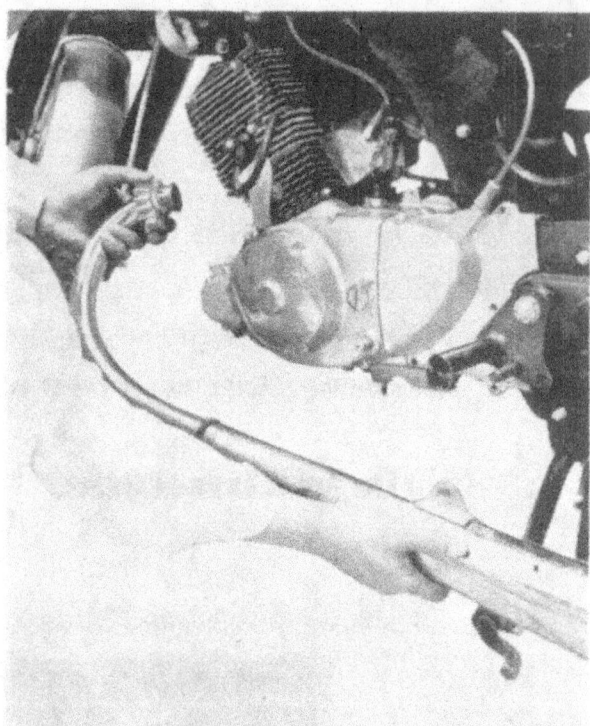

Fig. 8. Removing exhaust pipe and muffler

(3) Remove the carburettor covers. (Fig. 5)
(4) Take off tool box in order to remove the air cleaner element with the tool tray board. (Fig. 9) The air cleaner will be disconnected from the carburetter rubber tube by inserting left hand through frame under the carburetter and unhooking the clip on it.

Fig. 9. Attachment of tool tray board

(5) Unscrew the wire harness holder nut and release the clamp (Fig. 10) and discounnect all the wiring. (Fig. 11)
(6) Remove the chain case cover (Fig. 12) and disconnect the drive chain at the joint link (Fig. 13). Then take out the chain case cover (B) (Fig. 14) and unhook the clutch cable end from the clutch arm.

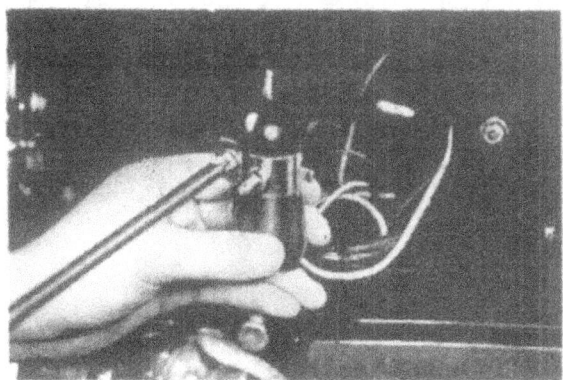
Fig. 10. Releasing wire harness holder clamp

Fig. 11. Disconnecting wiring

Fig. 12. Removal of chain case cover

Fig. 13. Disconnection of drive chain joint

Fig. 14. Removal of chain case cover B

Fig. 15. Unscrewing carburetter mounting nut

(7) Seperate the carburetter by unscrewing the mounting nut to the cylinder head. (Fig. 15)

(8) On the right hand side of the engine dismount the electric starter switch located on the right side of the frame, and disconnect the starter motor cable. (Fig. 16) Previous to this procedure, remove the battery unscrewing the clamp bolt and terminals of battery. (Fig. 17).

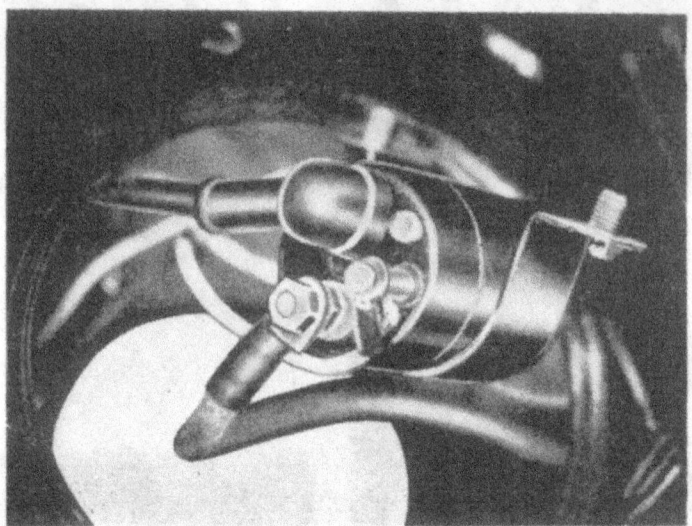

Fig. 16. Removal of starter switch

Fig. 17. Location of battery

Remove the kick pedal from the kick shaft on the right side of engine. Remove right side step plate and the brake pedal for CB92. (Fig. 18)

(9) Remove the spark plug cap at the end of the secondary wire and release the wire from the hole between the cylinder head fins. (Fig. 19)

(10) Place a support of suitable height under the crank case to support the engine for the provision of removing the engine mounting bolts.

Remove all the nuts from those bolts shown in (Fig. 20) with numbers ①, ②, ③ on both side of frame.

Fig. 18. Removing right side step plate

Fig. 19. Release secondary wire

Fig. 20. Position of engine supporting bolts

Then draw out the bolt ① on both sides of the frame and the bolt ③ should follow, when the rear end of the engine will drop onto the stand. At last withdraw the bolt ② freely and place the engine on the stand wholely, with aid of hand.

II. Engine Installation

Engine installation may be accomplished with the engine parts assembled, such as its condition at removal.

The procedure may refer to the items in the paragraph of "Engine Removal" conversely if it is assumed that the word "remove" is replaced by "install".

Proceed as follows:

(1) Place the engine on a suitable stand and push the stand under the frame to the position where the installation will be convenient.

(2) Insert the front engine hanger bolt supporting the front end of the engine to coincide with the mounting holes. Insert the rear end mounting bolts on both side of the engine from out-side of the frame. In this case, care should be taken not to forget to place a battery ground bond strap on the right side upper bolt. Tighten the nuts most securely.

(3) Install the carburetter on the cylinder head.

(4) Install the battery with the battery clamp and connect the cable terminals to the battery.

(5) Connect the electrical wiring at connectors and install the clamp on the frame. Connect the starter motor cable at the starter switch which should be fixed on the inside of the frame.

(6) Place the chain case cover behind the chain at rear end of the crank case and join the drive chain with joint link. The direction of the joint link should be inserted so that the slit end will point in the opposite direction to the rotation of the chain.

(7) Hook the clutch wire end to the clutch lever and set the clutch cable holder between the crank case rear-end, and the inner chain case cover. Install the outer chain case cover.

(8) Attach the air cleaner element to the connecting rubber hose and assure the fitting of the set rings and the insertion of the plastic tubes being brought from the carburettor and the vent hole on the cylinder head. Fix the air cleaner side-cover to the frame.

(9) Install the brake pedal and the right side step-plate on the frame. (CB92) Install both side mufflers and exhaust pipes. Install the step bar (STD) or right side step-plate (CB92), change pedal, kick arm, carburettor covers, tool box and battery box cover.

(10) Fill the engine crankcase to the specified level with the proper oil indicated in Section IV 16.

(11) Tune up the engine as detailed in chapter IV.

III. Engine Disassembly

Engine disassembly is presented in the sequence to be followed when the engine is to be completely over-hauled after removal from the frame (Fig. 21). The operations of the procedure pertinent to the clutch repairs, repairing of the starting motor and its devices, and the governor or A.C. dynamo repairs are also applicable seperately with the engine in the frame, provided that wherever necessary the part of the engine parts to be worked on is first made accessible by removal of engine parts.

Fig. 21. Engine complate

When the disassembly operations are performed, it is assumed that the oil has been drained prior to starting.

1-2. CYLINDER HEAD AND CAM CHAIN

The cylinder head is made of aluminum alloy casting in which the valve guides and valve seats are inserted by "shrink fit." For the method of fitting, the cylinder head is required to expand under the temperature of 200~250°C in a furnance for the insertion of inserts at room temperature.

The valves, rocker arms and cam shaft are located on the cylinder head and driven by the cam chain from the crankshaft.

Domed shape combustion chambers are provided for the improvement of efficiency.

The cams for CB92 and CA95 are different from the standard model.

For engines after the serial number CB92E-010511 and CA95E-010139, a tachometer cable adapter is provided on the R. cylinder head side cover, and a tachometer drive gear is machined on the end of the cam shaft.

If it is desired to install the adapter on the earlier engines, the cylinder head should be replaced due to uninterchangeable. (Fig. 24)

I. **Removal of Cylinder Head**

(1) Remove the contact points cover and disconnect the green colored electric wire at the junction on the plate (Fig. 22). Then the left crank case cover with attached contact plate will be removable by unscrewing the cross-recessed screws retaining the cover.

(2) Remove the 8mm bolt that attaches the spark advancer. In this operation apply a hammer on the end of wrench by an impact anticlockwise, otherwise the bolt will not release owing to its rotation in the same direction as the crankshaft.

Fig. 22. Primary wire at contact breaker

Fig. 23. Removing A. C. dynamo rotor with extractor

(3) Remove A.C. dynamo rotor with the extractor as shown in (Fig. 23.) After the rotor has been removed, remove the woodruff key wedged into the crankshaft.

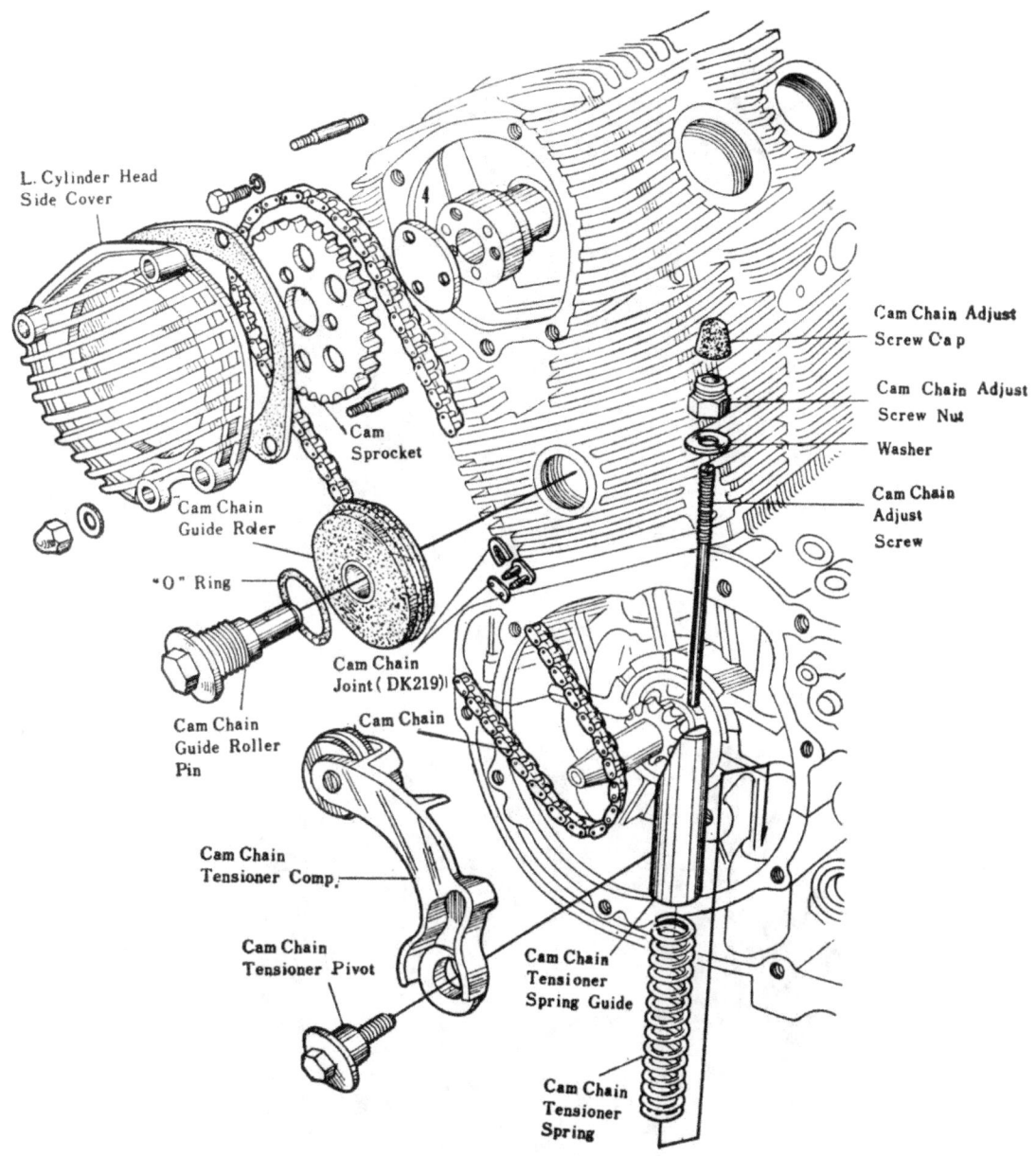

Fig. 24. Exploded view of cam chain system

(4) Remove the four (4) starter motor mounting bolts (6 mm) at the front end of the crank case (Fig, 25) and take out the starter motor from the chain by twisting the sprocket end of the motor towards the A.C. dynamo.

Previously remove two clamps retaining starter motor cable under the crank case. (Fig. 26)

In this case, if the starter motor sprocket set-ring pliers are available and there is no intention of disassembling the crank case further, remove the set ring fixed on the starter motor shaft for the preparation of the removal of the starter chain.

Fig. 25. Removing starter motor

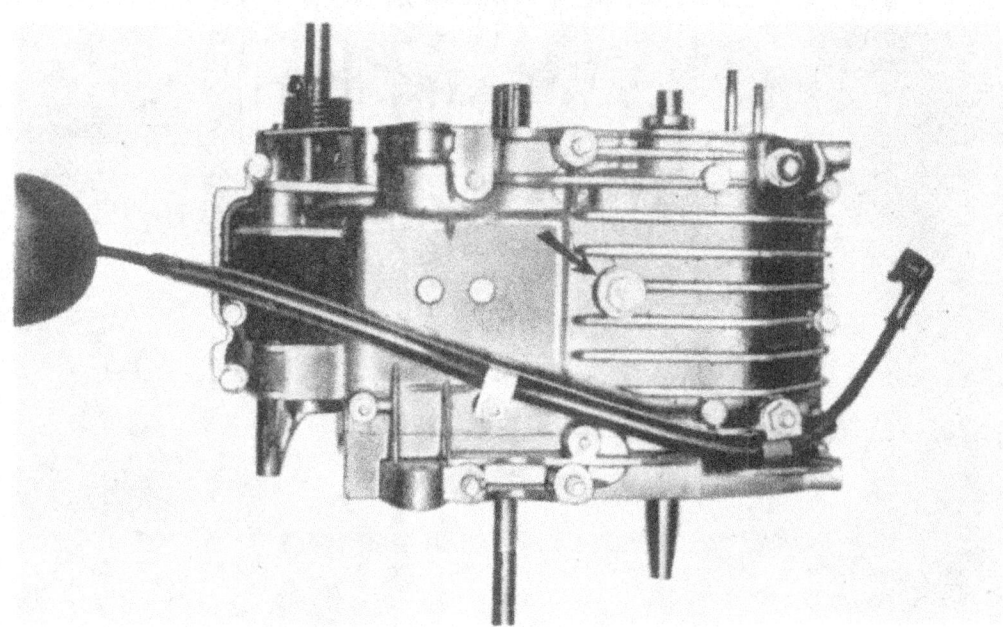

Fig. 26. Position of clamps under crank case

(5) Remove the ignition coil, (① in Fig. 27) attached on the right side of crank case for only engines up to the serial number C92E-937064.

Remove the cross head screws (five 6×30mm and one 6×24mm) and pull out the A. C. ② dynamo starter base along with the starting chain and the sprockets

— 12 —

as a unit, then the starter motor sprocket will pull out concurrently with the other sprocket.

Fig. 27. Location of ignition coil and A.C. dynamo

(6) Remove the cam chain tensioner pivot bolt marked with an arrow in Fig. 28 and take out the cam chain tensioner. For accessibility in doing this, previously screw-in the cam chain tension adjusting screw attached to the upper crankcase at the bottom.

Fig. 28. Cam chain tensioner privot bolt (arrow mark)

— 13 —

(7) Rotate the crank shaft until the cam chain joint appears on the side of the crank case where the cam chain tensioner rubber roller has been contacted. Then, remove the chain joint and seperate the chain.

(8) Remove the cylinder head cover by releasing six (6) nuts on it, (Fig. 29), and the cylinder head may be taken off from the crank case as refered in Fig. 30.

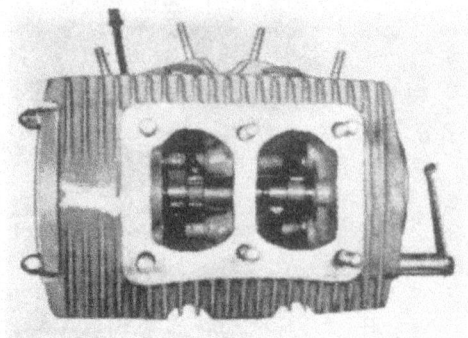

Fig. 29. Removal of cylinder head cover nuts

Fig. 30. Removal of cylinder head and gaskets

(9) The procedure for disassembling cylinder head should be accomplished as follows. (Fig. 31)

    9-1. Remove L. cylinder head side cover and rotate the cam sprocket with rotating handle provided in the service tool kit until the chain will be released from the cam sprocket.

    Remove the cam sprocket from the cam shaft unscrewing 3 bolts.

    9-2. Loosen all tappet adjusting screws so that every valve may be set free from rocker arms.

9-3. Remove distributor cap and rotor from the engines provided with distributor. Remove the R. cylinder head side cover.

For the CB92 and CA95 engines attached with tachometer drive gear.: Remove the tachometer gear box cap and gear bushing retaining bolt. Pry out the oil seal located on the entrance, with a driver. Then withdraw the bushing and gear shaft. (Fig. 31, 32)

Remove four screws, one of which is located behind the gear bushing, and take off the R. cylinder head side cover by rotating. (Fig. 33, 34)

9-4. Remove both end set rings fixing the rocker arm clamp pins using thin nose pliers (Fig. 35) and drive out the rocker arm clamp pins by tapping from one side (Fig. 36). The rocker arms should be taken out from the tappet holes.

Fig. 31. Location of tachometer gear box

Fig. 32. Removing tachometer drive gear

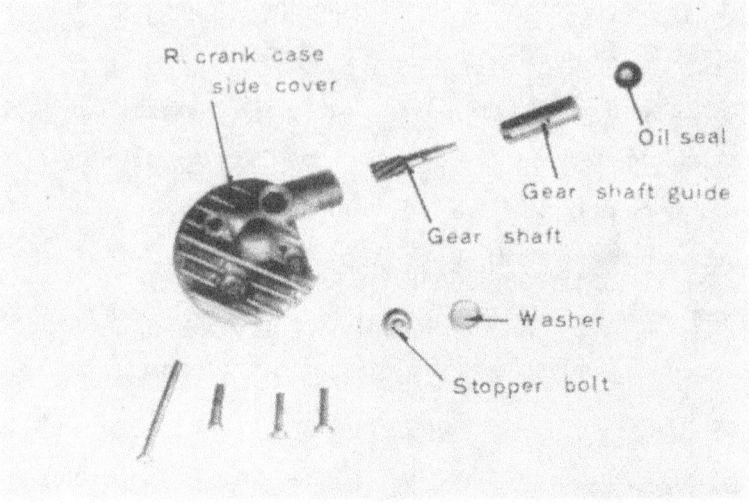

Fig. 33. Display of tachometer gear box

Fig. 34 Cam shaft gear

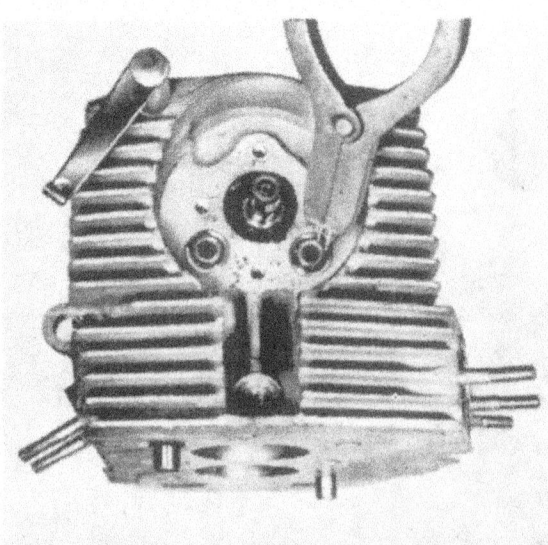

Fig. 35. Removing set rings of rocker arm clamp pins

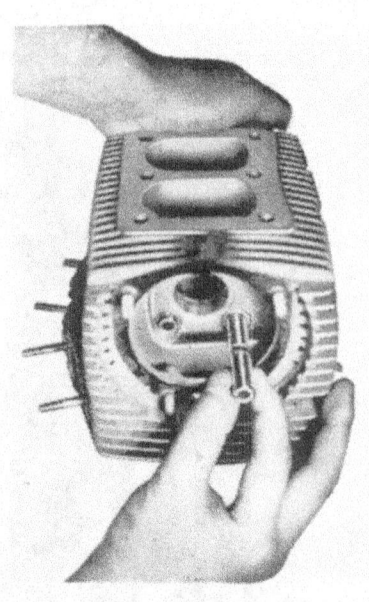

Fig. 36. Withdrawing rocker arm clamp pin

9-5. Pull out the cam shaft assembly from the opening in the cam chain side of the cylinder head.

(10) Remove valves and springs

With the valve spring compressor which is used to hold the valve between its arms, compress the valve springs by means of turning the handle and remove the valve cotters from the top of the valve stems. (Fig. 37)

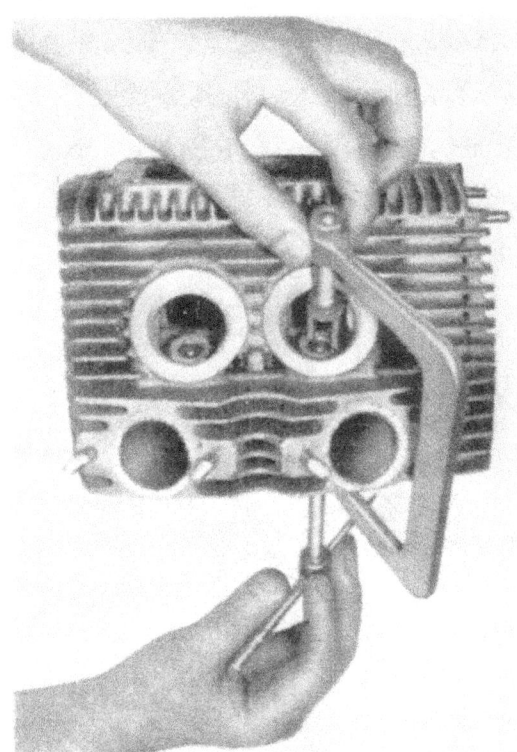

Fig. 37. Removing valve cotters using spring compressor

Remove all valves and tag to indicate the location of each in the cylinder head.

II. Inspection and Repaire

(1) Cylinder head

Remove all carbon deposited on the combustion chamber and/or the valves with a suitable scraper. Cleanse all the parts with solvent.

1-1. Replace the cylinder head if blown out, or warped 0.004″ or more over full length of head gasket surface.

If the warpage is under the above amount, the distortion may be removed by means of rubbing the surface of the head on a flat iron bed by the medium of lapping compound. Also check the manifold surface and correct it as deemed necessary.

1-2. Inspect the valve seat for burns, pitting or wear, and reface. If valve guides are to be replaced, this must be done before refacing the valve seats.

The tools for this purpose consist of the cutters with angle of 30° 90°, and 120°.

First of all apply the 90° angle cutter for correcting the seat angles on both inlet and exhaust until the faults disapper on the surface, and measure the seat width which should be within 0.04"–0.06" (1.0–1.5 mm) after refacing.

If it is measured more than the above amount and the valve seems to be deeply seated in the valve seat, reface the top of the seat with 120° cutter. Measure the width again and if it is still excessive apply the 30° cutter to correct the width finally.

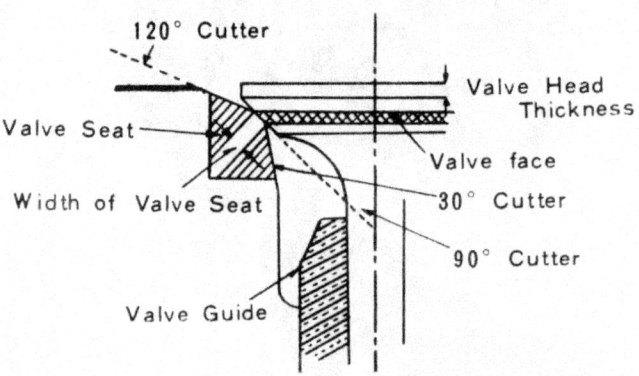

Fig. 38 Cutting angles of valve seat and valve

Do not cut more than necssarry to reduce the valves seat to the specification. The valve seats are "shrink-fitted" in the cylinder head, therefore, do not attempt to replace them.

1-3. Measure the inner diameter of the cam shaft bearing and replace the head which is worn, or excessively out-of-round.

(2) Valve guides

Check valve guide bores in the head with "go" and "no go" gauge, if available. The inside size may be referred in the specification P. 156. Any valve guide which is broken or has worn causing excessive valve stem to guide clearance must be replaced. The guide is shrink-fitted in the cylinder with temperatures of 200°-250°C, and if it is required to replace the guides in a workshop where a suitable furnace is not available, replacement of the complete head is advisable.

On the middle of the inlet valve guide, a slit is cut around which is lead to atmosphere through a drilled hole in the head. Therefore, care is necessary that the holes coincide with each other in case of replacement.

This device is provided to prevent oil invading through the guide and valve stem clearance. (Fig. 38-1)

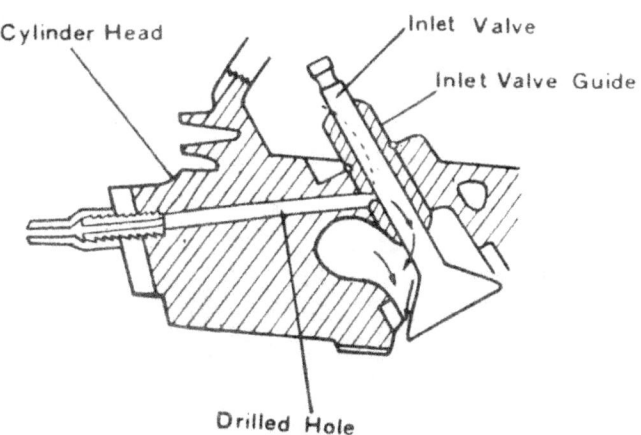

Fig. 39 Section view of air vert of valve guide

(3) Valves

Replace the valves which are deemed unserviceable due to excessive burning, warpage or wear, determined by visual inspection.

Measure the valve stem diameter and the head thickness to ensure that it is in accordance with the Specification (P. 158).

Replace valves having worn stems or heads, which are unserviceable. (Fig. 40)

If valve refacer is available, reface the valves until traces of wear will disappear around the head.

Then the valves must be lapped into the valve seats, using a suitable lapping compound after the valve seats are serviced. Do not exceed in lapping but cease as soon as an even face seating is observed around the valve when compound is wiped off cleanly.

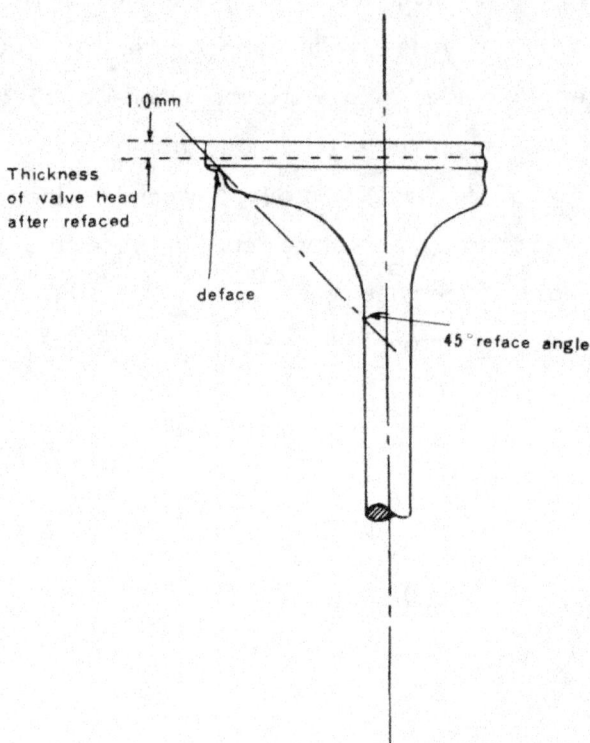
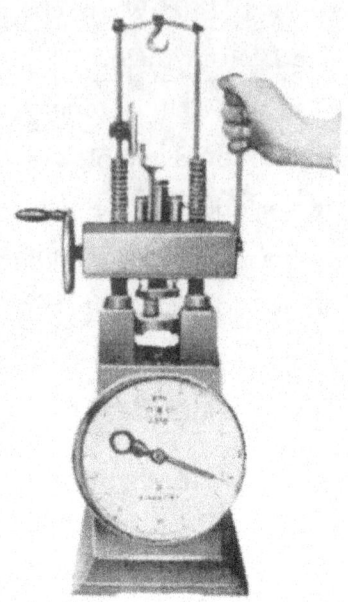

Fig. 41 Using valve spring tension gauge

Fig. 40 Refacing of valve seat

(4) Valve Springs

Measure the valve spring height and rightangleness by scale when it is placed free, and if springs are found to exceed tolerances in the condition out of the Specification (P. 159), replace rhem.

Test for tension using valve spring tension tester. Replace springs that are not within specifications (P. 159). (Fig. 41).

(5) Oil seals

For the type of engine which has a distributor (up to E No. C92E-737064) and the CB92 and CA95 engine with a tachometer gear box attached, check the oil seal on the right side cover for appearance of any seepage of oil. Replace oil seal which is observed as leaking.

(6) Valve rocker arms, and clamp pins

Chech and replace rocker arms where defacement of the portion contacting with the cam exceeds more 0.05 mm (0.002").

Check outer diameter of clamp pins and the clearance of the rocker arms to ensure that they measure within the Specification (P. 159). Replace any of them found to be unusable.

(7) Cam shaft

The features of the cam are shown in the fig. 42 and the cam shafts of various timmgs (STD. and Super Sport) are as follows.

Model used on	C92, C95	CB92, CA95	Accessory for racing and the latest CB92
Parts NO	921416	B921916-IIA	YB921416A Provided with tachometer drive gear

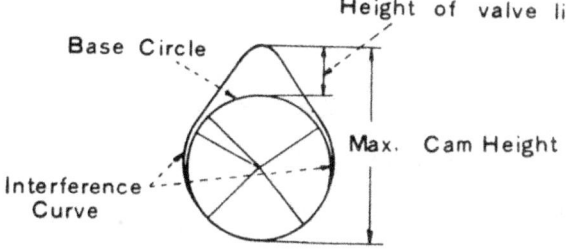

Fig. 42 Cam profile

Measure the max. height of cam and outer diameter of bearing journals to ensure that is within the Specification (P. 159).

Replace cam shaft having worn places.

(8) Cam sprocket and cam chain

Visually inspect the gear cogs for excessive wear and crack, and if a special micrometer for measuring diametrical distance between valleys of cogs is available, measure the distance refering to the Specification (P. 159).

Replace sprocket with excessive wear or crack. Measure the cam chain for total length when a weight of 5Kg is applied to an end. (Fig. 43)

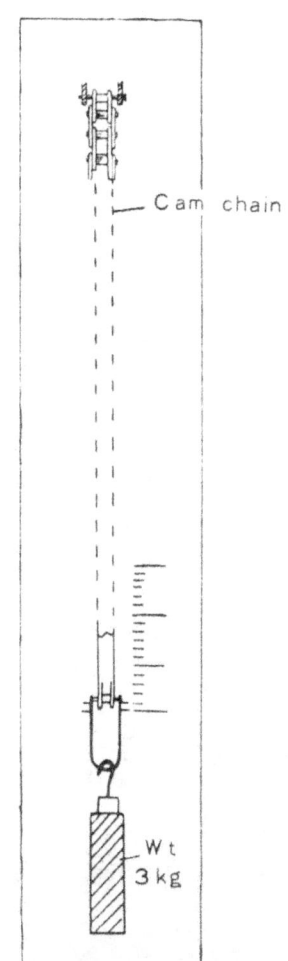

Fig. 43 Measuring overall length of chain

Replace chain if the total length is more than specification (P. 159).

III. Assembling and Installation of Cylinder Head

(1) Insert the valves in their own valve guides which have been lapped together. Do not mix them.

Place the valve spring seat, inner valve spring, outer valve spring and valve spring retainer over the valve guide.

Compress the valve springs using the valve spring compressor until the slit of the valve stem is observed above the retainer, and set the valve cotters using the thin nose pliers. Remove the spring compressor and tap the valve spring seat to ensure the cotters are set accurately.

(2) Install the rocker arm side collar and the rocker arm, with the rocker arm clamp-pin inserted through the head. Install the set rings on both ends of the clamp pin and ensure the fittings by means of tapping slightly on the clamp pin.

(3) Install the R. cylinder head side cover against the packing which is positioned on the head, and tighten with screws.

Use a new packing and apply a thin coat of Gasket Paste to make oil-tight.

(4) Install the cam-shaft holding the slipper ends of the rocker arm up and attach the cam sprocket and spacer plate behind to the cam shaft with three 6 m/m bolts. One of threaded holes which is the nearest to the timing mark on the sprocket is off-set, therefore, it is necessary to coincide the holes.

For the engines which are provided with a distributor, and after the electric rods of

Fig. 44 Installation of cam chain to cylinder head

the rotor and distributor cap are polished with fine emerypaper, install in their positions and fit the cap with a clamp fixed by one of the side cap screws.

For the Super Sport engine, install the speedometer cable gear shaft with the bushing on the cable side and retain with the setting bolt.

(5) Hook an end of the cam chain to the cam sprocket and rotate the sprocket using the cam shaft rotating hadle, until the inlet side of the chain end becomes 6" (15 cm) less then the other end when they are hanging down. (Fig. 44)

(6) Place the cylinder head completely on the cylinder on the head gasket, cam chain case packing, and 10 mm O-ring for the oil passage, while the chain is introduced along both sides of the chain guide roller in the cam chain case of cylinder. Install cylinder head cover packing and the cylinder head cover and tighten the cylinder studs with flat washer and nuts. For the right rear nut which is dome headed, apply a coat of gasket paste. It is important that all the nuts should be tightened gradually in the sequence of the numbers in (Fig. 45, 46) up to the torque of 10 to 15 ft-1b is reguired by each.

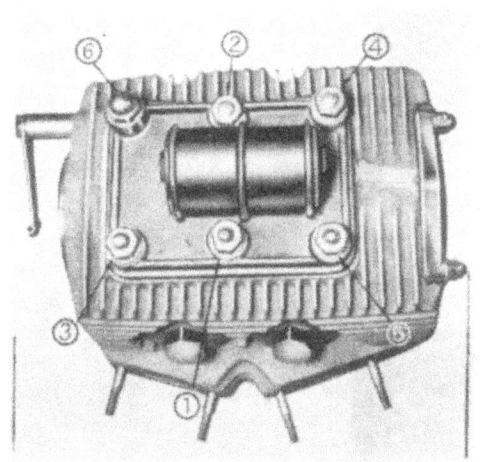

Fig. 45 Tightening order of cylinder stud nuts

Fig. 46 Checking tightening torque for stud nuts

(7) For jointing of the cam chain, set the timing marh "O" on the cam sprocket so that it coincides with the notch mark on the cylinder head just above where tne left side cover packing is attached.

Bring the mark on the timing sprocket of the crank shaft to the lowest part of the center line of both sprockets. Note that the key-way of the crank shaft is on the opposite side to the mark. (Fig. 47)

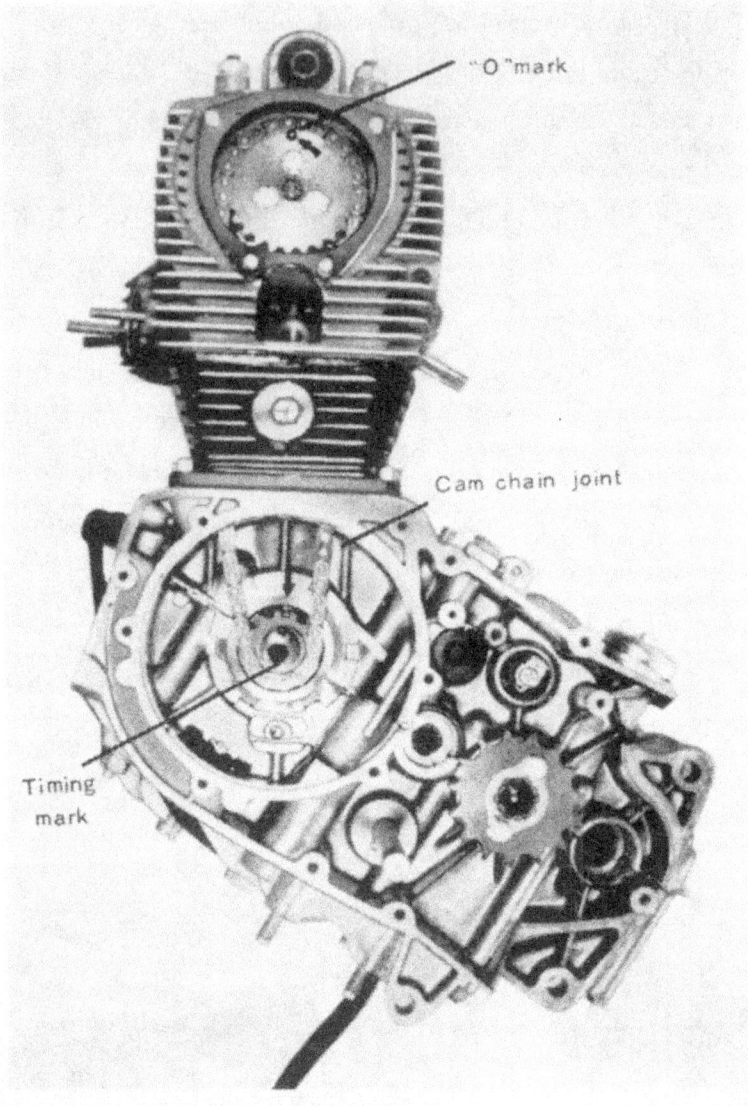

Fig. 47　Setting timings of sprockets

Fig. 48　Adjusting cam chain tensioner

— 24 —

Then the chain is joined at the position indicated by arrow in Fig. 47 taking care that the slit end of the clip face is towards the timing sprocket.

(8) Install the cam chain tensioner with the pivot bolt and turn the crank shaft somewhat in the direction of engine rotation.

Loosen the cam chain tensioner adjusting bolt which is assumed to have been screwed in all the way when disassembled, until the moment the cam chain tensioner guide separates from the end of the adjusting bolt. (Fig. 48)

Secure the tightening of the lock nut. (Refer to the details in P. 161).

(9) Install the A. C. dynamo stator base and complete the assembling with reference to the (P. 103).

1-3. CYLINDER, PISTON AND PISTON RING

The cylinder is integrated in the cylinder block made of special cast iron, and the bore is finished with a honing machine to the accuracy of within 0.0004" (0.01 mm) of taper, or out of round. Right rear cylinder stud hole commonly performs the function of oil passage lead to the cylinder head.

The cam chain is enclosed in the chain case located left side of cylinder block.

The piston is of high silicon aluminum alloy and the crown is domed. It is a oval shape and taper ground piston with a relief area on both sides of position pin hole. Two compression rings keep compression tight and an oil ring prevent oil from pumping up.

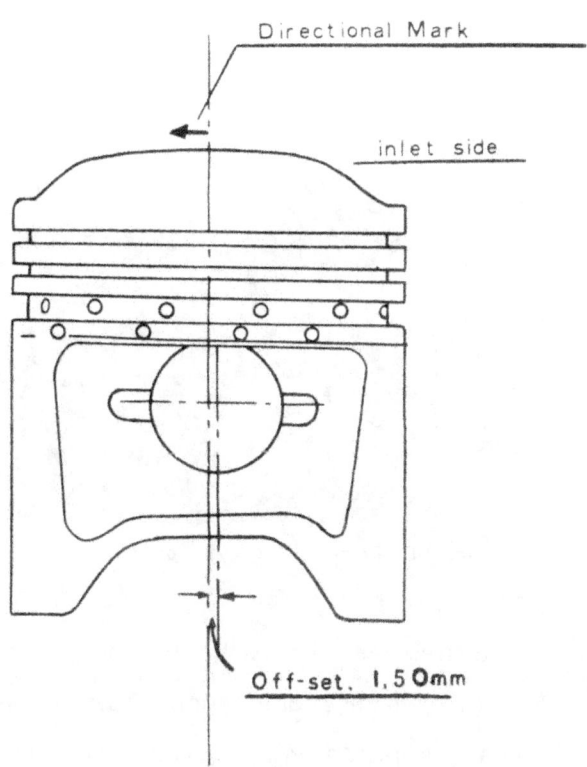

Fig. 49 Location of piston pin bole

The piston pin is finished very precisely and is fitted, (Fig. 49) off-set by 1 mm, on the inlet side of the piston center line.

I. **Removal of Cylinder & Pistons**

(1) After removal of the cylinder head, and removal of the two 6 mm stud nuts located on the left side foot of the cylinder, the cylinder block can be lifted from the crank case over the stud bolts. (Fig. 50)

Fig. 50 Removing cylinder head

Fig. 51 Removal of cylinder head

(2) Remove both outside piston pin clips with the sharp thin nose pliers and draw out both piston pins, (Fig. 52) which enable removal of the pistons from the rods.

(3) Remove the piston rings from piston-ring grooves : expanding with fingers or a special tool if available.

Fig. 52 Removing piston pin clip

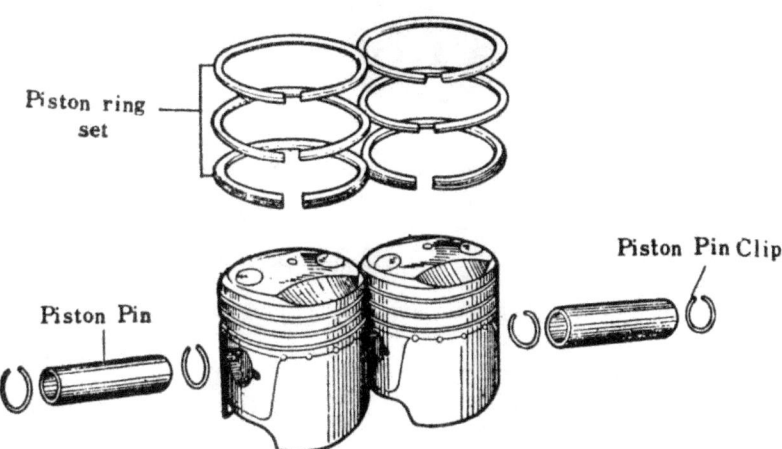

Fig. 53 Exploded view of pistons

II. Inspection & Repair of Cylinder, Pistons and Rings.

(1) Remove all carbon from the crown or grooves of the pistons.

(2) Check flatness of mating surface of the cylinder with a straight edge and thickness gage. Re-grind or recondition the surface if it is marred by 0.002" (0.05 mm).

(3) Check the cylinder bores with cylinder bore gauge for out-of-round and taper to establish whether the bores require reboring or honing. The decision should be made according to the Specification of (P. 155). (Fig. 54)

(4) Cylinder reboring and honing

If the cylinder bores are scored or if they are tapered or out-of-round in excess of 0.002" (0.05 mm), they may be honed to recondition the wall to enable new piston rings to seat properly.

To recondition a cylinder bore that is out-of-round or tapered no more than the limit of the wall may be removed by reboring.

— 27 —

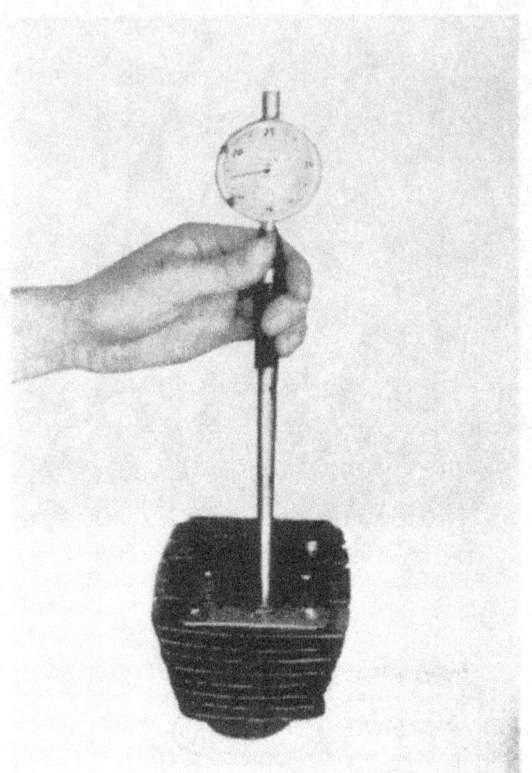

Fig. 54 Measuring cylinder bore

Pistons and rings are available in 0.15, 0.30 and 0.45 mm (0.006", 0.0118" and 0.0177") over size, therefore, the minimum amount of material to be removed by reboring or honing is determined from the original diameter of the cylinder bores plus the amount of oversize in diameter of oversize pistons to be fitted. Both cylinders must be reconditioned to the same size in diameter in consideration of balance.

In case of reboring, that thickness of material of wall to be removed by honing of an amount up to 0.0008" (0.02 mm) must be retained. Honing is necessary in any case for final finishing.

Finishing tolerance of recondition must be within 0" to 0.004" (0 mm to 0.01 mm) plus the amount of oversize.

(5) Pistons

Examine the pistons for fractures or scores on the surface and replace if necessary. Whenever the cylinder is submitted for reboring, new oversize piston must be used.

(6) Measure the piston's ground diameter in direction along the piston pin hole and at right angles to it with a micrometer. Replace the pistons deformed by the amount exceeding the specifications (P. 156). (Fig. 55)

Specified clearance between the cylinder and piston should be 0 to 0.0012" (0–0.03 mm).

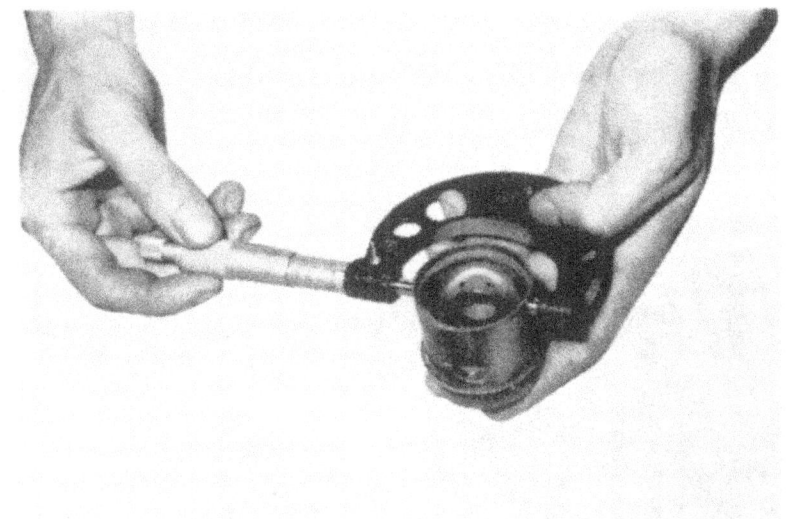

Fig. 55 Measuring piston diameter

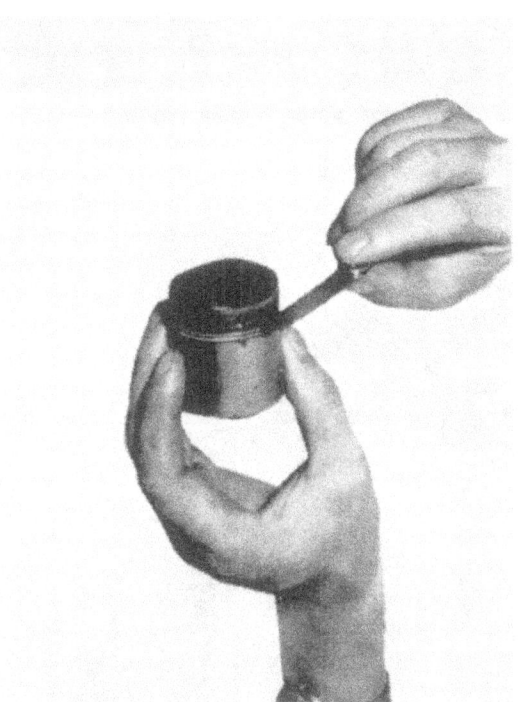

Fig. 56 Measuring clearance between piston ring groove and ring

(7) Measure the piston ring side clearance with the new rings installed in the grooves using the feeler gage, (Fig. 56).

Replace the pistons having clearances more than the specification (P. 156)

(8) If any tolerance existing is felt by hand when radially moving new ring fitted in the piston, replace the piston.

(9) Piston Rings

It is desirable to replace the piston rings whenever the engine is overhauled.

In this event, the fitting to the pistons should be undertaken as follows:—

9-1 Position each ring squarely in the cylinder bore, approximately one inch down from the top of the cylinder. Measure the piston ring end gap with a feeler gage. The gap must be 0.008"–0.02" (0.2 mm–0.5 mm) for both compression and oil rings. (Fig. 57)

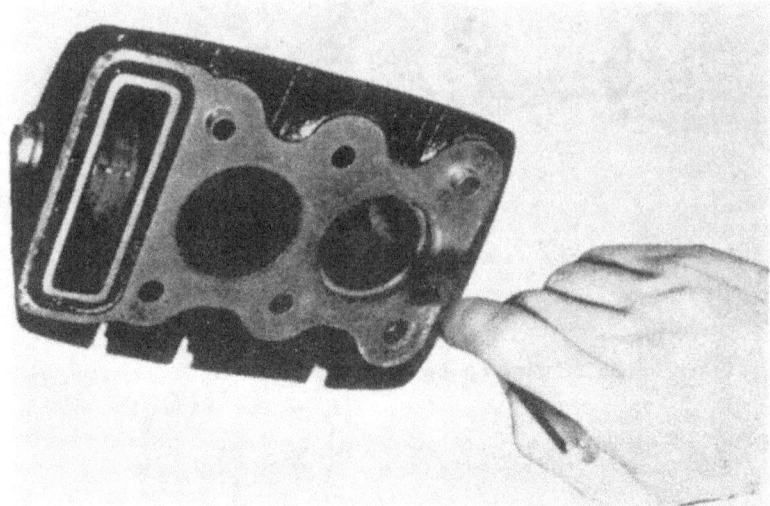

Fig. 57 Measuring piston ring end gap

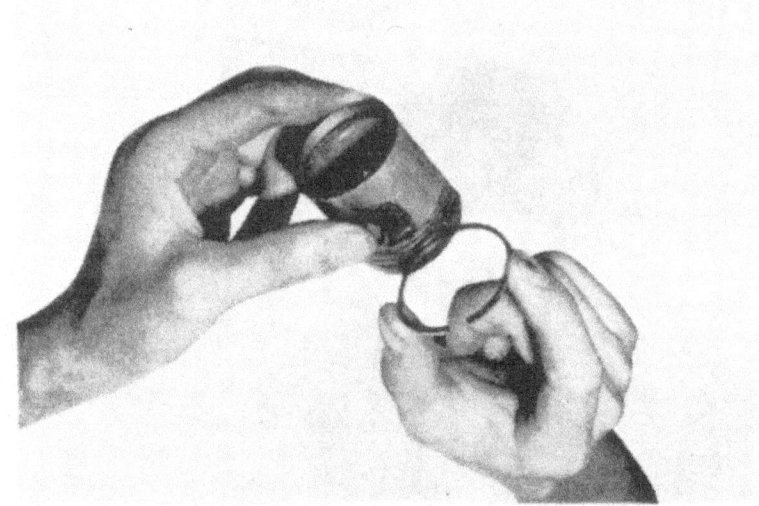

Fig. 58 Checking fit for ring in piston groove

9-2 If the gap is less than 0.008" file squarely at ends of piston ring with a fine file to obtain the proper gap.

If the gap is more than 0.02" replace the new ring. Oversize rings are available as mentioned previously.

9-3 Before fitting the new rings in the new piston ring grooves, externally roll the ring in the groove around the piston to make sure they freely operate in the grooves without obstructions. (Fig. 58)

9-4 Especially take care not to fit the rings upside-down for this may result in the faulty performance.

The shapes of the ring cutting sections fitted correctly in the piston are shown in the Fig. 59 and the visual indicator is determined by the manufacturer's mark punched on the top side with such letters as TP or KR Fig. 59.

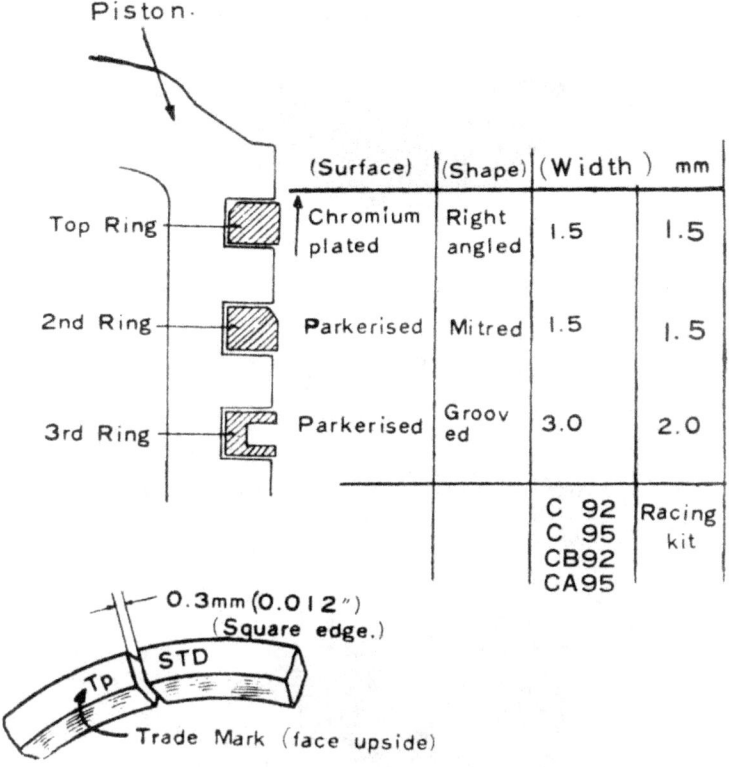

Fig. 59 Section view of piston rings and marks on ring

(10) Measure outside diameter of the piston pin and replace if it is worn or out-of-round. This can be determined by comparing with the original size in the specification (P. 157).

III. Installation of Piston and Cylinder

(1) Fit the piston rings into the piston ring grooves using a ring expander or both hands. Do not fit rings in reverse.

(2) Install the piston pin clips in the piston pin bore of right side for the left piston and left side for the right piston and push in the piston pins through the connecting rods to which the pistons are to be fitted. Install the outer end of the piston pin clips on both pistons. The pistons should be installed to the connecting rods as the stamped arrow mark on the top indicate the front direction. (Fig. 60)

(3) Place the packing on the crank case and tap two dowels in the cylinder where the one is on the oil passage and the other is in a diagonal position. Keep the pistons at the top dead center by placing a wooden block between piston skirts and gasket which was previously positioned on the crank case upper end. Fit piston ring com-

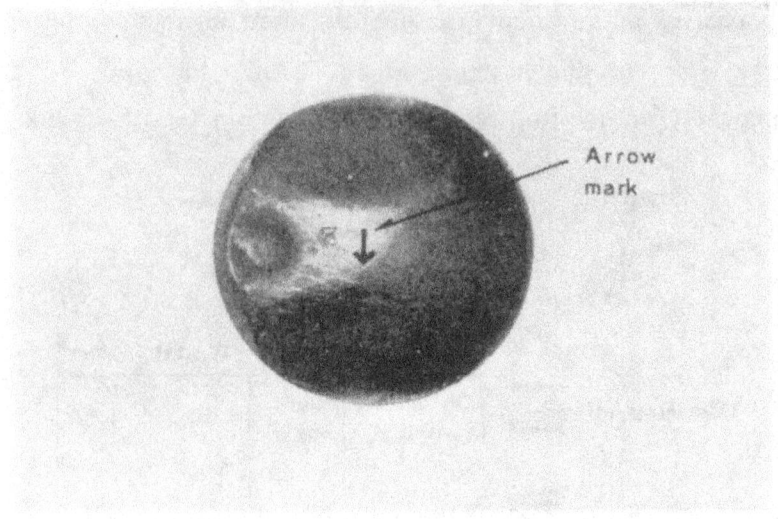

Fig. 60 Top view of piston

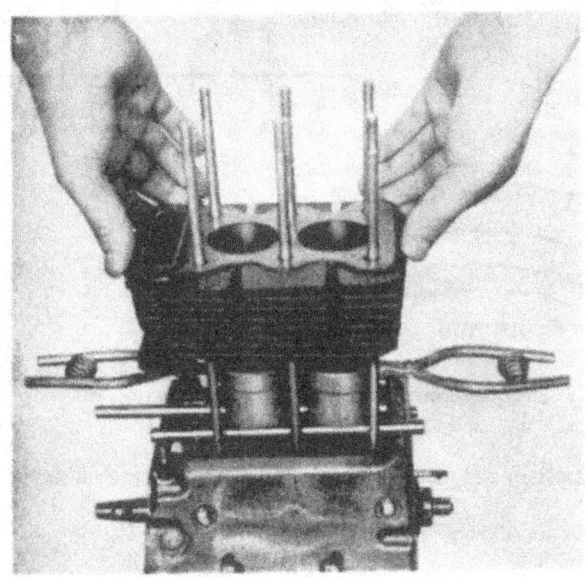

Fig. 61 Installing cylinder

pressors around both piston rings which are to be compressed.

Then, install the cylinder block onto the pistons, gently tapping the cylinder block with hand to it force down. Take out the ring compressor and wooden block, after having fitted the piston rings into the cylinder. (Fig. 61)

(4) Position cylinder head gasket, cam chain rubber packing, and "O" rubber ring around the dowel pin of oil passage.

Before placing the gaskets, 3 dowel pins should be tapped into the cylinder.

(5) Locate the cylinder head and tighten the stud bolts on the head (refer to P. 162), then tighten 6 mm stud nuts fixing the cylinder cam chain case to the crank case.

— 32 —

1-4. CRANK SHAFT AND CONNECTING ROD

Two types of crank shaft are available, one of which is for standard engine and the other is common to the CB92 and CA95.

The standard has two main ball bearings which support the crank shaft and one crank pin press-fitted to the right and left crank shaft and two intermediate balancer weights. The main bearings have altered to one of a thicker outer race from C92F-939667. On the other hand the CB92 and CA95 has two ball bearings and an intermediate roller bearing for support of the crank shaft, and left and right crank pins integrated with their balancer weights and to which their respective crank shafts are press fitted. At both sides the completed crank shafts are press fitted with center crank shaft. Connecting rods and the big end rollers have been modified twice in the standard and Super Sports, therefore, there are 3 kinds of these parts exclusively available in accordance with the engine numbers. (Fig. 59, 63)

The main ball bearings have a groove around each race and are push fitted to the crank shaft. On the right end, the drive gear is fitted onto a spline and locked with a nut. On the left end the timing sprocket is fitted with a dowel pin.

In engines after the serial No. C92E-931006 C95E-912778 a helical drive gear is provided instead of spur gear for earlier model. (Fig. 64)

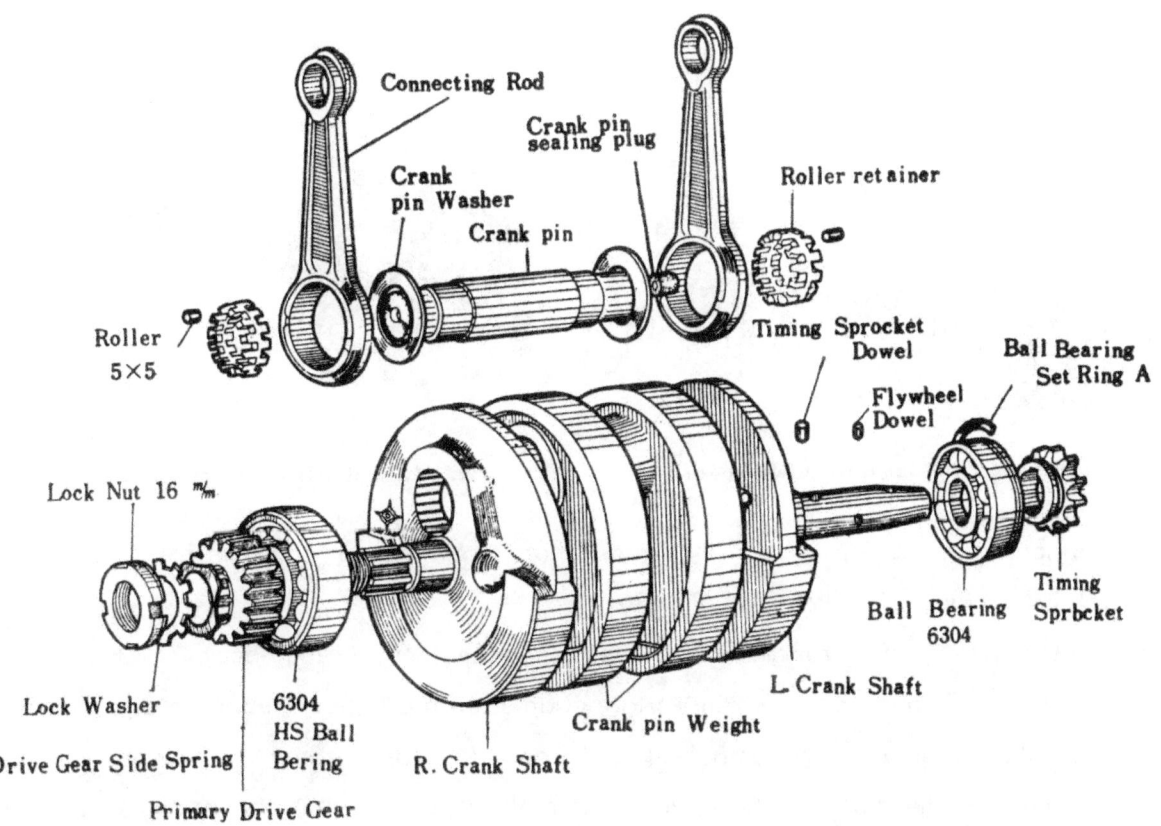

Fig. 62. Exploded view of crank shaft (standard model)

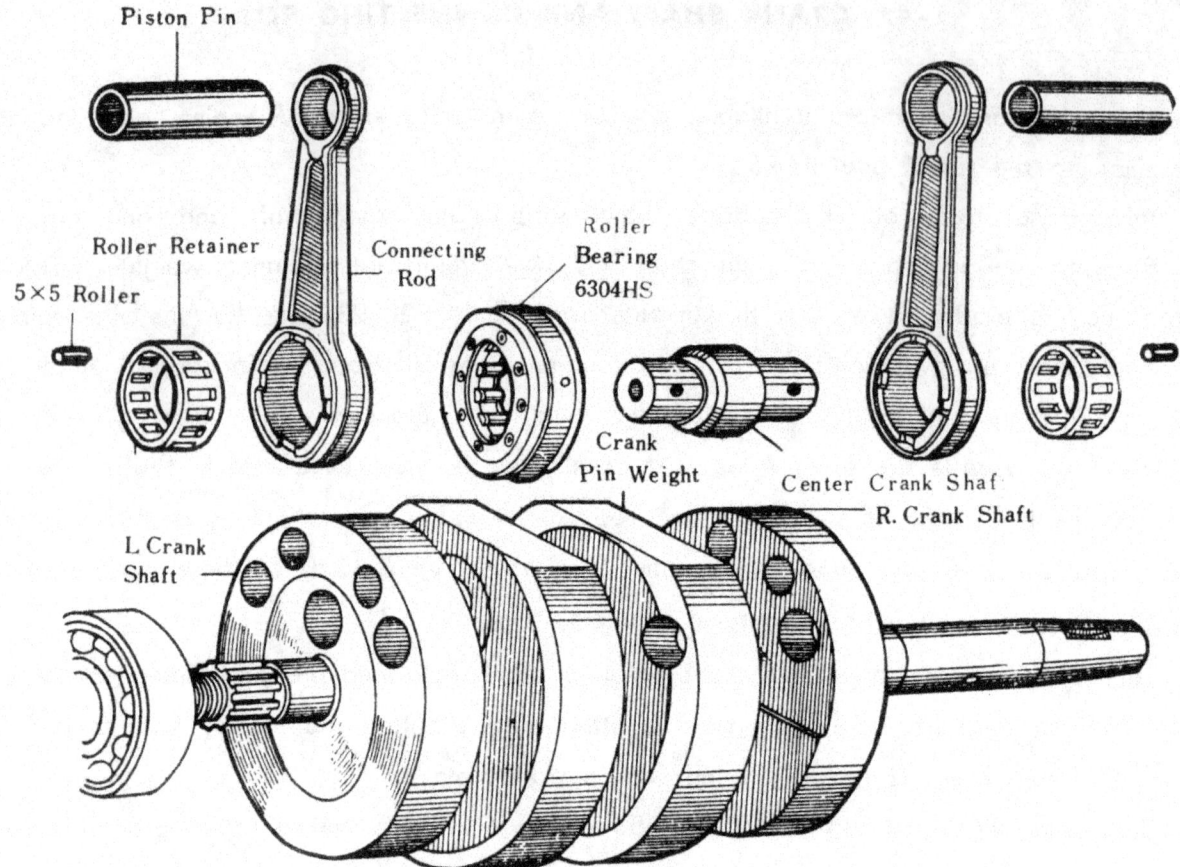

Fig. 63. Exploded view of crank shaft (CB92 & CA 95)

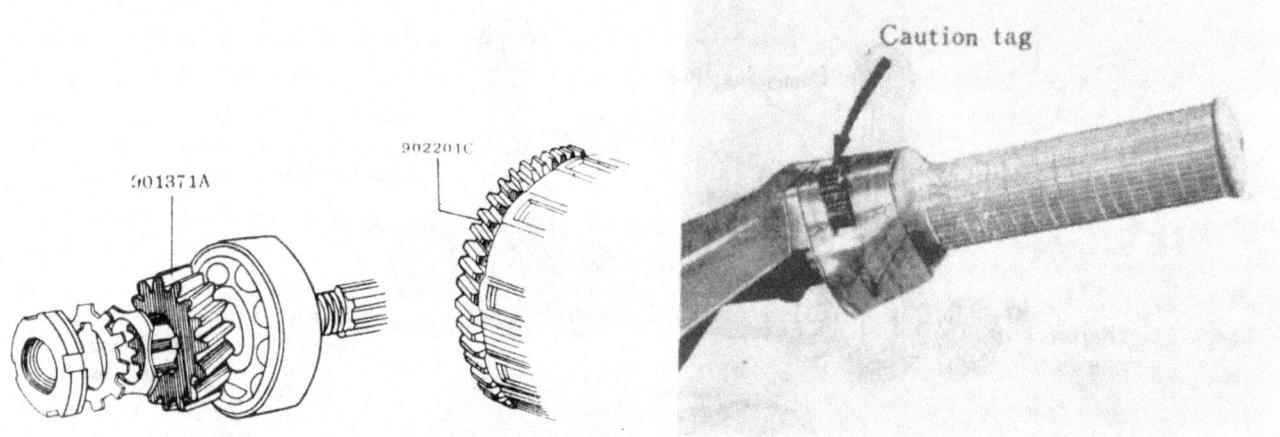

Fig. 64. Helical drive driven gear   Fig. 65. Instruction of anti-thrust rubber piece

Filtered lubricant is fed into the right crank shaft in which a passage for it is drilled and then led to the crank pin. (Refer to P. 57)

For the prevention of the crankshaft from thrusting impact arising due to the axial play existing, while handling freight or transportation an anti-thrust piece rubber is attached between the head of the dynamo rotor clamp bolt and contact breaker cover. The tag of notice for this is attached on the starter button, in which it is mentioned that the rubber piece should be removed before starting the engine. (Fig 65)

I. **Removal of Crank Shaft**

(1) Start disassembling from the condition where the cylinder and pistons are stripped as mentioned in the previous paragraph.

(2) Remove the right crank case cover, oil filter and the clutch assembly (P. 42)

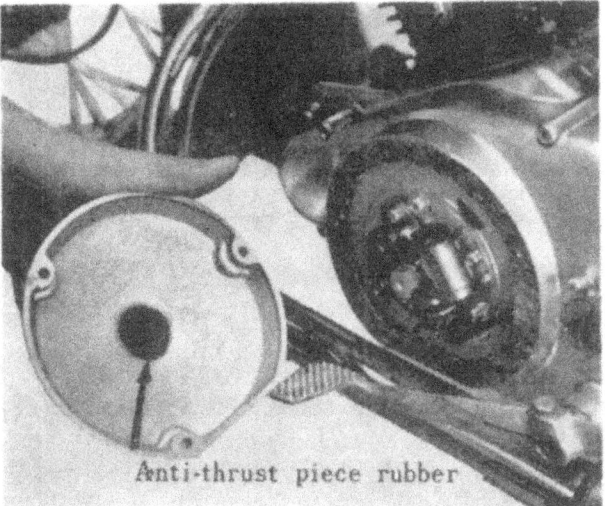

Fig. 65' Anti-thrust piece,

Fig. 66. Removal of under crank case

Remove the oil pump with clutch outer.

(3) Unscrew three 6 mm and two 8 mm nuts retaining the upper crank case.

(4) Place the crank case upside down and remove six 8 mm stud nuts, two 6 mm stud nuts and six 6 mm bolts.

(5) Remove the under crank case giving a gentle tap with wooden hammer. (Fig. 66)

(6) Remove the crank shaft assembly.

(7) Take out the timing gear with Extractor. (Fig. 67)

(8) With a small chisel and hammer, straighten the lock plate at the drive gear retaining nut. Remove the nut lock plate, washer and gear.

(9) Both side main bearings can be pryed out using Bearing Extractor.

II. Inspection and Repair of Crank Shaft.

(1) Cleanse all the parts with cleaning solvent and wipe dry.

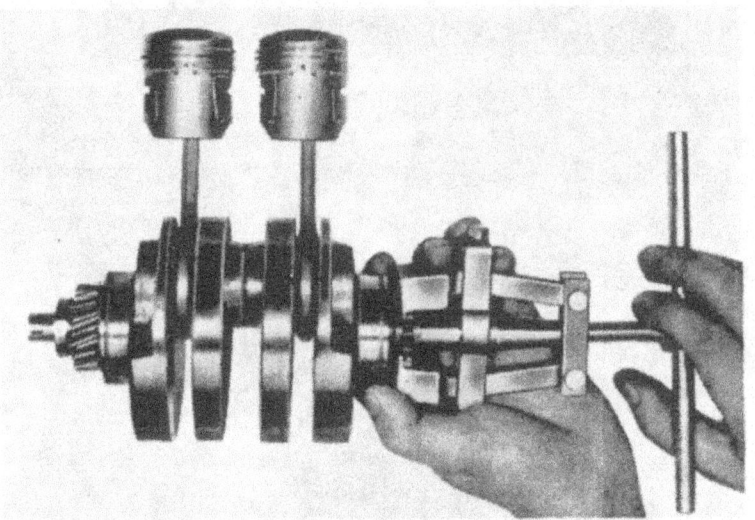

Fig. 67. Removing timing gear with extractor

(2) Main bearings

2-1. Hold the main bearing inner race with hand and rotate outer race forcing with other hand in order to check smothness of rotation or noise incurred. Replace the bearings which turn with excessive noise.

2-2. Mount the bearings on the crank shaft, with the crank shaft supported by V blocks at the balancer weight. Set the dial gauge at zero on the surface of the outer race of bearing and force the outer race up and down radially to measure the amount of free play. Maximum allowable free play is 0.0002" (0.005mm). (Fig. 68)

2-3. Visually inspect on the surface of the crank shaft journal, on which the ball bearing is mounted. Replace the crank shaft if any defacement or distortion appears.

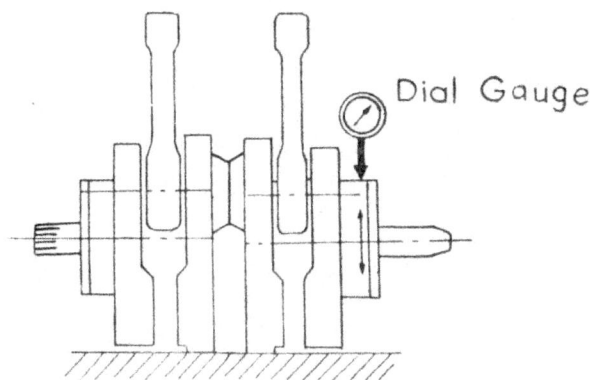

Fig. 68. Measuring run-out of main bearing

(3) Connecting rods, crank pin and large end bearings

3-1. Measure the inside diameter of the small end of connecting rods, replace the connecting rods when disassembling the crank shaft if they exceed the specified limit.

3-2. Place part of the balancer weights of the crank shaft on V-blocks and measure the maximum amount of big end axis play by forcing the connecting rod vertically up and down. Use of the dial gauge is advisable for this purpose and the measurement should be done in the direction of small end and the right angles to same. Overhaul the crank shaft if the amount of play is more than 0.0002" (0.05mm). (Fig. 69)

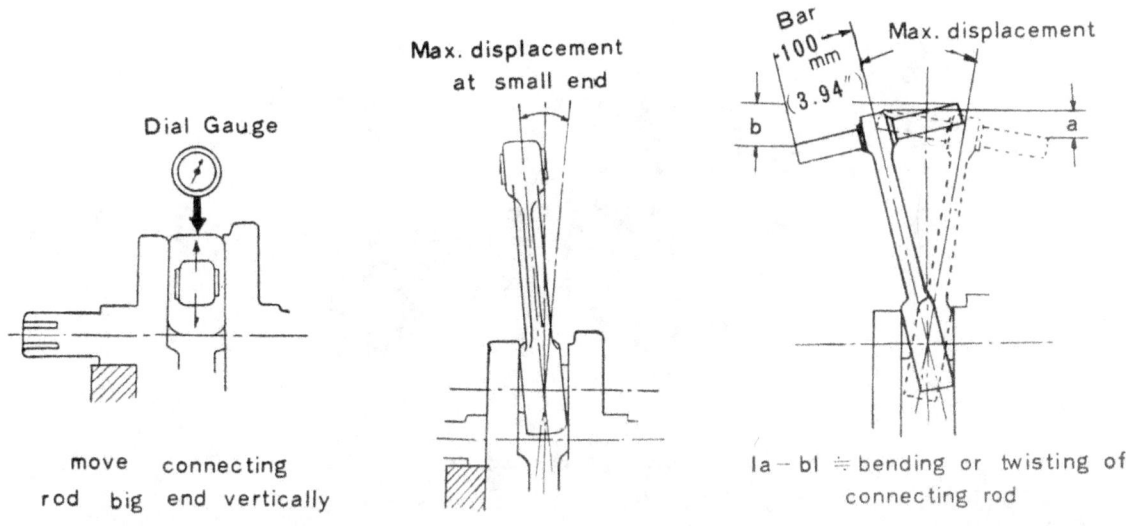

Fig. 69. Measuring radial play of connecting rod big end.

Fig. 70. Measuring swing of connecting rod.

Fig. 71. Measuring distortion of connecting rod.

3-3. Measure the axis play of connecting rod big end located between the crank shaft and balancer weight. Maximum allowable play is 0.04" (1mm), therefore, overhaul the crank shaft if it exceeds this specification.

3-4. Hold the big end at the center of the circle and swing the small end to the axis of the crank shaft. Maximum allowable limit is 0.2" (3 mm), therefore overhaul the crank shaft if it exceeds this amount. (Fig. 70)

3-5. The total amount of distortion consisting of bending twisting and uneven defacement in the connecting rod is measured by the amount of discrepancy between both ends of a 200mm fittable bar inserted in the small end of the connecting rod, when it is swung as in the paragraph (3-4). If it exceeds 0.08" (2 mm), disassemble the crank shaft and inspect. (Fig. 71)

3-6. After the crank shaft has been disassembled, trace the cause of the faults by measuring the parts including connecting rod big end, connecting rod rollers and crank pin. The maximum allowable limits are listed on P.157 to which they can be referred. Replace the parts rejected and also those parts which have any surface flow.

(4) Measuring crank shaft run-out

For checking run-out of the crankshaft, place main bearings on V-blocks. Locate a dial gauge at the ends of crank shaft where spline or taper are not machined, and gently rotate the crankshaft reading amount of run-out in the gauge. Maximum allowable amount is 0.0012" (0.03mm) for newly assembled. (Fig. 72)

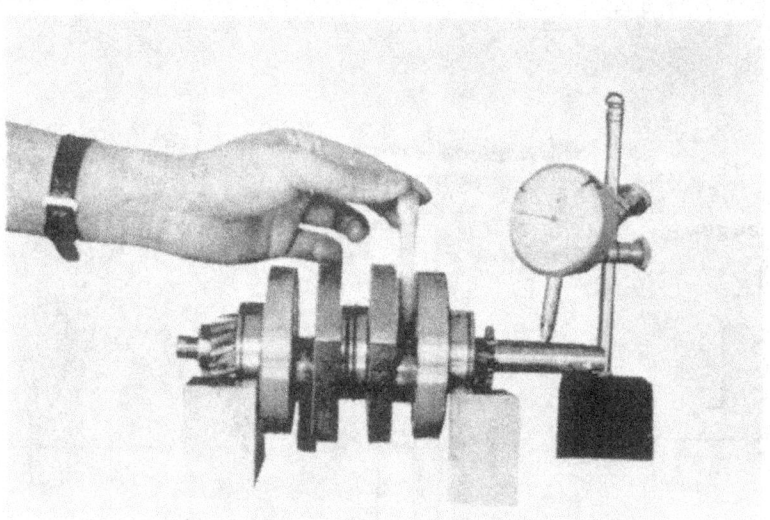

Fig. 72. Measuring crank shaf trun-out

(4') Center bearing

The center roller bearing on the crank shaft of CB92 & CA95 is able to be measured in accordance with the procedure of paragraph 3-2.

Disassemble the crank shaft if it has play in excess of the amount of more than 0.002" (0.05mm). Measure and check the fault after disassembly.

(5)   Disassembly of crank shaft

Using special jig provided, and 10 to 15 ton press, the crank pin will be pushed out from the crank shaft and balancer weight.

Place the crankshaft on the hydraulic press and support one of the balancer weights fimly.

Drive out the crank pin with an aid of a suitable arbor which is smaller than the crank pin in diameter, applying hydralic pressure.

(6)   Assembling crank shaft.

Using the same hydraulic press and a specialized jig for assembling. First, press the crankpin in the R. crankshaft and install connecting rod with rollers and press the balancers in. Then assemble the L. crank shaft and connecting rod roller by holding the balancer weight firmly. Attention should be recalled so that the oil hole in the crankshaft coincide with the crankpin.

III. Installation of Crank Shaft

(1)   Place the upper crank case on a block with inside facing upward.
(2)   Position the complete crank shaft on which the main bearings are installed, with the connecting rod hanging downwards. In this position, grooves on the main

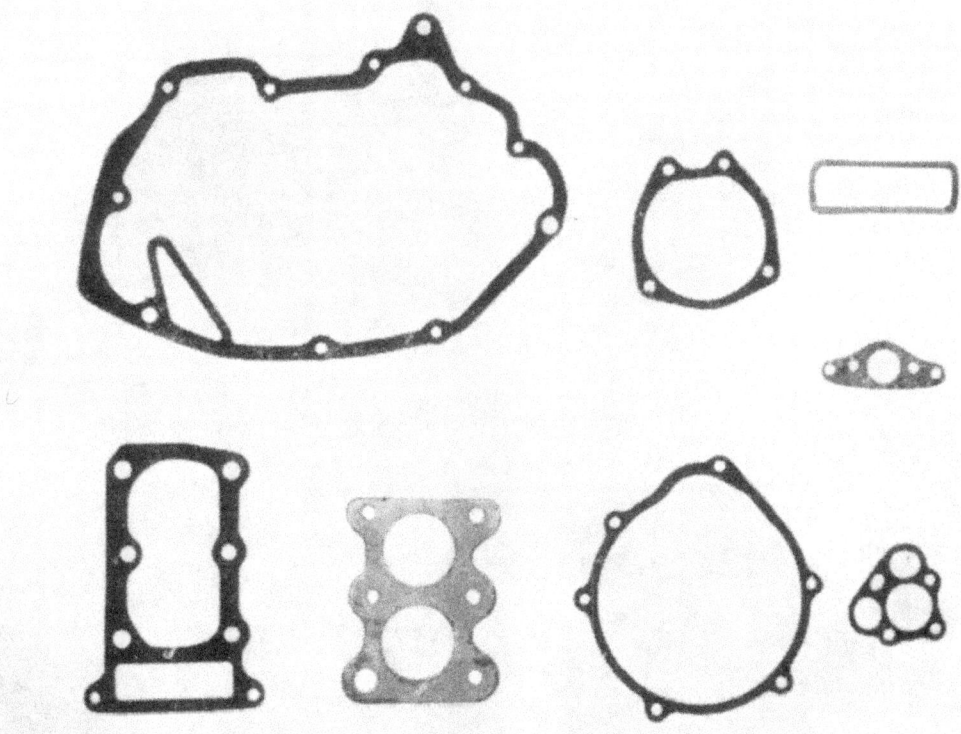

Fig. 73. Gaskets and packings for engine assembling

bearing and bearing housing on the crank case should be coincided by means of set rings inserted between them. Set a dowel pin between crank case intermediate housing and center roller bearing for the models CB92 and CA92.

(3) Apply a coat of Gasket Paste (liquid gasket) on the mating surfaces.

(4) Place the under crank case on the upper crank case, when it is assured that the transmission gears and shifting devices have been completely assembled. (Refer to P. 55). Before covering the under crank case, ensure that the oil seperating plates are fixed in. (Fig. 74)
Tighten all the nuts and bolts.

(5) Install the right crank case cover, left cover, cylinder and cylinder head with all their internal mechanisms.

(6) All the gaskets, except liquid gasket required to be replaced upon completion of assembling the engine are as follows. (Fig. 73)

MEMO

1-5. CLUCH

The clutch with its four facings and discs is located on the right end of the transmission main shaft of gear box and fixed with a set ring on the end. Primary drive gear is fitted on the clutch outer by 6 rivets through the medium of damping rubbers which prevent shocks being transmitted to gears arising from acceleration and deceleration.

Pressure applied on the clutch lever is converted to axial longitudinal power by means of the action of the clutch lifter thread, and it is in turn conveyed to the clutch at the right side of the crank case. Then the clutch disengages the engine torque which is transmitted as shown by the arrow line in (Fig. 74). The clutch plate is dipped in the right crank case cover oil sump and this enables an increase of the clutch efficiency.

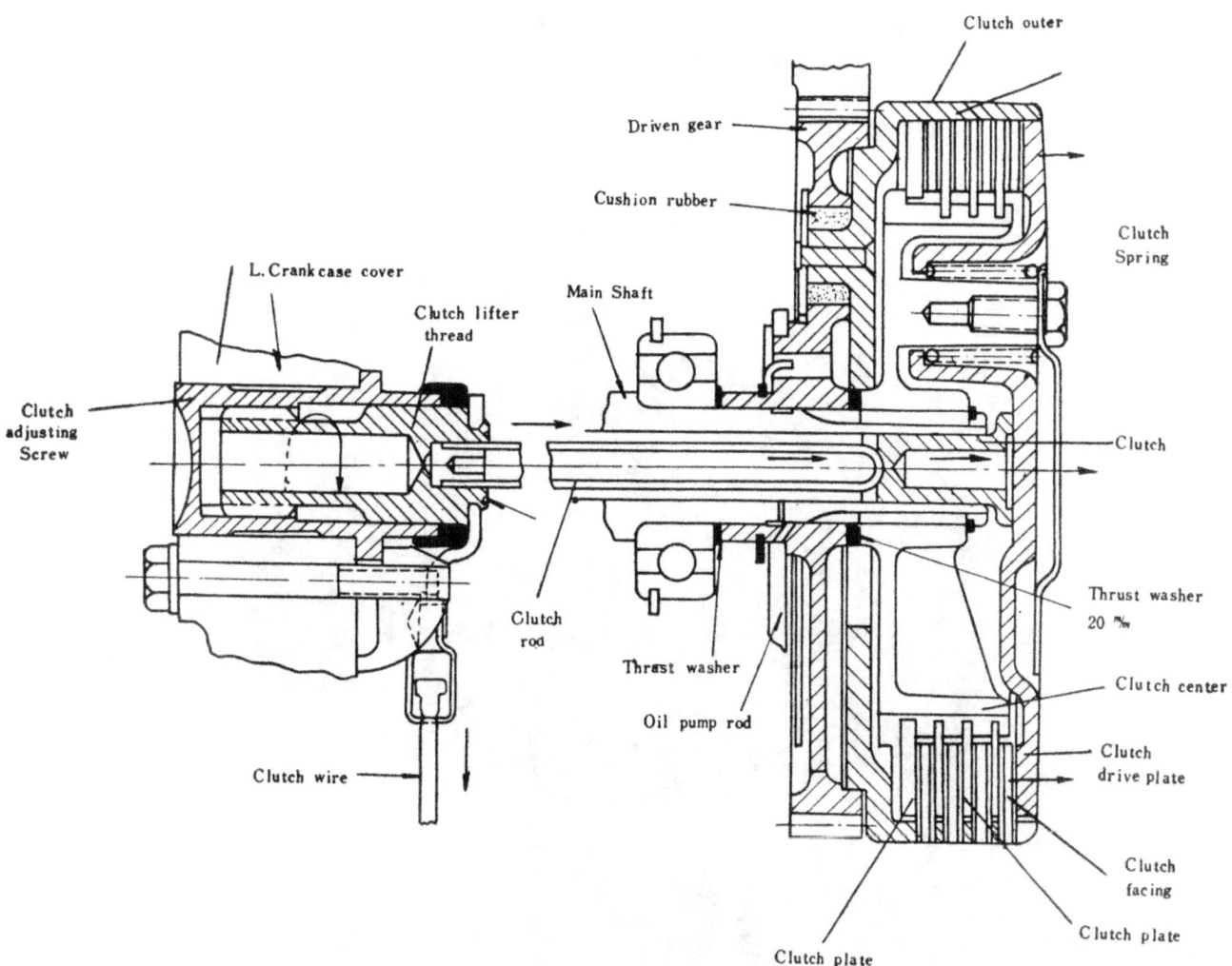

Fig. 74 Sectional view of clutch ass'y.

I. **Disassembly of Clutch**

   (1) Remove the R-crank case cover, unscrewing the 11 cross screws there-on.

   (2) Remove the oil filter cage which is inserted over the end of the crank shaft.

   (3) Remove the four 6 mm bolts retaining the clutch plate. (Fig. 75). Then take apart the clutch plate and clutch springs.

Fig. 75 Clutch retaining bolts

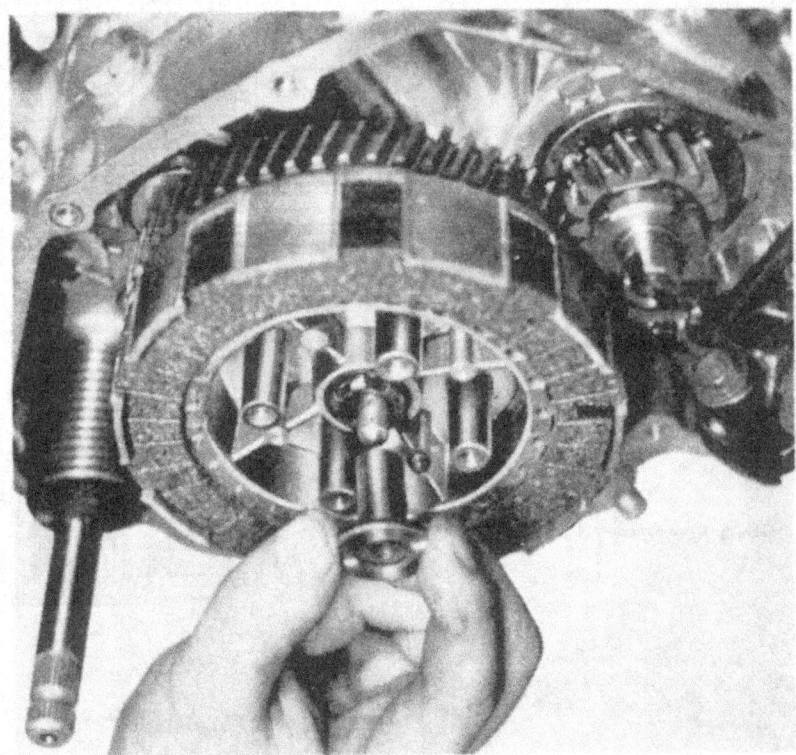

Fig. 76 Removing clutch lifter joint

   (4) Draw out the clutch lifter joint piece (Fig. 76) and the clutch lifter rod complete.

   (5) Remove the set ring at the end of the transmission main shaft using set ring remover. Then the clutch center may be removed. (Fig. 77)

(6) Remov the the plunger oil pump mounting stud nut and holding bolt.

(7) The clutch outer and the oil pump is removed as a unit, pulling them out together. Remove thrust washers.

(8) Separate the oil pump plunger arm and piston from the oil pump body.

(9) When required to remove the pump arm from the clutch outer, remove the set ring mounted behind it with a set ring remover. (Fig. 78)

Fig. 77 Removing clutch center retaining set ring

Fig. 78 Removing oil pump rod set ring

(10) At the left side of the engine, remove the L. crank case cover. Remove the 6 mm bolt retaining the clutch adjuster fixing piece, when the clutch adjuster complete may be removed from the cover. (Fig. 80). Unhook the clutch lever spring from the cover.

(11) Unscrew the clutch lifter thread complete from the adjuster. (Fig. 79)

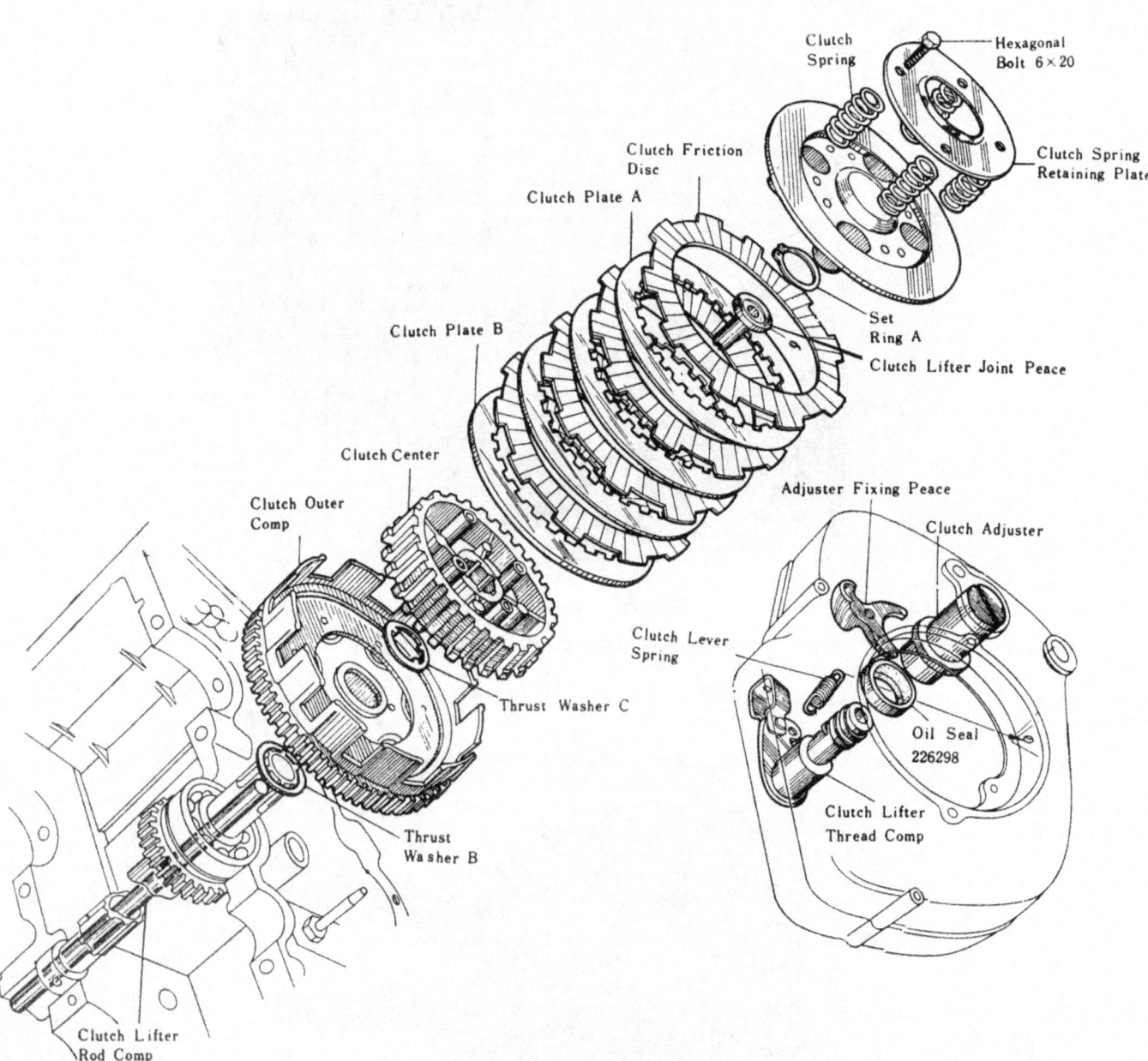

Fig. 79 Exploded view of clutch

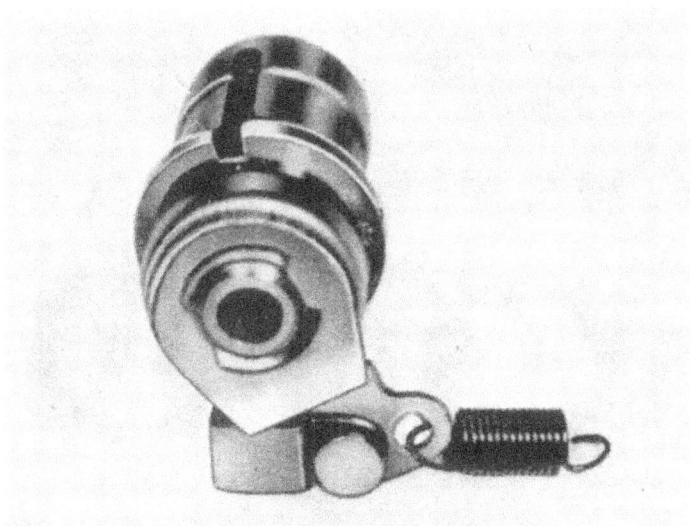

Fig. 80 Clutch lifter thread complete

II. Inspection and Repair of Clutch

(1) Visually examine the outer appearance of all composite parts for damage or flaws. Replace faulty parts.

(2) Measure inside diameter of the clutch outer and replace if it does not meet the specification (P. 159).

(3) Measure the thickness of clutch plate and facing for wear corresponding to their specification. Measurement of surface distortion of these parts is done by placing them on a surface plate and checking any clearance existing on or around the circumference of the clutch-plate visible between the flat surfaces.
Ammount of distortion which may be allowed to the limit is mentioned in the specification (P. 160).

(4) Measure free height and squareness of all clutch springs and replace if any of them are beyond the limits of the specification (P. 160).

(5) Check the general condition of the drive and driven gears, back lash between them and inspect for evidence of excesive wear. Replace excessively worn, damaged gears.

(6) Replace the oil seal fitted in the lifter thread adjuster if any tendency of oil seepage appears.

III. Assemhly of Clutch

(1) If it is assumed that the gear shift arm and kick starter spring and other relevant parts are completely provided on the crank case, the clutch assembly should be commenced. (Fig. 81)

(2) Insert 20 mm thrust washer on the transmission shaft, position the oil pump gasket

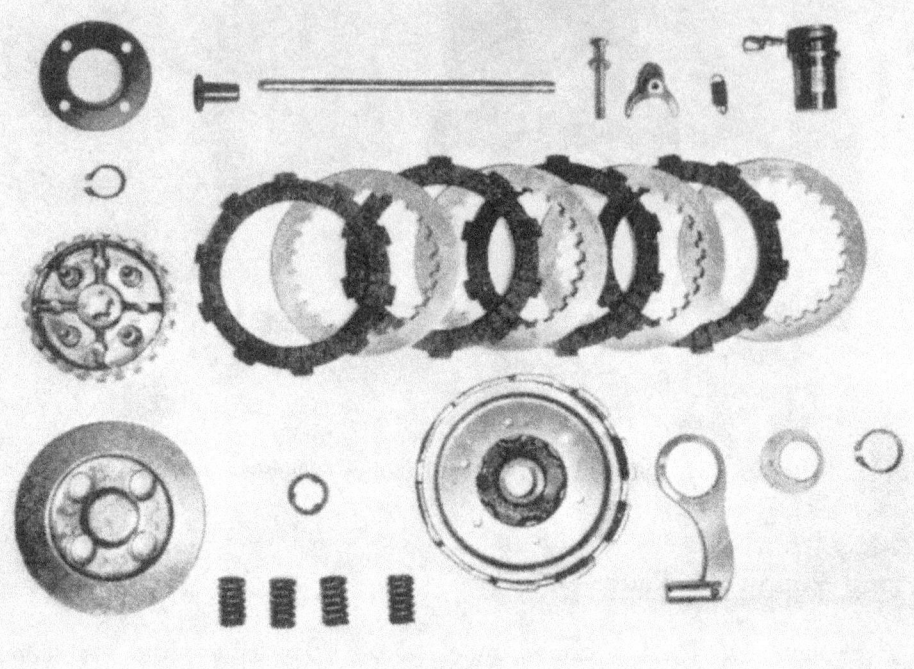

Fig. 81 Disply of clutch parts

and install the clutch outer with oil pump body as a unit.

Install the clutch outer complete and fix with the set ring onto the transmission shaft. Tighten the oil pump stud nut and bolt.

(3) Set the clutch plate B to the bottom and alternately install four clutch facings with three clutch plates A.

(4) Insert clutch lifter rod complete and the joint piece in the transmission main shaft. Install the clutch pressure plate and clutch springs on the extrusions of the clutch center. Tighten firmly the springs and retaining plate with four 6 mm bolts.

(5) Insert the oil filter complete over the crank shaft and install the right cover with its packing.

(6) Fix the clutch adjuster assembly onto the L. crank case cover and hook the return spring.

Apply grease into the adjuster through the nipple using grease gun.

(7) Adjust the clutch referring to (p. 160).

1-6. TRANSMISSION AND KICK STARTER

The transmission gear box is compactly enclosed in the crank case and the power produced by crank shaft is transmitted to the gear box through the train of helical gears.

Input shaft is called the transmissions main shaft and output is transmissions counter shaft on which the drive sprocket is attached. The four gears on each shaft usually mesh each other and are manually shifted in or out of the forward gear ratios by mechanical linkages of the shift arm, shift drum and shift fork. The gears are cut into spur gears and hardened to provide long trouble-free service.

Operation of gear change

Two kinds of changing mechanism are applied on the Benly, one of which is the so-called "rotary type gear change" and the other is "return type gear change." The former type is effected on the Benly standard up to engine No. C92E-12000 and the latter is provided on the standard engines after the same number, and on CA95, CB92. As for the shifting operation applied on the change pedal, the differences between them are as fhllows:—

Rotary system: (with none stopper)

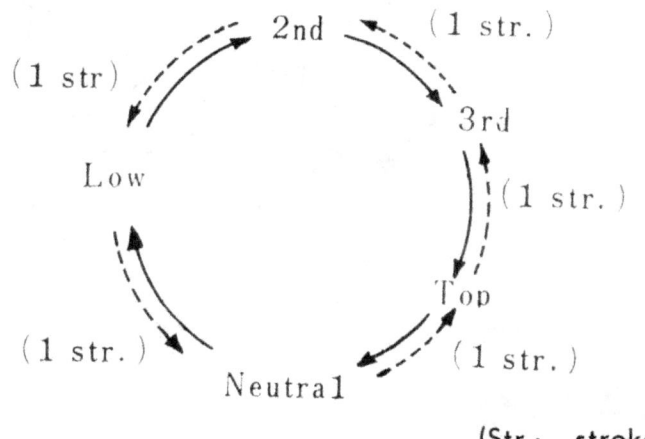

(Str.: stroke)

Return system: (with Stopper)

(Stopper) Low⇆Neutral⇆2nd⇆3rd⇆Top (Stopper)
　　　　　 1/2 str.　 1/2 str.　 1 str.　 1 str.

In the rotary there is no final position of shift through successive positions, while the return system is comming to an end after the top gear is reached.

Manual force applied by the foot is transformed into the rotary motion of the shift drum which operates two shift forks fitting into grooves on the drum. (Fig. 82)

The rotary motion of the shift drum is turned in the axial motion of the shift forks effected by the cam action of the grooves on the drum, and the drum is interlocked by the stopper. Actually, the gear shifting is operated by the main shaft 3rd gear and counter shaft 2nd gear, both of which are commected with the shift forks. The respective gear positions and the positions of shifting are shown in the pictures following.

(Fig. 83, 8,4 85, 86, 87)

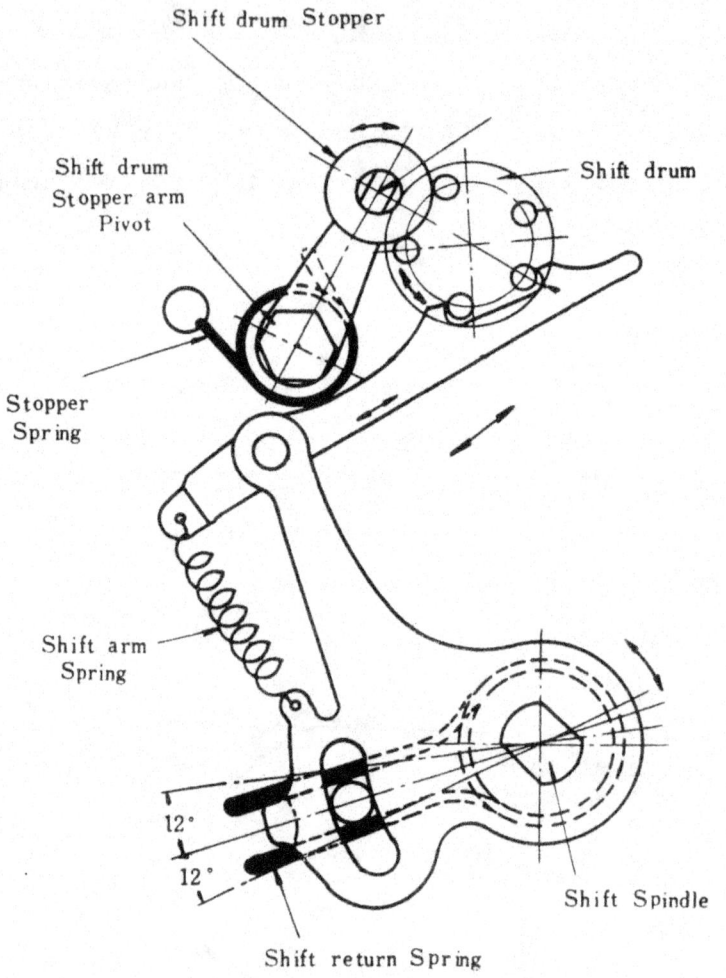

Fig. 82 Mechanism of change lever

Fig. 83 Neutral

Fig. 84 Low gear

— 48 —

Fig. 85 Second gear

Fig. 86 Third gear

Fig. 87 Top gear

Operation of kick starter

The kick starter is provided at the rear end of the gear case and its pinion gear is meshed with the low gear of the counter shaft introduced to the main shaft and crank shaft. When the kick pedal is depressed the ratchet pawl on the ratchet engages with the starter pinion and rotates the crank, othewise, the pawl rests on the starter spindle bushing preventing interference with the pinion. (Fig. 88)

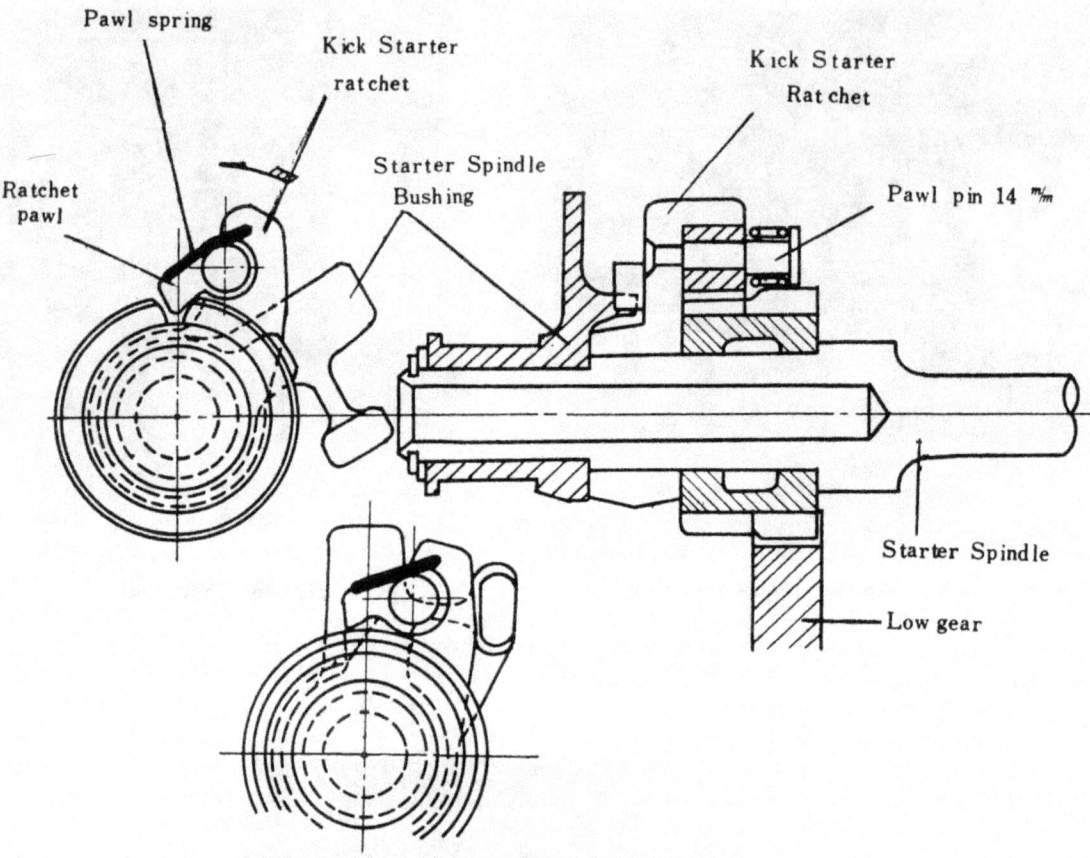

Fig. 88 Mechanism of kick pinion

Gear ratios

Gear teeth numbers for gear trains and their gear ratios are follows.

	Standard (C92-C95)	CB92 CA95
Drive Gear	16	16
Driven Gear	62	62
Gear ratio to transmission	3.875	3.875
Transmission main shaft gear	14 T	14 T
〃 2nd	18	19
〃 3rd	18	19
〃 4th	25	25
Counter shaft gear	22	22
〃 low	34	33
〃 2nd	29	29
〃 3rd	25	24
Gear ratios; at Low gear	2.61	2.36

2nd	....	1.61	.... 1.474
3rd	....	1.19	.... 1.043
Top	....	0.88	.... 0.840
final drive sprocket	....	15	.... 15(CB 92) 18 (CA 95)
final driven sprocket	....	60	.... 36(CB 92) 40 (CA 95)
Secondary gear ratio (final drive)	....	2.67	.... 2.93
Kick pinion	....	18	 19

I. Disassembly of Transmission and Kick Starter

(1) Place the engine upside down on a suitable stand and remove the under crank case after the parts enclosed in L. crank case cover and R. crank case cover have been removed. Unhook the coil spring attached on the upper crank case for kick spindle.

(2) Then the transmission shaft, counter shaft and kick spindle with their respective gears, bearing and bushing can be detached from the upper crank case. (Fig. 88) (Fig. 90)

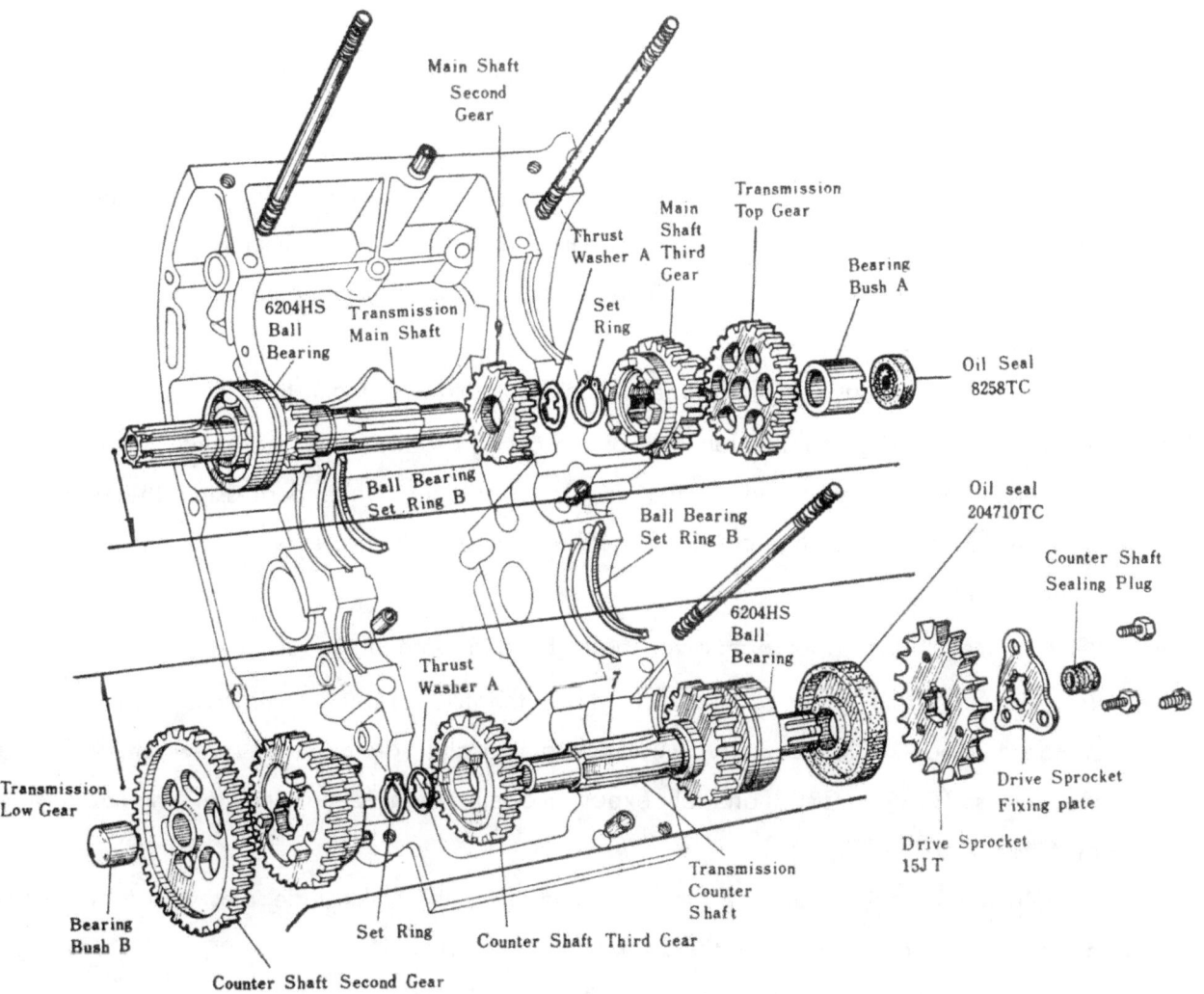

Fig. 89 Exploded view of transmission

Fig. 90 Kick starter ass'y.

Fig. 91 Changing links

(3) With set ring remover, remove the set ring attached on main shaft and counter shaft which retain the main shaft second gear and counter shaft third gear. Remove the sprocket by unscrewing the three fixing 6 mm bolts. (after Engine No. C92E-925610, they were altered to two bolts.)
Then the oil seals and main bearings can be extracted from their shafts.

(4) Remove the set ring on the left side of the change shaft. Then tap gently with wooden hammer on the serrated end of the gear shift spindle, while depressing the gear shift arm link (a) until the projection of the link will not interfere with the gear shift arm guide. (Fig. 91)

(5) Remove the shift stopper arm pivot bolt (b) and detach the stopper arm.

(6) Remove shift drum guide roller mounted on the top of the crank case (Fig. 92) for standard model. Remove two bolts retaining shift drum guide screw and take out the guides. (CA95, CB92 and all export models for C92 after the engine number of C92E-12001) (Fig. 93)
Straighten the lock washers folded over on the shift fork guide pins with a chisel and a small hammer and remove the shift fork guide pins.
Remove the neutral switch rotor from the end of the shift drum.
Then the shift drum is extracted from the upper crank case. (Fig. 94)

Fig. 92 Removing shift drum guide roller

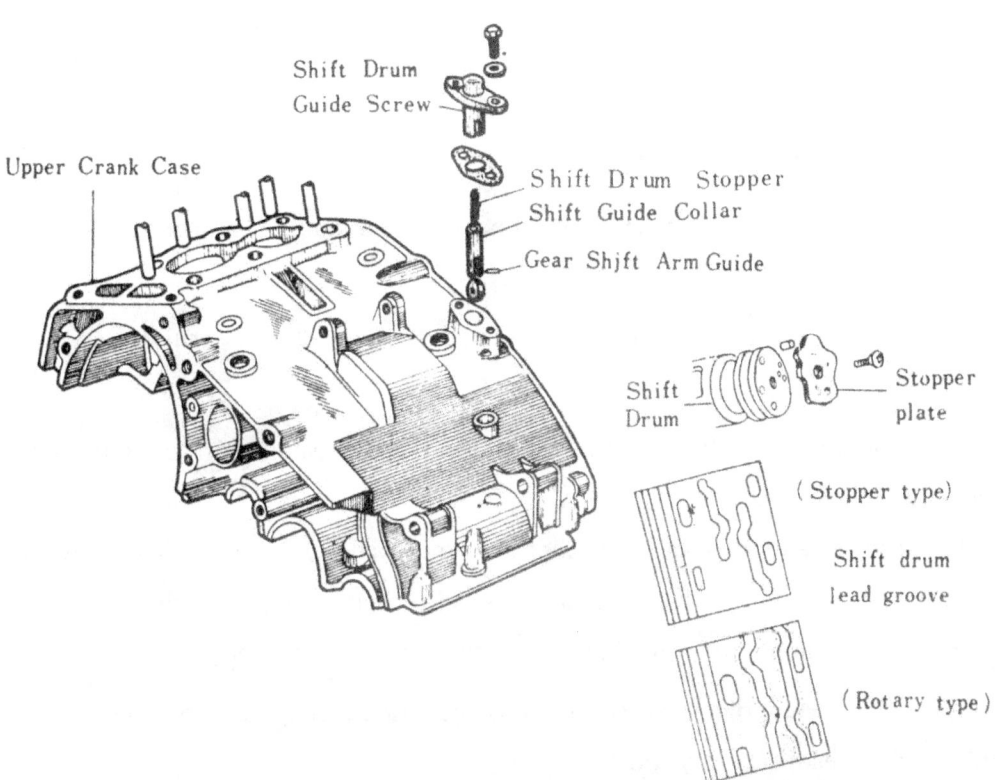

Fig. 93 Removal of shift drum stopper roller (CB92 & CA95)

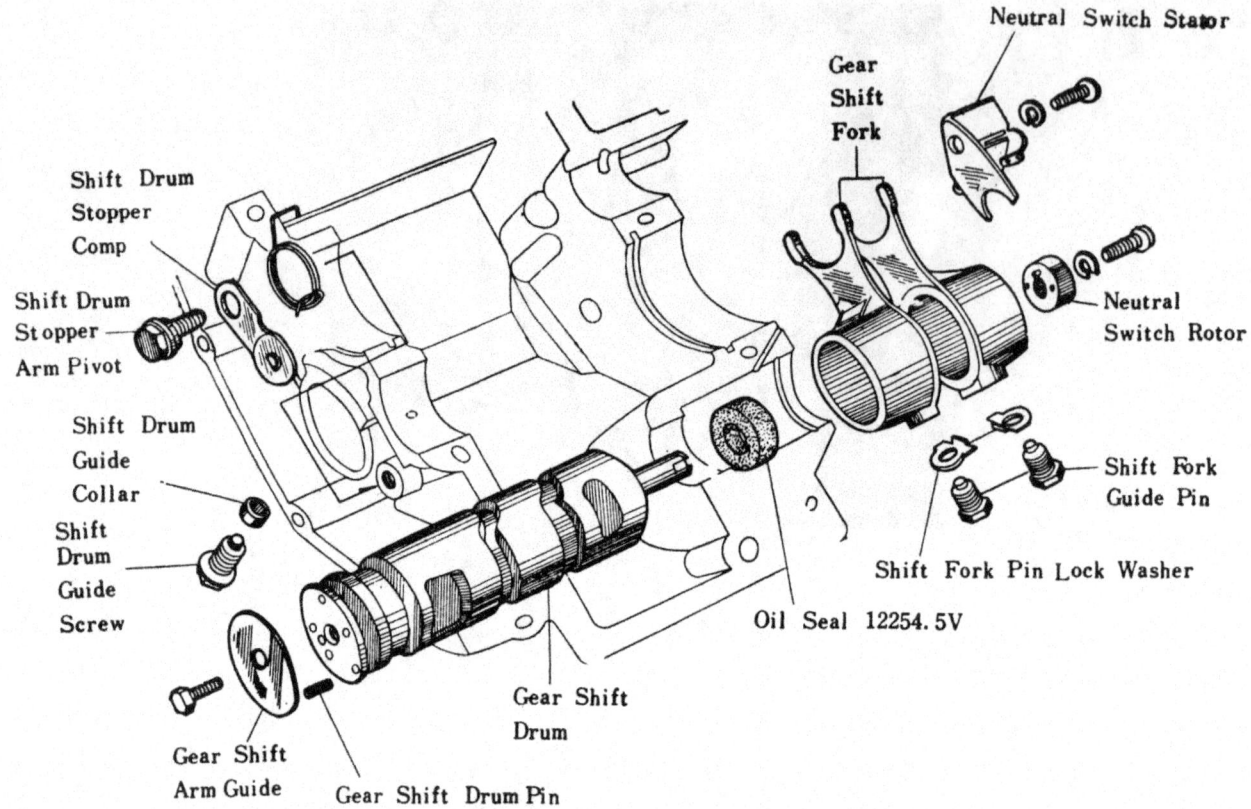

Fig. 94 Exploded view of shifting system

II. Inspection and Repair of Transmission

(1) Before disassembling the crank case check and examine for seepage or leak from the oil seals and blind plug. If any tendency of this appears, replace oil seals and plug.

(2) Inspect for excessive wear, crack or damage on all components and replace any faulty parts.

(3) The ball bearings on the counter shaft and main shaft can be checked for excessive wear as follows:
In the case where they are attached on their shaft, remove the outer race radially with finger pressure. If some play is felt in hand replace the bearing. Rotate the outer race by hand, and if there is excessive sound it must be replaced.

(4) Measure the inside diameter of the bushings according to the specifications replace the unsatisfactory parts.

(5) Measure the diametrical distance between valleys of gears and replace if this dimension exceeds the specification
Or measure distances of respective numbers of cogs in gears using micrometer for measuring teeth thichness (Fig. 95)

Fig. 95 Measuring thickness of gear teeth

III. Assembling of Transmission and Kick Spindle

(1) Shift drum

Place the upper crank case, inside uppermost on an engine assembling stand as it assumed that all studs, and an oil seal have been installed.

1-2. Insert the gear shift drum from the upper crank case large bore, introduce into the shift forks, and set the small end journal of the drum in the crank case.

The position of the shift forks must be face to face with each other as illustrated in (Fig. 94)

Insert the shift fork guide pins with folding washers so that they can be set in their respective grooves on the shift drum. Tighten securely and fold up the washers at a face of the bolt head (not at a corner). To coincide the faces do not rotate by unscrewing but always turn in the direction of tightening.

1-3. Install the neutral switch stator on the crank case and install the neutral switch rotor on the end of shift drum. (Fig. 94)

1-4. Insert gear shift drum pins into the large end of the shift drum and retain them with guide plate. Then attach the shift drum stopper with its spring in its position for standard C92 and C95.

1-5. Turn the crank-case upside-down and install the shift drum guide screw with collar.

For CA95 and CB92 model install the shift drum stopper complete with two bolts from the out-side of the crank case.

(2) Kick starter

Set the pinion gear, the kick starter ratchet, the kick starter bushing and thrust washer on the kick spindle shaft so that they are placed in the position as illustrated in Fig. 87 and retain the end with the set ring.

Place the kick spindle complete on the crank case so that the stopper of the starter spindle bushing is seating within the protrusions on the crank case inner surface.

(3) Counter shaft

    3-1. Tap the ball bearing onto the counter shaft so that the groove on the outer face comes closer to the gear.

    3-2. Slip the oil seal 204/710TC onto the counter-shaft taking care not to damage the lip.

    3-3. Slip on the counter shaft third gear and the thrust washer and hold them to the shaft with the set ring.

    3-4. Slip the second gear first, then the transmission low gear on to the shaft. Install the 14 mm bushing B on the end of the counter shaft.

    3-5. Insert a dowel pin and a ball bearing set ring on each side of the bores where the counter shaft and transmission shaft are resting.

    3-6. Place the counter shaft gear cluster on the crank case dent in the position so that bearing and a hole on the bushing coincide with their inserts.
         At the same time the counter shaft second gear (sliding gear) should be engaged in the respective shift fork.

(4) Transmission main shaft gear cluster.

    4-1. Tap the main ball bearing 6204HB on to the main shaft so that the groove on the bearing outer race positions inwards. Slide the main shaft second gear toward the main shaft gear so that the face without the projection encounters the gear. Retain the gear with thrust washer and set ring.

    4-2. Slide on the third gear, the top gear and the bushing on the shaft.

    4-3. Install the transmission gear cluster on the dent of the crank case such as was in the counter shaft.

    4-4. Place the oil seal 8258TC in the crank case dent at the end of bushing.

(5) Apply a coat of gasket paste on the mating surface and insert dowel pins (front and rear intermediate) and install the under crank case. Tighter all bolts and nuts firmly.

(6) Install the change return spring stopper pin on the outer side of undercrank case and insert the shift arm assembly through the bore of the crank case until correctly seated. It is assumed that the shift arm return spring and shift arm spring have already been attached.
Place the washer on the oil seal left side crankcase and install the set-ring onto the spindle shaft.

(7) Attach the shift drum stopper roller with the shift drum pivot bolt and spring in position. (standard engine previous to E. No. C92E-012001), insert the stopper roller with spring and guide in upper side of the crankcase, (for return type change)

(8) Complete assembly with the R. crank case cover, gear change arm and kick arm. Adjust the position of change pedal for CB92 as shown in (p. 137).

1-7. LUBRICATION AND BREATHER

It can be understood by referring to the **lubrication diagram** (fig. 96), that oil is pressure fed to the engine by means of the oil pump located on the right side of the crank case.

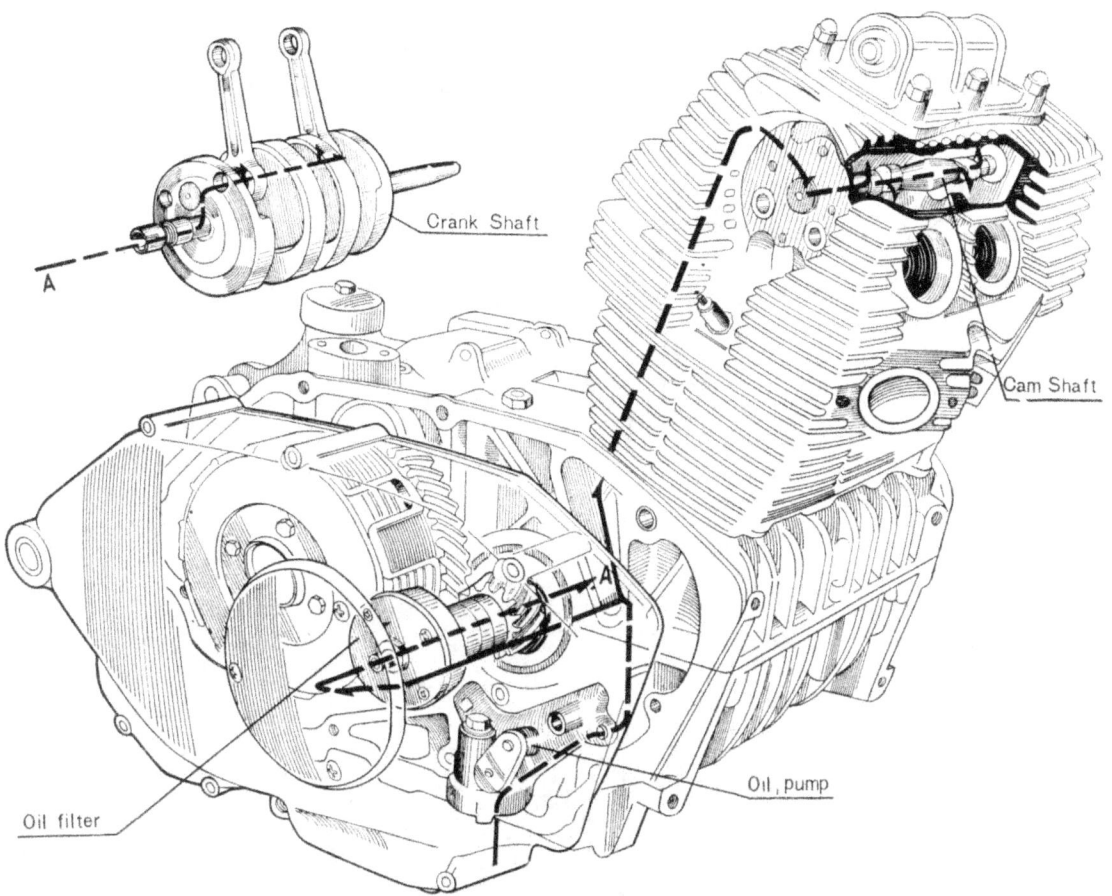

Fig. 96 Circulating diagram of lubricant

The plunger-type oil pump, cam operated by the crank shaft, draws oil through a submerged oil screen and forces it under pressure to a chamber located on the crank case cover and thence to the oil gallery in the cylinder and head. It is also introduced to the cam shaft and rocker arms, as well as to the oil filter, crank shaft, connecting rods, and bearings.

The cylinder walls, connecting rod, small ends and pistons are supplied with oil splash from spurt holes in the crank pins.

Centrifugal type oil filter fitted on the end of the crank shaft rotates and as a result, seperates particles of metal and sand mixed in the oil by centrifugal force, and the particles deposit around the wall and partitions in the filter.

The clutch and transmission are lubricated with oil splash originated by clutch and gear rotation. For the bushing on the counter shaft a slit is provided on upper side which enables it to collect oil for lubrication.

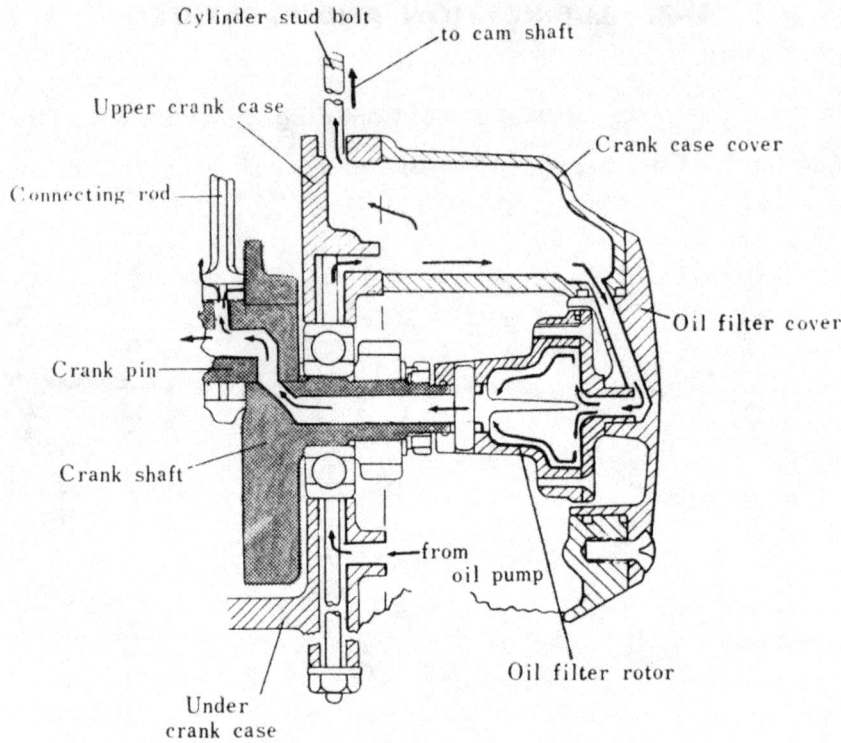

Fig. 97 Sectional view of oil filter

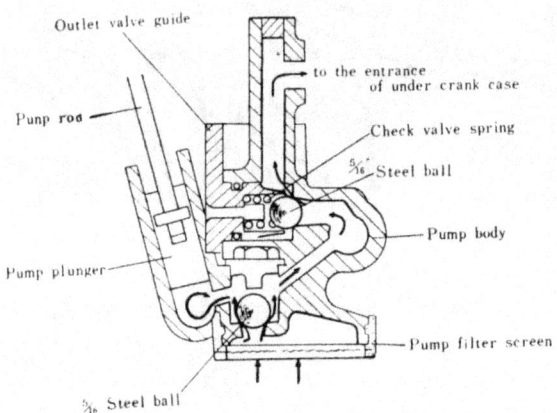

Fig. 98 Sectional view of oil pump

Oil collected in the sump which is part of the under crank case performs lubrication of the engine as well as the transmission.

The crank case ventilation is effected by the breather located on the crank shaft breather valve or on the rear end of the upper crank case (from No. C92E-937667 C95E-914982) for the purpose of discharging blow-by gas and water vapors which would otherwise contaminate engine oil and cause oil seapage though the packings or gaskets.

The old type breather was located on the L. crank shaft and discharge was by a gallery passed through the shaft in cooperation with a breather seal which had barriers in the lip for controlling the timing of discharge. (Fig. 99)

The other, the later type, is that the gas introduced in the gear case through the holes between crank chamber and clutch case is simply discharged from the breather funnel posessing an oil separator inside. (Fig. 100)

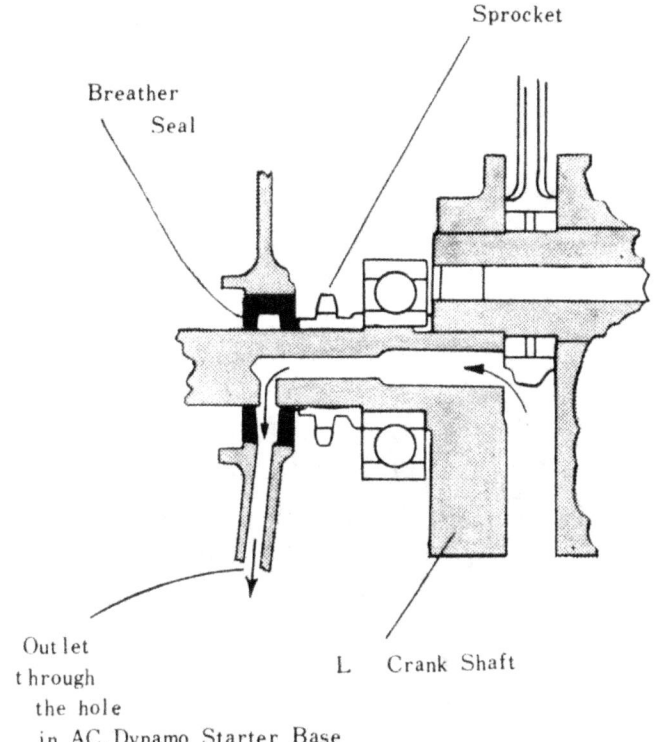

Fig. 99 Breather system for old model

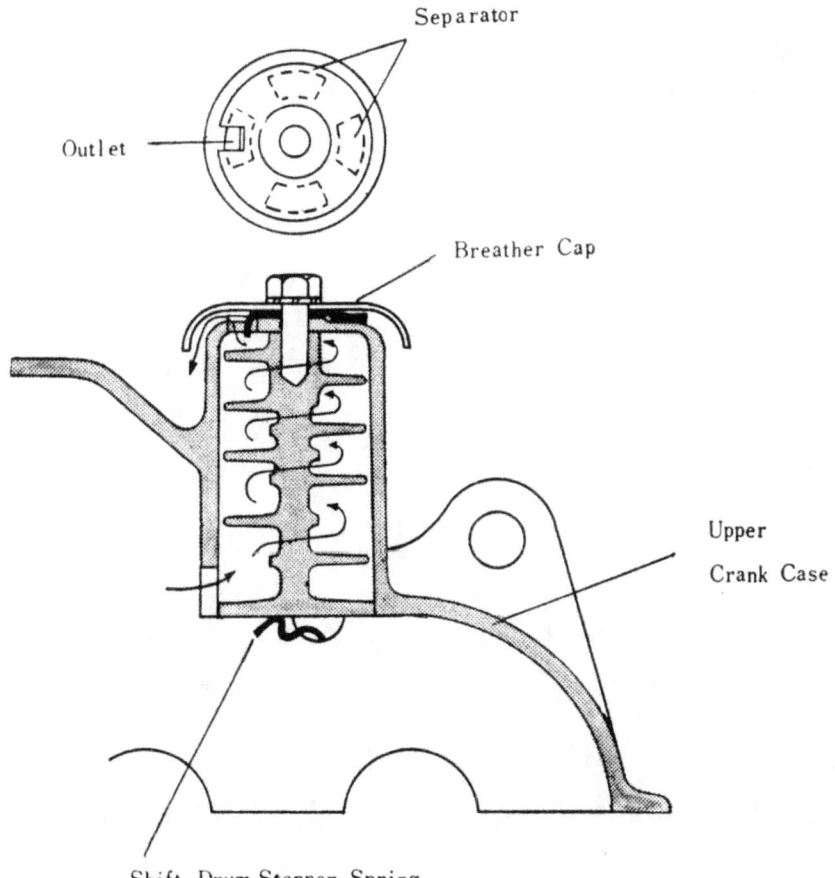

Fig. 100 Breather system for later model (from C92E-937667 C95E-914982)

I. **Disassembling of lubricating system**

(1) Oil filter

Remove three screws on the oil filter cover and pry out the cover using two screw drivers inserted in the slits.

Then extract the oil filter chamber with fingers and open the cover secured by 4 screws. (Fig. 101)

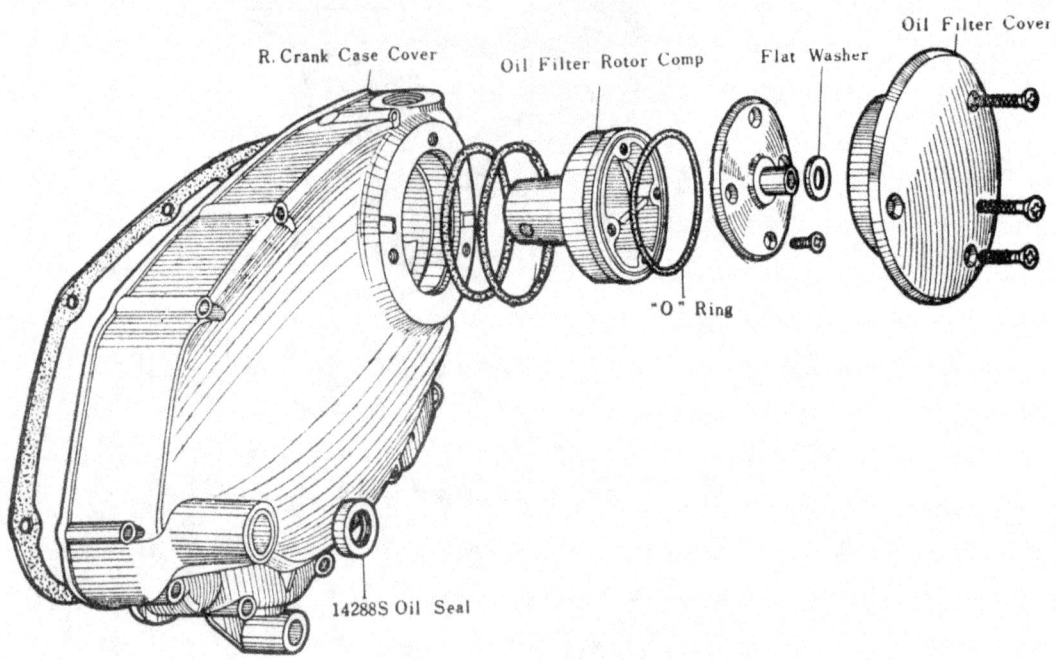

Fig. 101 Oil filter display

(2) Oil pump

2-1. Remove the R. crank case cover and remove the oil pump mounting nut and dismount the oil pump as a unit with clutch assembly.

2-2. Seperate the plunger piston from the pump body.

2-3. Disassemble the oil filter screen and valve guide complete with retaining spring and valve ball.

Remove suction valve bolt and take out the ball. (Fig. 102)

(3) Breather (Later type)

3-1. Remove the under crank case, all transmission gears and shift drum stopper roller spring. Remove the shift drum stopper spring which retains the barriers.

3-2. Remove the 6 mm bolt on the top and disassemble.

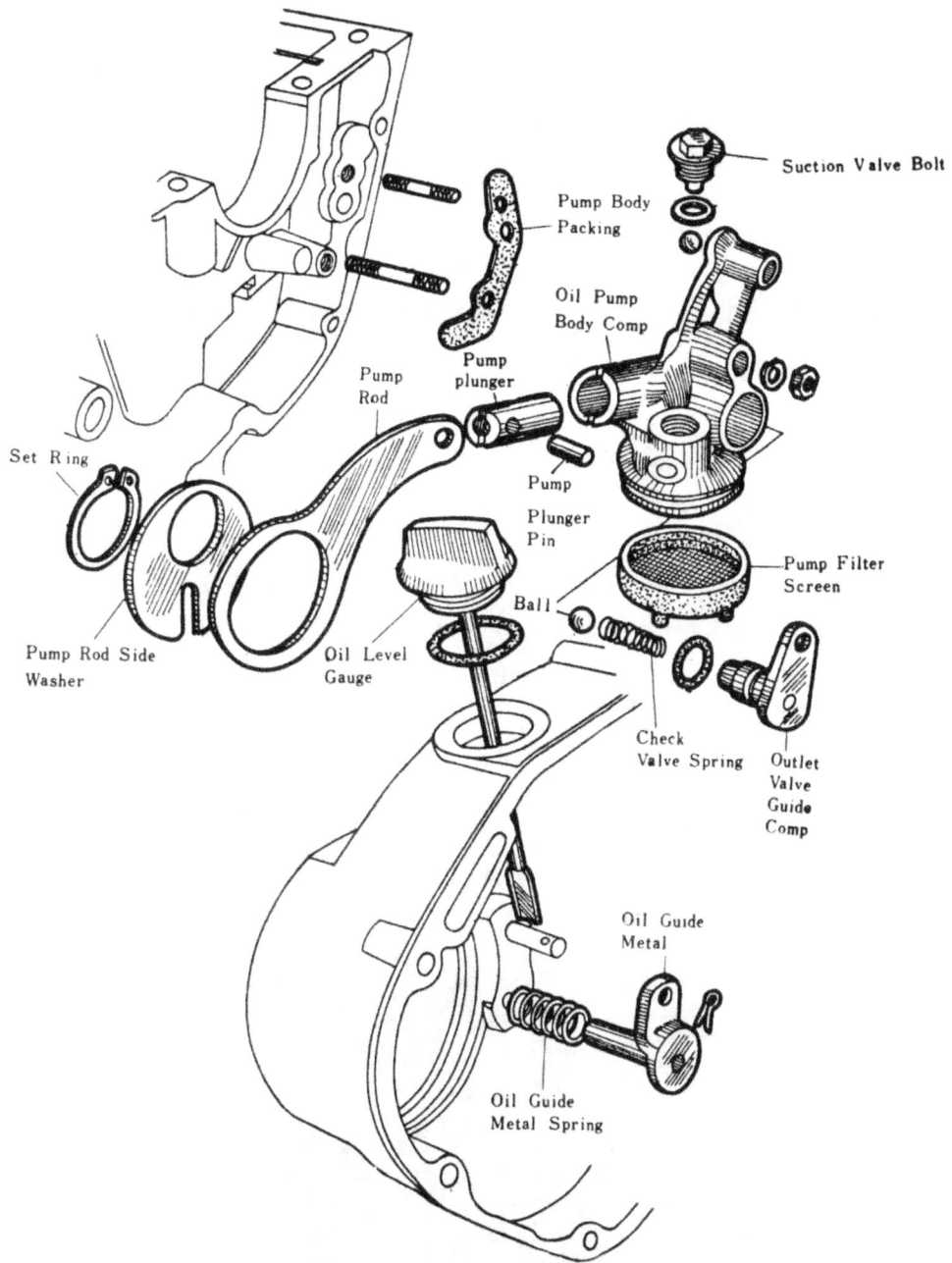

Fig. 102 Exploded view of oil pump

(4) Breather (Old type)

4-1. Remove the under crank case and crank shaft.

4-2. Draw out the breather seal from the crank shaft and examine the lips for wear or distortion.

II. Inspection and Repair of Oil Filter and Oil Pump.

(1) Clean thoroughly the parts with solvent, especially taking care with the inside of the filter.

(2) Measure the diameter of the plunger piston with micrometer and if go and no-go gauge is available check the inside diameter of the plunger body. Replace the pump of not complying with the specifications (P. 159)

(3) Visually examine the check valve balls and seats to ensure that they are in proper condition.

(4) After the pump is ressembled dip the oil pump screen in oil and work the pump by hand, checking the oil spurt out from the outlet hole on the valve guide.

(5) Replace rubber 0-rings and packings used on the oil pump.

III. Assembly of the Oil Pump and Oil Filter.

(1) Oil pump and oil filter

1-1. Place a new packing (gasket) on the correct position.

1-2. Assemble the oil pump body completely.

1-3. Attach the pump rod to the clutch outer with a set ring.

1-4. Mount the pump body together with clutch outer in position.

1-5. Secure with their respective bolts and nuts.

1-6. After the completion of the clutch assembly insert the oil filter body so that the pin across the bore of the filter meets the crank shaft slit. (Fig. 103)

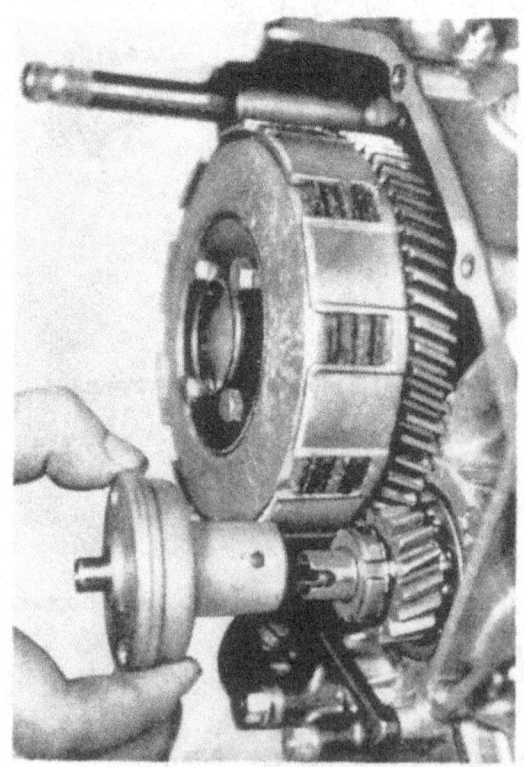

Fig. 103 Installing oil filter

1-7. Finish the assembly by attaching the R. crank case cover.

(2) Breather body.
- 2-1. Insert the oil separator into the chamber body, place the rubber valve and breather cap on the top, and tighten the separator with 6 mm bolt with the parts in position.
- 2-2. Before attaching the shift drum stopper roller insert stretched end of the roller stopper spring through the crank case to hold the oil separator.
  Fix the drum stopper roller with its bolt. (Fig. 104)

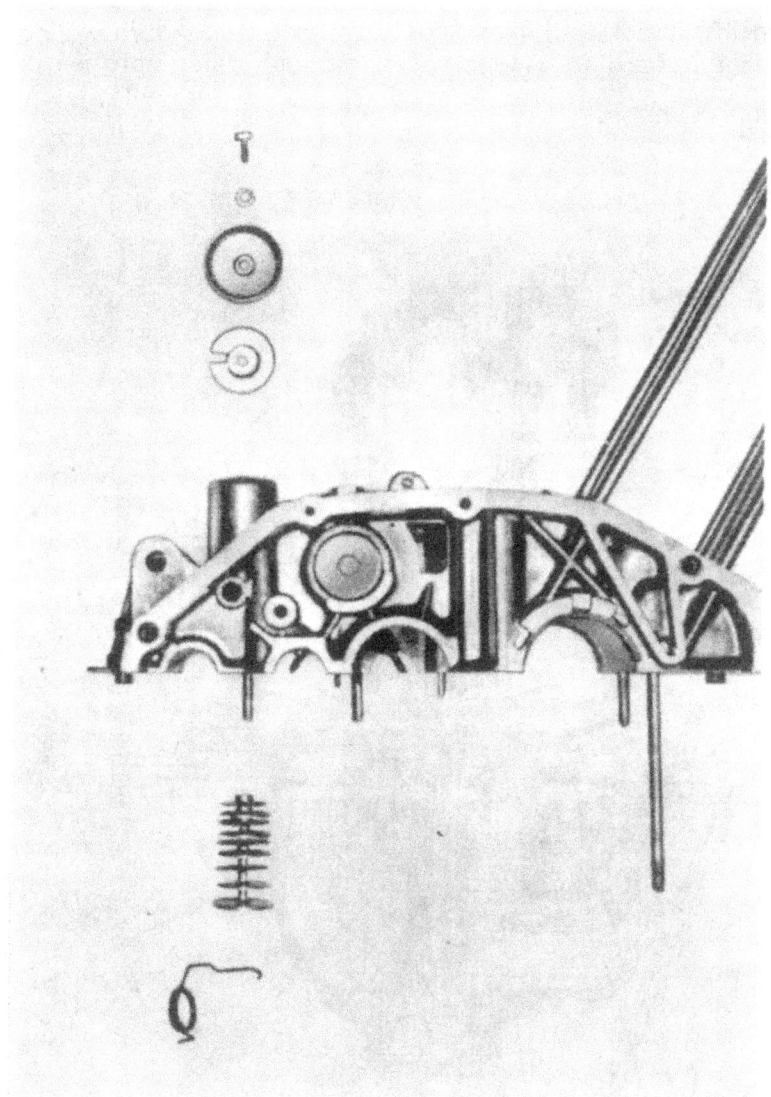

Fig. 104 Parts for funnel type breather

1-8. CARBURETTOR

The fuel is drawn into the sedimemt bowl which is combined with the fuel cock, and introduced to the carburettor through the rubber tube.

Two different types of carburettor are used, one of which is for standard and the other is for CB92 or CA95.

A special device as **power jet** is provided on the CB92 and CA95 carburettor for the purpose of increasing fuel supply at high revolutions.

A filter type air cleaner is used to prevent dust, dirt and other abrasive particles from entering the engine through the carburettor

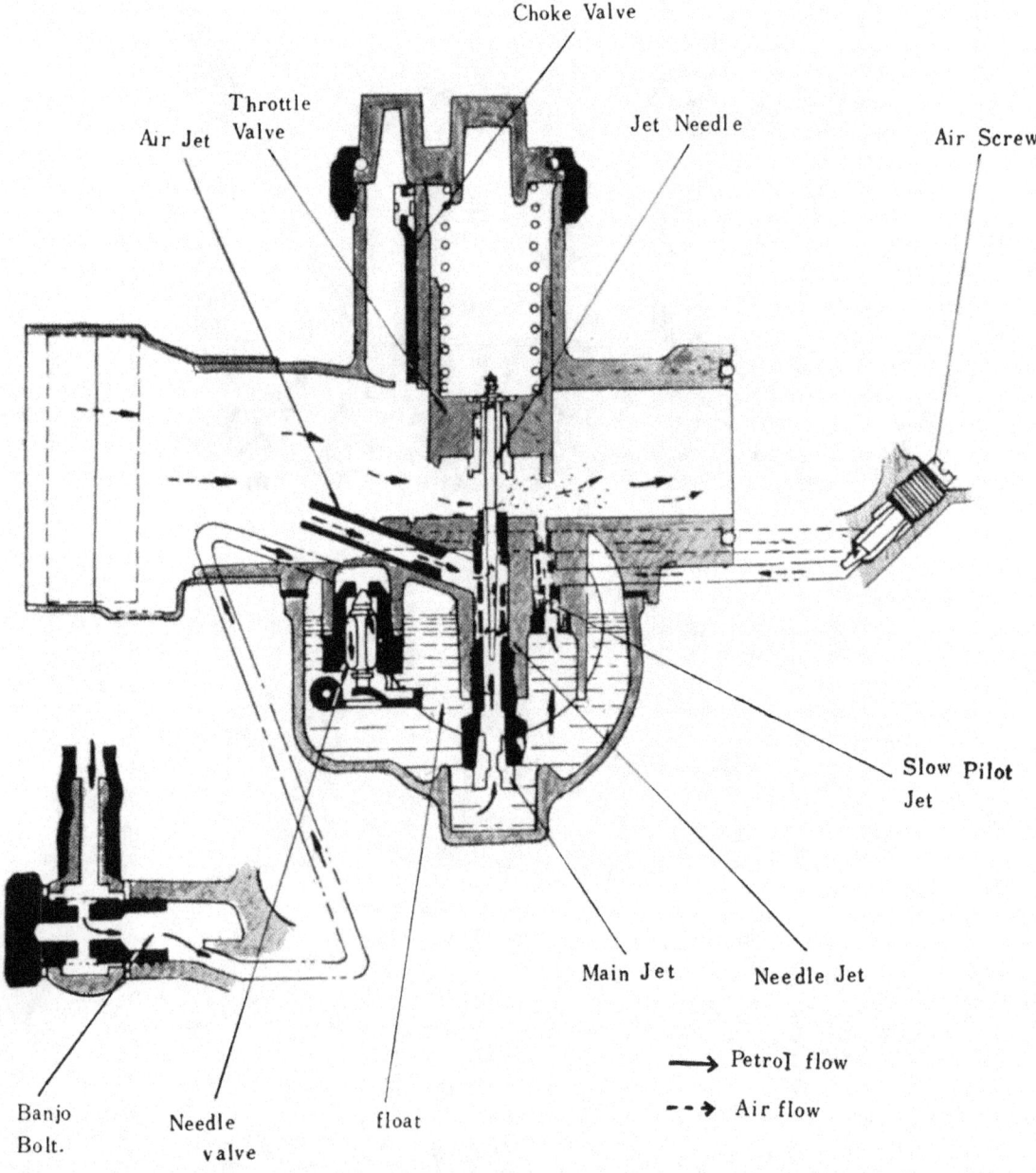

Fig. 105 Cutting view of over flowing pipe

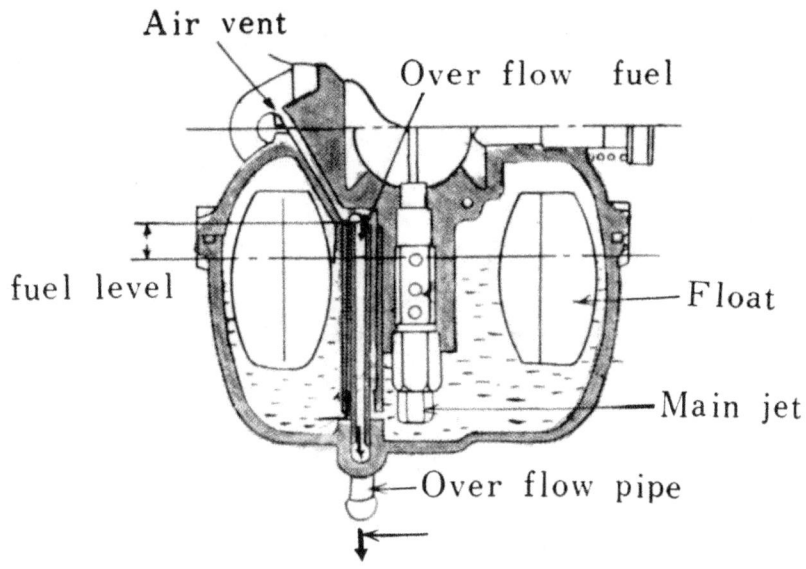

Fig. 106 Sectional view of carburettor

The fuel supplied from the tank is collected in the fuel chamber up to a constant level and sucked into the cylinder through two nozzles for standard, and three nozzles for CB92 and CA95.

The nozzles are called main jet and slow jet for both models, with additional power air jet for CB92 and CA95.

The slow jet acts mainly at the throttle oppening up to about 1/8, and the main jet which is controlled by the jet needle operates from the same opening to full throttle. The power jet works at 6000 rpm. or speed of 70 km/Hr with top gear. Therefore two kinds of adjustment are required separately for such as at low speeds and high speeds.

Sectional view of standard carburettor and its functions are illustrated by (fig. 106) and the setting sizes of their jets or nozzles are described as follows.

	C92	C95	CB 92 STD	Racing	CA 95 STD
Model of carb.	PW18HOV18	PW20HOV20	PW18HA3	″	PW20HA3
Main Jet	#90	#95	#85	″	#95
Air Jet	#150	″	#150	″	#150
Jet Needle	1.8331-3	″	18401-3	18401-4	18401-3
Throttle Valve	#2	″	#2	″	#2
Oppening rate of Air Screw	1½	″	1½ open	″	1¼ open
Slow Jet	#60	″	#35	″	#35
Power Jet	—	—	#200	″	#130
Power Air Jet	—	—	#160	#140	#130

Fig. 107. shows the section of the power air jet for CB92 and CA95

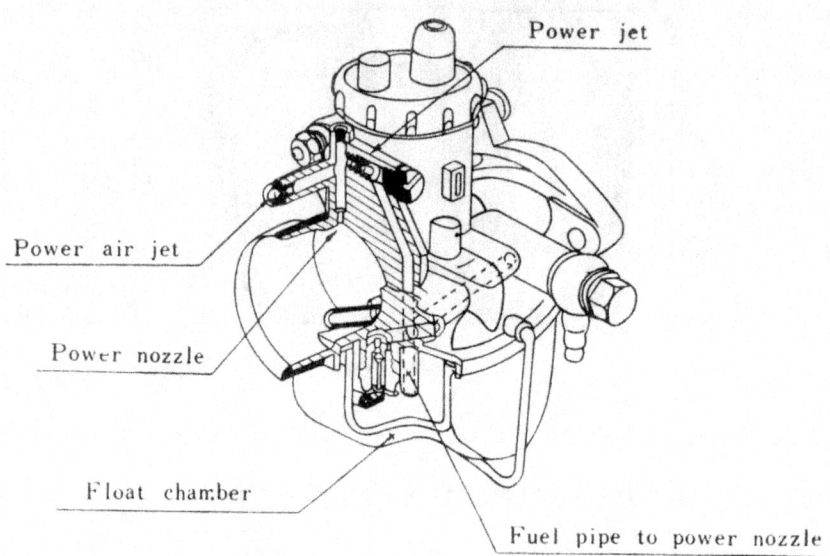

Fig. 107 Cutting view of power jet

I. Disassembly of Carburettor

(1) Shut off the fuel cock turning the tap to "stop" and take off the rubber tube from joint pipe at the carburettor.

(2) Unscrew the throttle top cap and draw out the throttle valve, remove the neddle clip plate fitted on the bottom of throttle valve dent and unhook the throttle wire end notch from it.

(3) Remove the rubber connecting tube clip at the intake port.
Remove two stud nuts where mounting on the cylinder and remove the carburettor assembly.

(4) Unhook the float chamber set clip to remove the float chamber body.
Drive out the float arm pin and remove the floats and needle valve.
Using 8 mm socket wrench, remove the valve seat.
Main jet may be removed with screw driver.
Remove jet needle holder and needle jet with 6 m/m socket wrench.
Remove the slow jet and power jet (for CB92, CA95) with a suitable driver.
Remove the air screw and throttle stop screw.

II. Cleaning and Inspection of Carburettor

(1) Clean all the parts with petrol paying careful attention not to damage the nozzles.

(2) Blow out all drilled passage in the carburettor body and all jets with compressed air. Visually inspect all jets for clog and remove any obstacle by compressed air. Do not use metal needle or other tool for stick.

(3) Inspect the tips of air screw, jet needle and float needle valve for defacement. Replace the parts having defacement.

III. Assembling of Carburettor

(1) Install all jets in their respective bores in the carburettor body and ensure that they are correctly fiitted into interior.

In this case attention is directed that headed screws are not damaged.

Whenever the carburettor is opened up, replace the packing (or gasket) or rubber O-rings.

Before installing the float chamber body inspect the height of float according to the paragraph regarding adjustment.

(2) Mounting on engine

Pass the throttle wire end through carburettor top, top cap, throttle valve spring and throttle valve to recess and install the jet needle with clip attached to the third place of notch from the top and fit the clip plate into the throttle valve.

Insert the throttle valve in the bore of the carburettor body and screw down the top cap compressing the spring.

Then mount the carburettor to the cylinder head stud and tighten with nuts evenly.

Connect the fuel rubber tube back to the connecting pipe.

Install connecting rubber tube to air cleaner completely and secure with clip ring.

IV. Adjustment of Carburettor

(1) Adjustment at high speed

When the throttle valve opening is from full to 1/2 open the fuel supply is controlled by main jet. Therefore, examine the performance and function when running at full throttle by closing the choke lever a little. In this case the phenomena can be read as follows:

1-1. If the speed increases, the mixture may be too weak and a larger size of jet is required.

1-2. If the speed decreases, the size of main jet may be either correct or too large, attempt the same test with a smaller size jet until the proper jet can be selected.

(2) Adjustment at intermediate speed.

When the throttle opening is from 1/8-1/2 way, the fuel supply is controlled by the height of the jet needle and the area of cutaway of throttle valve.

1-1. If the engine exhibits a tendency to exhaust black smoke and it is believed that mixture, is too rich, lower the jet needle by one notch, that is to say, the clip on the notch should be raised by one step.

1-2. At the instant of accelerating or while cruising with constant speed of abt. 1/2 opening of the throttle, and the engine happen to be misfiring, probably the mixture is be too lean, raise the jet needle position by one knotch.

The number marked on the throttle valve represents the size of cutaway area, and the large number is used for reducing the rate of petrol mixture, on the contrary, rich mixture is provided by the smaller number. But when adjusting the carburettor by the throttle valve, pay attention not to disturb the performance for less than 1/8 opening as this adversely effects the mixtures.

(3) Adjustment at idling speed

In the event of adjustment of throttle valve opening below 1/8, it should be born in mind that the fuel supply is controlled by pilot air adjusting screw and the cutaway of the throttle valve.

1-1. Mixture rate in the range will be adjusted by the pilot air screw. By tightening the screw, a rich mixture should be obtained and counterwise, the weaker.

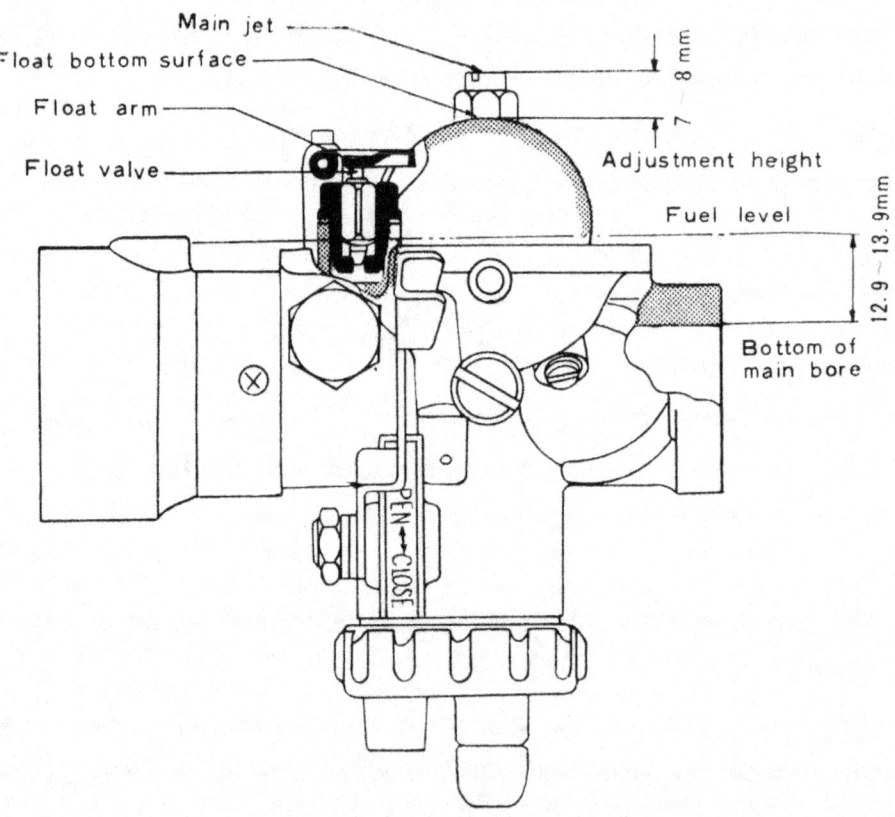

Fig 108 Adjusting float level.

1-2. The cutaway is requested to be replaced when the adjustment by the pilot air screw is deemed insufficcient from various points of view.

(A) Adjustment of float level

Place the carburettor upside down as illustrated in (Fig. 108), and measure the distance from the bottom face of the main jet to the float surface. When the float is supported with fingers until the float arm is about to touch the top of the float valve, the distance should be 7-8 mm (0.28~0.32 in), and if it is more or less than this amount, adjust the height, raising or bending the float arm carefully.

Once the distance aforementioned has been determined the height of the fuel level is correct.

The height of the level is 12.9 mm-13.9 mm (0.514~0.554 in) measured from the bottom of the bore for model PW 180 V 18 A 1.

MEMO

II CHASSIS

The frame and fork of all models are made of pressed steel in two halves welded together as a single unit.

For the standard model, the handle bar is of pressed steel, and for CB92 and CA95 is of steel pipe. Consequently, front and rear directional indicating winker lights are abolished on the model CB92 and CA95, while the standard is equipped with winker lights which are operated by a switch on the handle bar.

Front and rear suspensions are pivoted and are of swinging arm type, supported by coil springs internally, and provided with hydraulic shock absorbers.

All bushings of pivoted portions are rubber except front arm link pivot metal bushing.

Both front and rear tires are sized 3.00"×16" and the rear wheel is driven by the drive chain through the medium of rubber dampers.

The drive chain is concealed by the chain case which protects it from dust.

II-1. HANDLE AND VARIOUS CONTROLS.

The pressed steel handle bar for the standard model is fixed by two studs through rubber cushions, while the CB92 and CA95 pipe handle bars are fixed to the front forks with handle bar pipe holders.

The clutch and front brake cables for CB92 and CA95 are provided with grease nipples and adjusters of free play.

Fig. II-1. Handle bar (C92 STD)

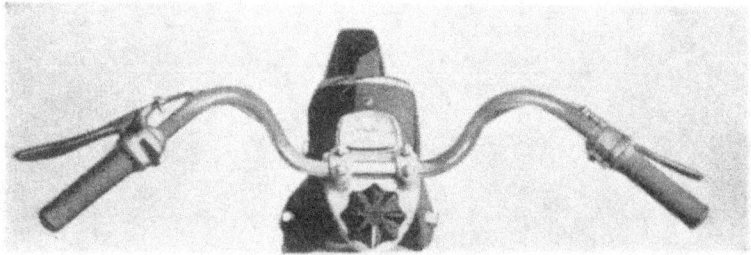

Fig. II-2. Handle bar for for CA95

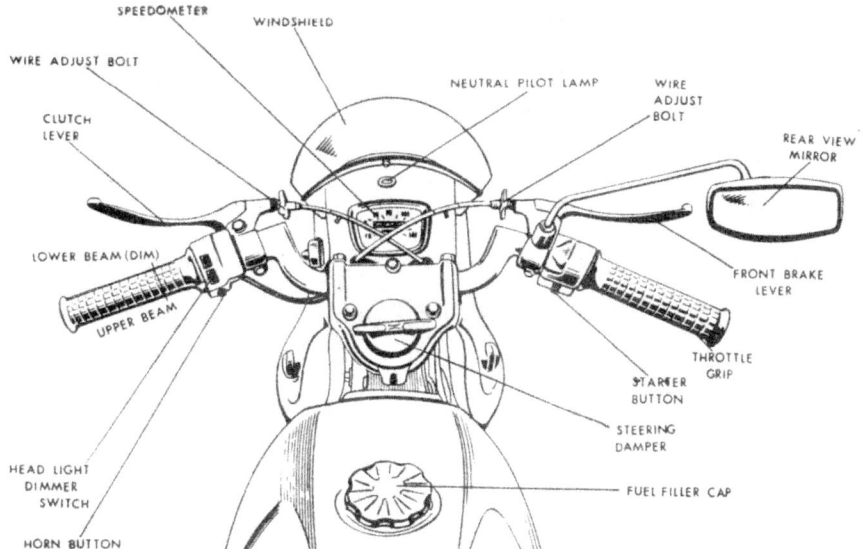

Fig. II-3. Handle bar (CB92)

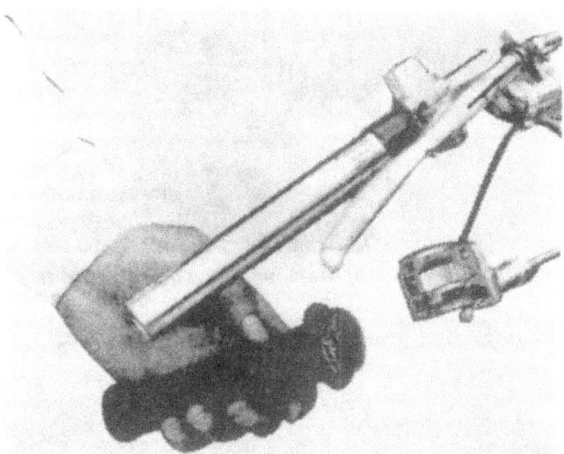

Fig. II-4. Removing throttle grip and stater button metal

Fig. II-5. Removing handle bar mounting nuts

1. Disassembly of Handle Bar.

— 71 —

(1) Remove the throttle, clutch, and front brake cables at the attachments to both handle levers and throttle control. The procedure for removing the throttle control is to begin with disassembling the starter button metal base and drawing out the throttle grip from the handle bar.

(2) Remove head light, behind the light, and disconnect the wiring which is relevant to the electrical operating switchs located at each end of the handle bar.

(3) Remove two mounting stud nuts under the handle bar (C92STD.).

(4) Remove the handle damper assembly, the handle bar pipe holder by withdrawing the retaining two 6 mm bolts and two 8 mm bolts. (CB92, CA95)

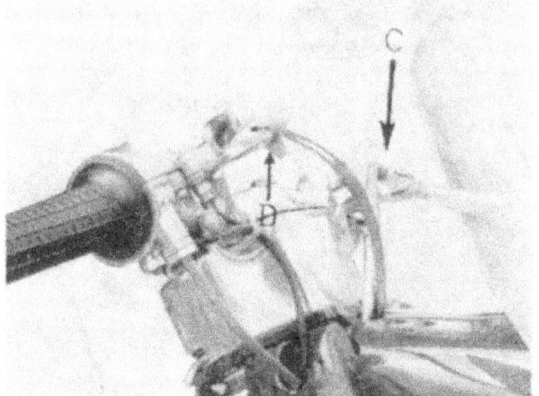

Fig. II-6. Wire adjusters on the control cables

Then the handle bar should be removed with the wiring of the electrical operating switches still attached.

II. Assembly of Handle Bar

(1) Place vibration damping rubber onto the stud bolts welded under the handle bar and install handle bar to the fork top bracket. (C92STD)

(2) Set one half-piece of the handle bar pipe holder and secure with, tightening screws. Then place the handle bar and the other half of the holder in position and tighten the bolts at the most suitable position of the handle bar (CB92, CA95).

(3) Complete assembling by attaching throttle, clutch, and front brake cables and handle levers. Connect the wiring in the head light case with their respective colors. Check and adjust free play and operations for the control cables.

(4) Special attention is required when passing control cables and electric wiring through respective openings in the handle bar, that the coverings of cables and wires may not be injured.

(5) Lubricate the control cables periodically. with cable lubricator if available.

II-2. FRONT FORK

The bottom of the steering columm (stem) is welded to the pressed steel front fork. The steering column rotates on the steering center line. Through the medium of ball races located at the top and bottom of the frame head.

The maximum steering angle is fixed by the stops on the steering column base. the angle of caster is decided by the welded angle of the column to the front fork.

Front forks for the standard model and CB92 or CA95 are not interchangeable and accordingly top bridge plates are not the same.

On the CB92 and CA95, the steering damper is provided for optional adjustment of the tightness of steering according to the road surface condition.

The head light case, front fender and handle bar lock are attached on the front fork. (Fig. II-7, II-8)

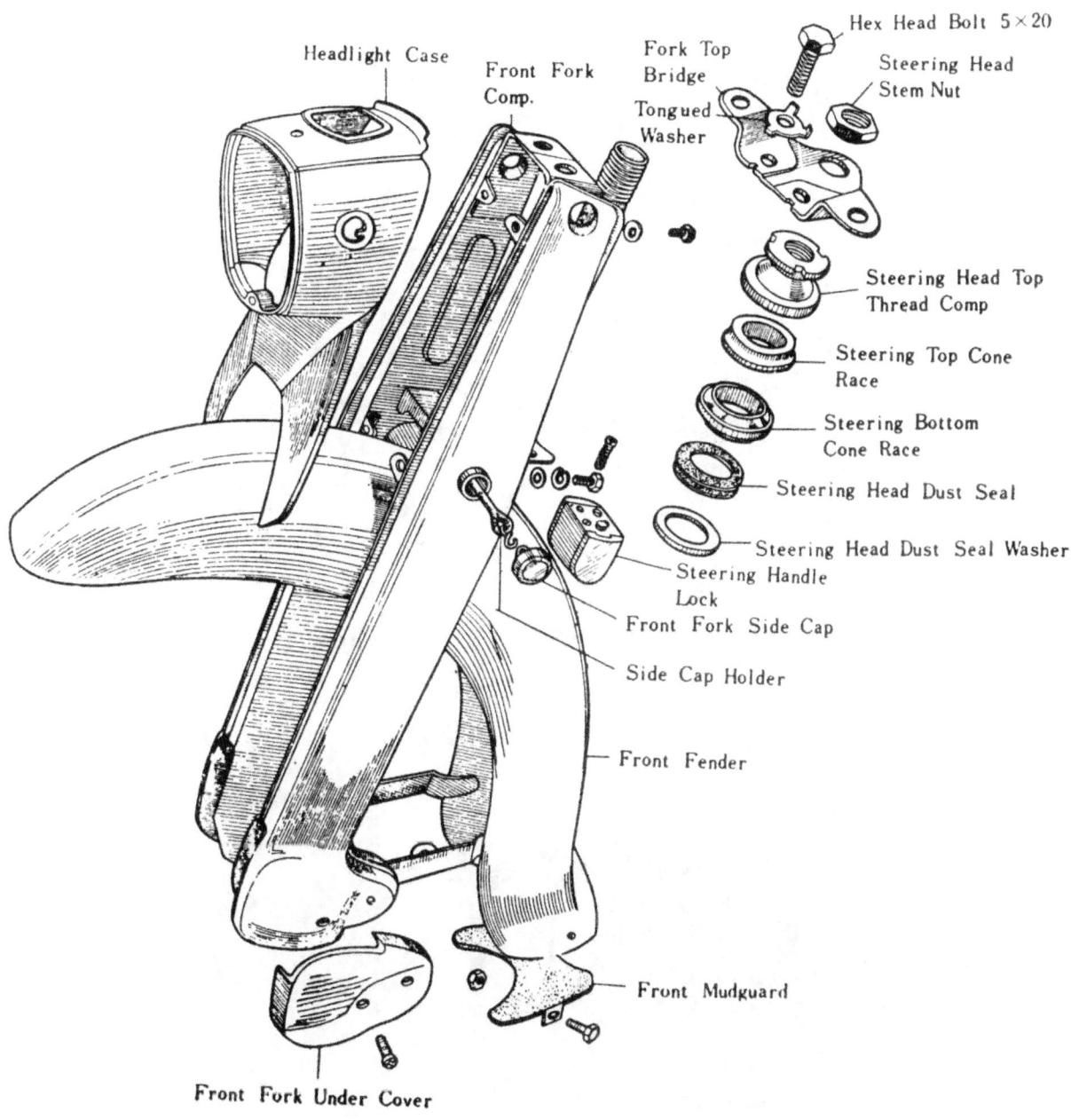

Fig II-7. Exploded view of front fork (C92)

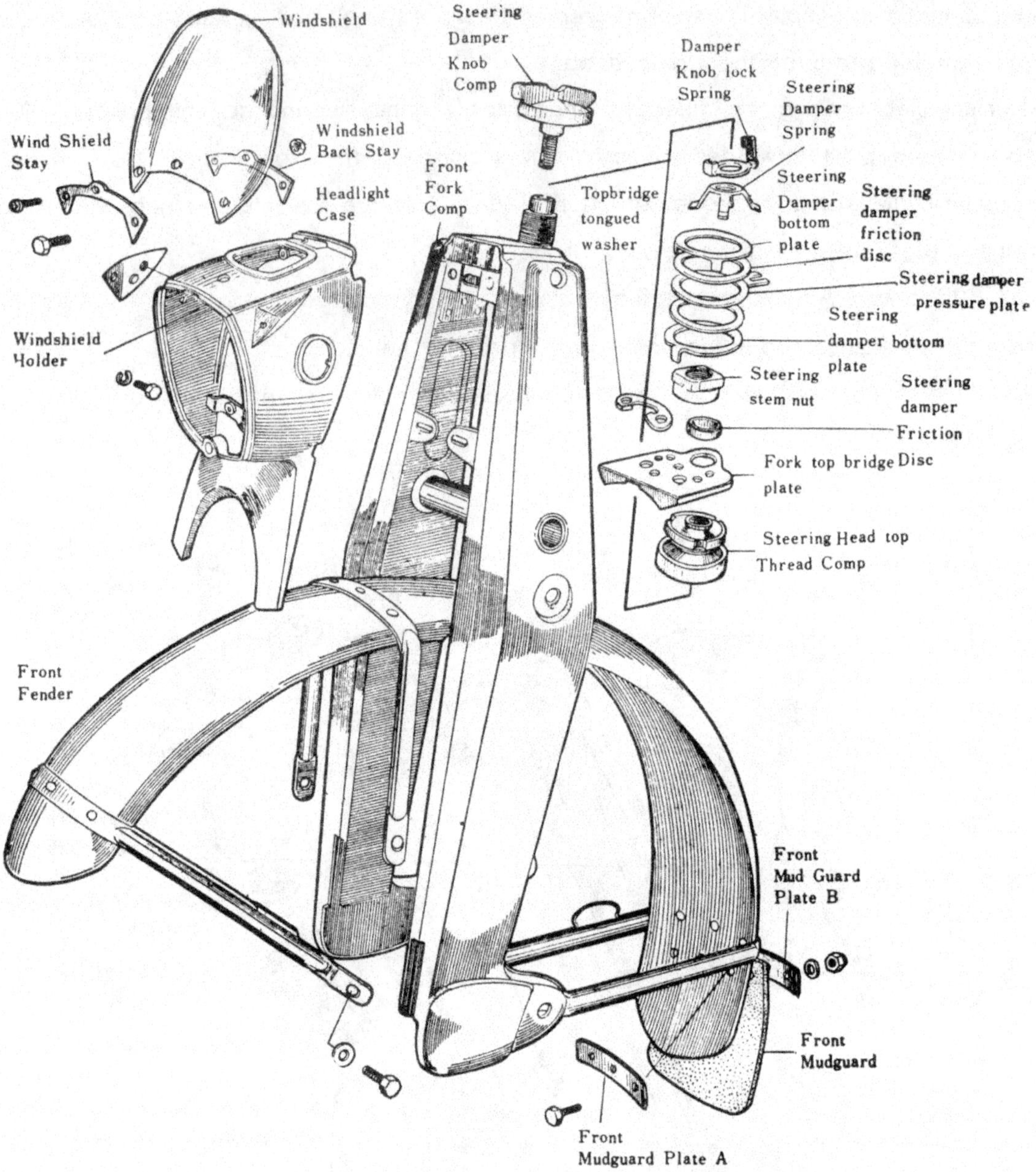

Fig. II-8 Exploded view of front fork (CB92)

1. Disassembly of front fork

(1) Remove front wheel (P. 85) placing a suitable support under the crank case.

Fig. II-9. Display of steering damper friction plates. (CB92 CA95)

(2) Remove the steening handle damper for CB92 and CA95. (Fig II-9)
Remove the steering handle, cushions and fender.

(3) Straighten the folding washers located on the fork top bridge plate, with a chisel and hammer, and remove the two bolts retaining the front fork and one big nut for the steering column. Then the fork top bridge plate should be taken off. (Fig. II-10 for standard model) (Fig. II-11. for CB92, CA95)

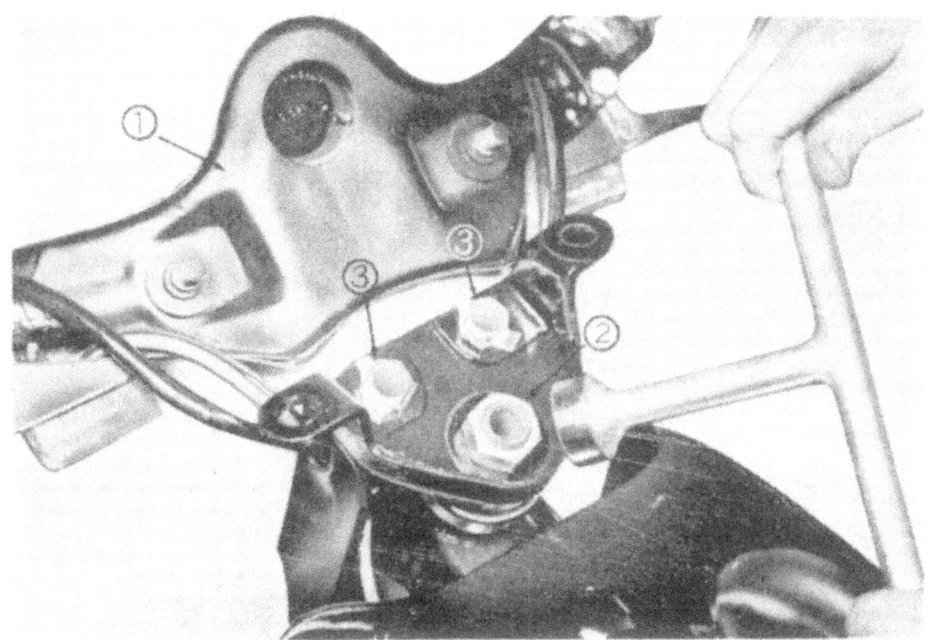

Fig. II-10. Removing steering stem nut (C92)

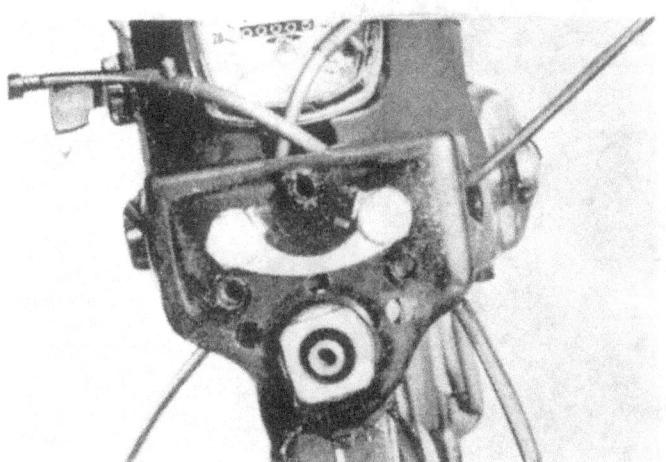

Fig. II-11. Steering stem nut and top bridge plate bolts (CB92)

Fig. II-12. Removing steering top adjusting nut and top race.

(4) Remove the combination switch from the head light case.
(5) Supporting the front fork assembly with one hand, unscrew the steering head top thread using a pin spanner and remove the top ball race. Then the front fork assembly may be taken out from under the head pipe. (Fig. II-12)
(6) Remove the head light case and the front fender from the fork.

— 75 —

1. Repair and assembly of the front fork.

    (1) Replace damaged or worn steel balls.

    (2) Replace damaged or defaced steel ball races.

    (3) Replace excessively twisted or bent front fork or steering column. If a special inspecting or truing jig is available, the checking is a simple matter but a rough check may be made using height gauge and flat surface bed.

    (4) Repack grease in the ball races fltted in both ends of the frame head pipe with medium toughness fibre grease and position all balls in grease to facilitate reassembly.

    (5) Install the front fork complete after ensuring that the dust seal washer, dust seal and the botton race are on the column. Place the top ball race over the upper balls and tighten with the top threaded cap.

    (6) Tighten the top threaded cap until looseness of steering stem has disappeared when shaking the fork to front and rear, and up and down.

    (7) Position the fork top bridge plate, tighten with the top bridge plate bolts and the column nut firmly, and fold up the washers. Check the steering ability by turning the fork to right and left sides. It should turn easily so that the fork continues to move when given a slight touch. Adjust the tightness if nessary. (Fig. II-13)

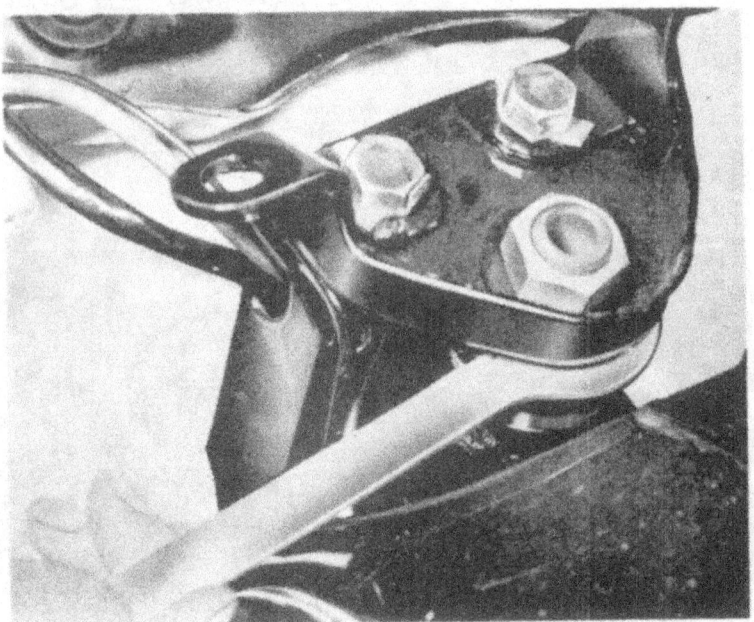

Fig. II-13 **Adjusting tightness of steering bearings.**

    (8) Attach all other parts such as the head light case and fender.

II-3. FRONT CUSHION

The front spring provided with the oil damper containing oil is installed inside the front fork. (fig. II-14) Construction of the springs and dampers are as shown in (Fig. II-15)

I. **Disassembly of front cushions**

(1) Remove the upper bolts and the pivot bolts of the front arms. Then the springs (cushions) may be withdrawn with the front arms. Remove the under bolts.

(2) Lift up the caulking at the end of the damper rod. Unscrew the bottom metal by holding the damper rod with a driver. Then remove the lock nut from the damper rod, and take out the coil spring with spring case.

(3) Interior of the damper piston is not recommended for disassembly and if there is any oil leakage or other defects are found, replace with a complete set of cushions.

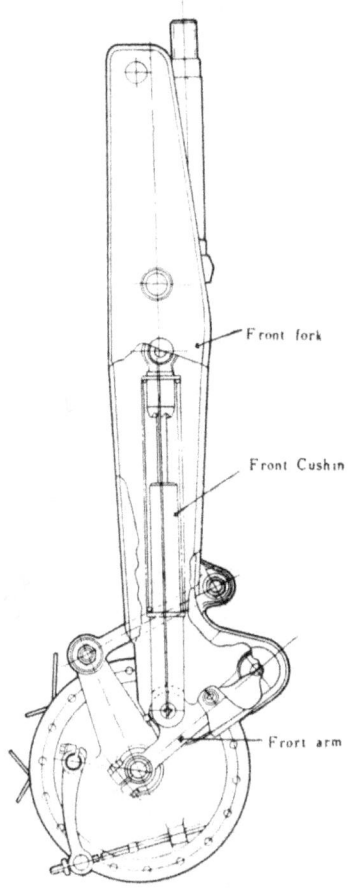

Fig. II-14. Construction of front fork cushion

II. **Inspection & reassembly of front cushions.**

(1) Measure the inside diameter of front arm pivot bore and the outsider diameter of pivot collar. Replace the part excessively worn.

(2) Measure the free length of the coil spring, tension and rightangleness. Replace the spring, if it does not agree with Specification (p. 161).

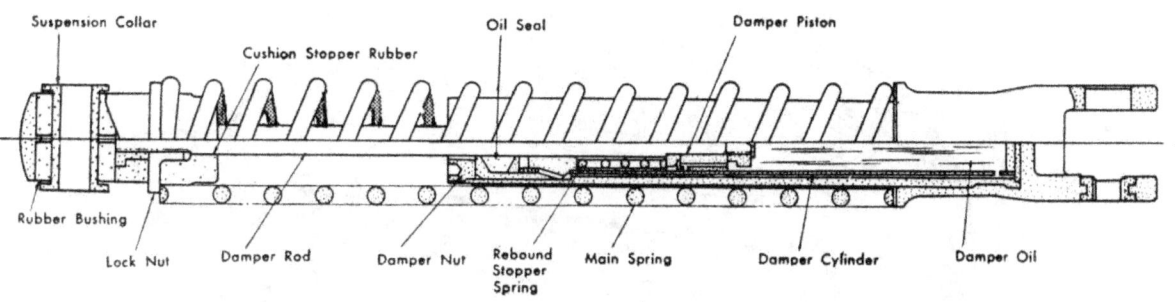

Fig. II-15 Front cushion ass'y.

(3) Visually inspect the rubber bushings and stopper rubber for damage or distortion. Replace the faulty parts.

(4) For reassembling the cushion, pull out the damper rod as far as possible and install the spring and spring case over the rod. By compressing the spring, install the lock nut on the end of the damper rod and screw-in the lock nut to the end, holding the shaft with driver. Install the bottom metal securely and caulk the end of the rod to the bottom metal.

11-4. REAR FORK AND REAR CUSHION

The front ends of the rear fork are supported from the frame with pivot bolt and the rear ends support the rear cushions. (fig. 11-16, 11-17) The shape of the cushion for CB92 is different from the standard model and the strength of the spring is adjustable in three steps.

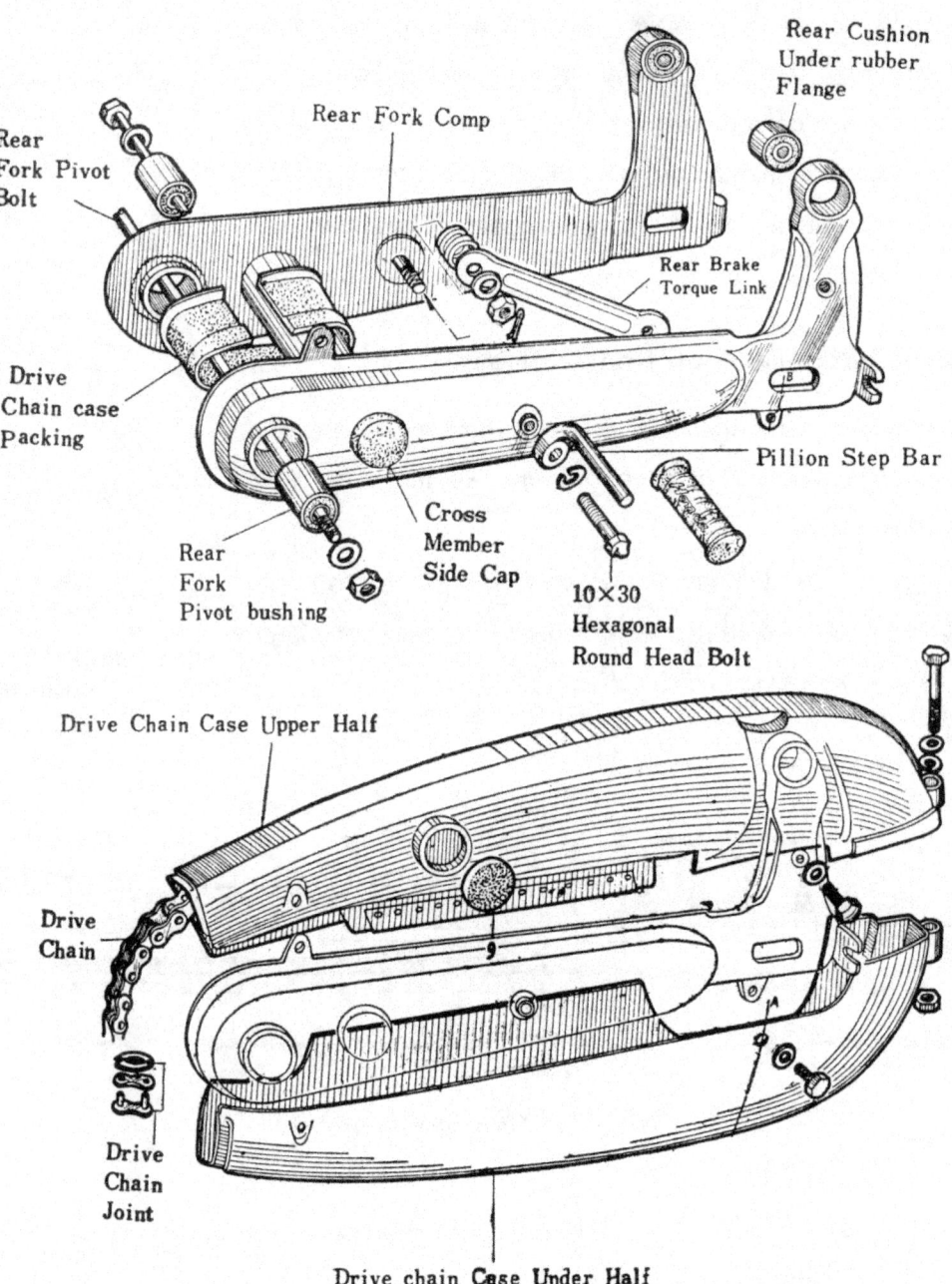

Fig. 11-16 Exploded view of rear fork and chain case (C92 & CA95)

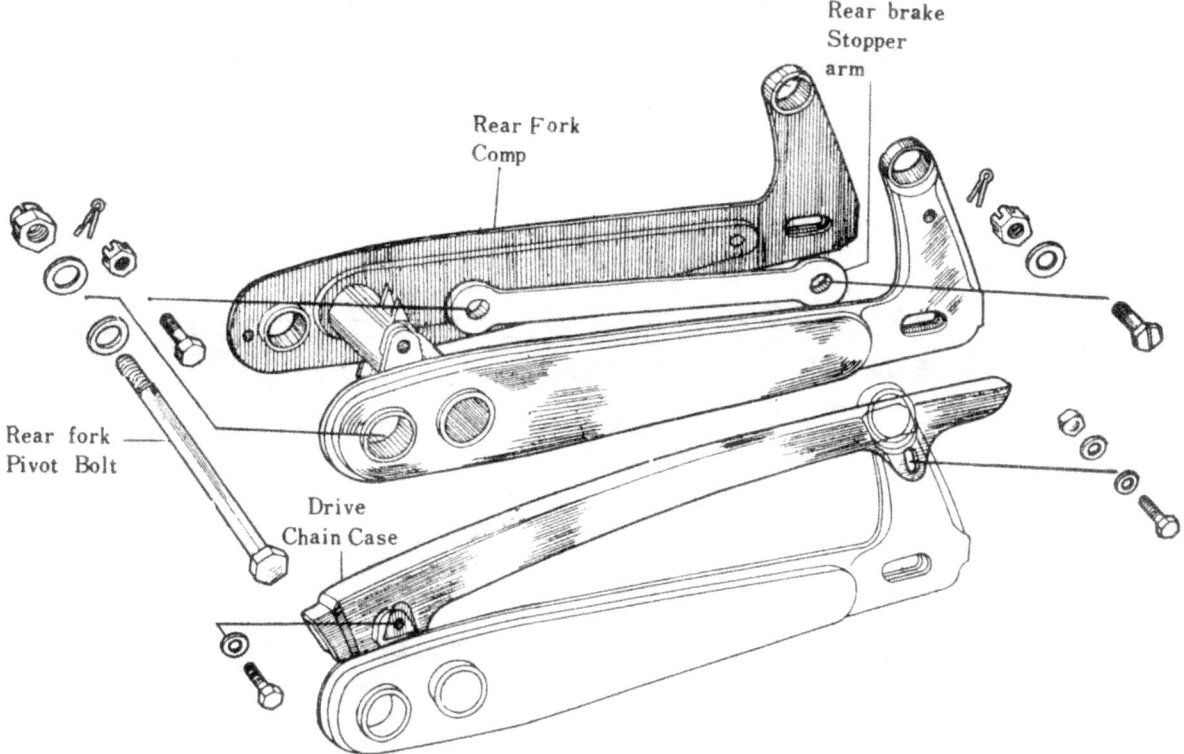

Fig. II-17 Exploded view of rear fork and chain cover (CB92)

A. REAR FORK

I. Disassemble

(1) Remove rear wheel and hub.

(2) Remove top and bottom chain cases and chain (C92 & CA95). Only top chain case and chain (CB92).

(3) Remove the lower cushion mounting bolts.
Remove rear fork pivot bolt nut, withdraw pivot bolt and take out the rear fork.

II. Inspection

(1) Visually inspect deformation or wear in rubber bushings and chain case packing. Drive out the defective bushing with driver and hammer and install the new bushing with press.

(2) For checking distortion or twist, insert a long bar which fits closely to the pivot bushing and support both ends with V-block on the flat surface.
Insert another bar through the rear end opening where the rear axle is installed and support the center of the bar at a point. Measure the difference between both ends with height gauge.
Use square gauge for checking twisting.

B. REAR CUSHION

Construction of the rear cushion is referred to in the sectional view of (Fig. II-18).

Spindle oil is contained in the cylinder and the effect of absorbing shock is shown by the action of piston and rod. The cushions for CB92 are not covered with cases and the tensions of their main springs are made adjustable by three steps

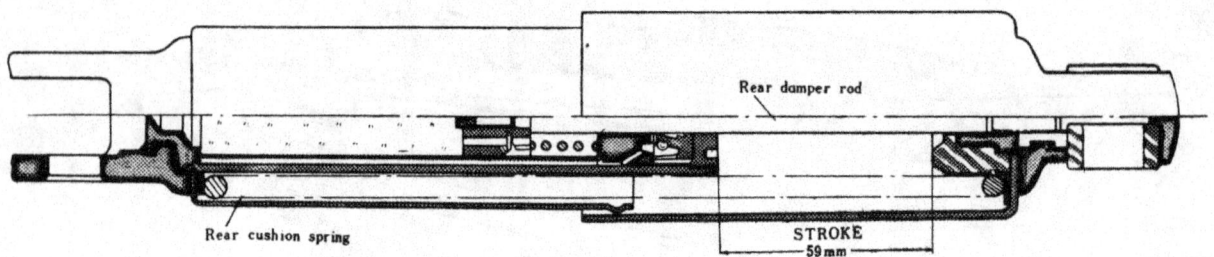

Fig. II-18   Rear cushion ass'y.

I. Disassembly of rear cushion

(1) Remove the rear cushion by removing upper and bottom support stud nuts or bolts.

(2) Remove the two cross head screws attached on the bottom metal.

(3) File the caulked part of the damper rod lock nut and remove it. In this case, hold the end of rod with screw driver to prevent turning. Then the case, spring and dampers are removed. (C92, CA95)

(4) Draw out the notch pin from the upper joint and remove it by un-screwing. Set the spring tension adjusting notch at the bottom. Compress the main spring with a spring compressor and take out the upper spring retainers and the set (for CB92)

II. Inspection and assembly

(1) Measure the free height and right angleness of the main spring, and replace the part if exceeding the limits of specification (p. 161)

(2) Replace the damper as a complete assembly if the damper rod is defaced or if oil leaks from the rod.

(3) Replace the stopper rubber if it has deteriorated or is damaged.

(4) Reassembly is done as follows :—
Pull out the damper rod all the way and install the main spring onto the damper. Fit the damper rod nut while compressing the spring. Tighten the nut, place the under case and tighten the lock nut. Attach the bottom metal. (C92STD. & CA95)
Compress the spring with the seat, screw in the upper joint to the rod and insert the pin through the joint and rod, then set the rear cushion spring retainers.

(5) Adjust the spring tension according to the riding purposes, that is for touring or racing, using pin spanner provided in tool kit. (Fig. II-19)

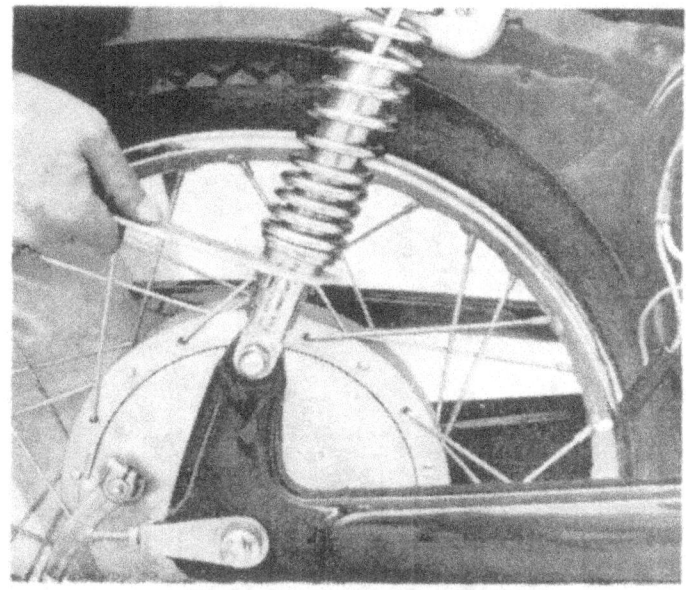

Fig. II-19 Adjusting tension of rear cushon spring (CB92)

II-5. REAR WHEEL AND REAR BRAKE

The rear wheel is driven by the sprocket attached on the flange through the rubber dampers. For C92STD and CA95 four semi-circular shape dampers are used and for CB92 there are four small round type rubber bushings. On both models, the rear wheels are removable without disassembling the rear flanges. (Fig II-20,)

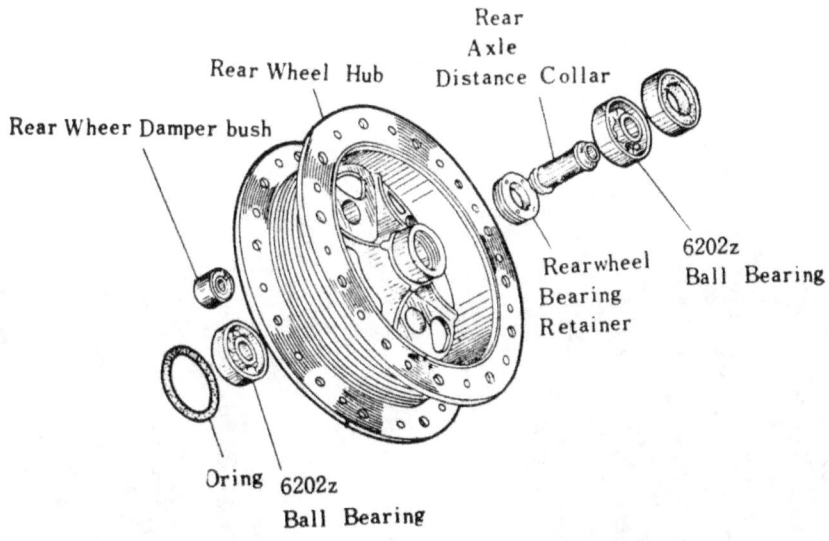

Fig. II-20 Rear wheel hub and damper (CB92)

Brakes are of a brake cam and an anchor pin for C92STD. model and CA95, but two anchor pins for CB92.

1. **Dissassembly of rear wheel**
   (1) With the stand in the standing position, remove the rear brake torque link bolt at at the panel and brake adjusting nut at the brake rod. Remove the rear axle and side collar.

— 81 —

Take out the brake panel with brake shoes attached. (fig II-21)

Fig. II-21. Removing rear wheel (C92 & CA95)

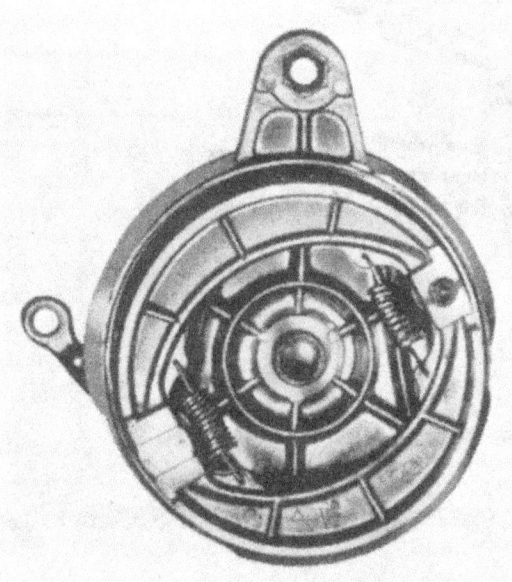

Fig. II-22. Rear brake shoes and panel (C92 & CA95)

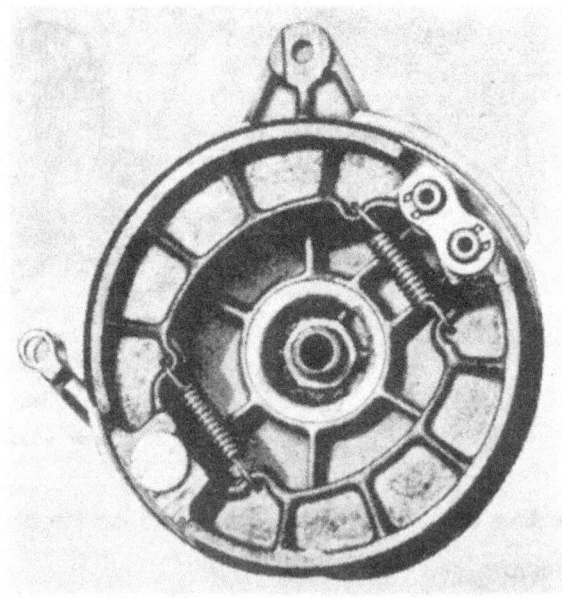

Fig. II-23 Rear brake shoes and panel (CB92)

Then withdraw the wheel from the flange and take out from the rear fork tilting the vehicle. (Fig. II-22, II-23)

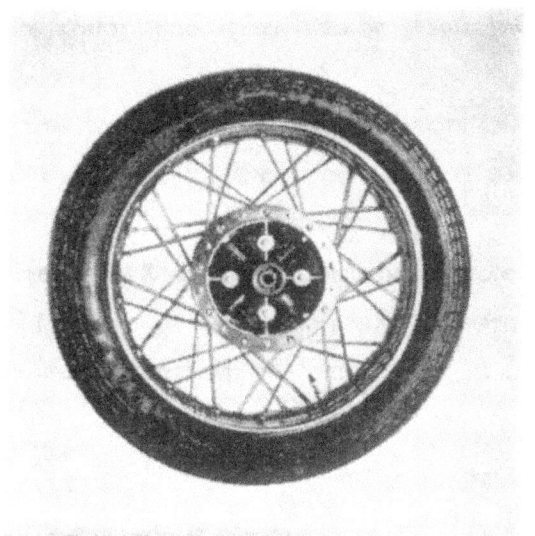

Fig. II-24. Rear wheel and damper (C92 & CA95)

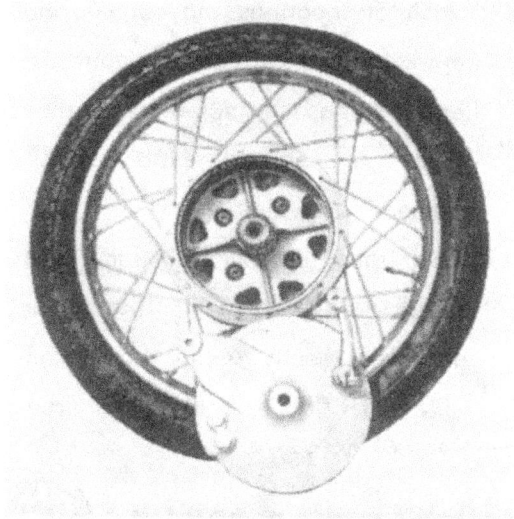

Fig. II-25. Rear wheel and damper (CB92)

(2) To disassemble the brake shoes, merely remove the brake springs (for C92STD. & CA95) and remove anchor pin set rings with a set ring remover, and the anchor pin washer. Then withdraw the brake shoes from the anchor pins. (for CB92) (Fig. II-24, II-25)

(3) The bearings can be taken off by hand but if tight, take it out tapping lightly on the inside. The oil seal can be removed at the same time.

(4) Wheel bearings and oil seal:-
Remove 6 mm bolts retaining the damper rubbers and take out the four pieces of rubbers. (for C92STD & CA95)
Drive out the rubber dampers with a driver and hammer or a press. (for CB92)

(5) Tyre and tube
Remove the tube valve cap and valve using the tip of valve cap to deflate tube of air. Lay the tire on ground and press the side of tire to force out the tire bead from the side of the rim. Insert two tyre levers between rim and tire bead, and pull tire bead out away from the rim plying with the lever all around.
Push the valve stem into the rim and take out the tube from the tyre. For preparation of repairing the tube a piece of rubber and rubber paste and scissors are provided in the tool kit.

II. Inspection and reassembly.

(1) Repair tyre and tube if necessary, and push the tube back in between the tyre and rim aligning tube valve with hole in rim and making sure that tube is not twisted. Using the tyre levers to pry the bead in the rim all around. Gradually inflate the tyre ensuring the bead fits into the rim up to the pressure of 32 lbs/in^2.

(2) Wash all bearings thoroughly and check for excessive radial play and roughness. Replace if it is in bad condition.

Repack grease completely on the bearings and fit into hub.

(3) Check oil seal and rubber "O" ring on the hub for distortion and replace if it is deemed unservicale.

(4) Install the rear axle through the bearings and hold the axle stationarly between blocks (refer to fig. II-26), set a dial gauge on the face of the rim and hub drum, turn the wheel gently with reading amount of run-out. If run-out of the drum exceeds 2.0 mm (0.08"), replace the drum.

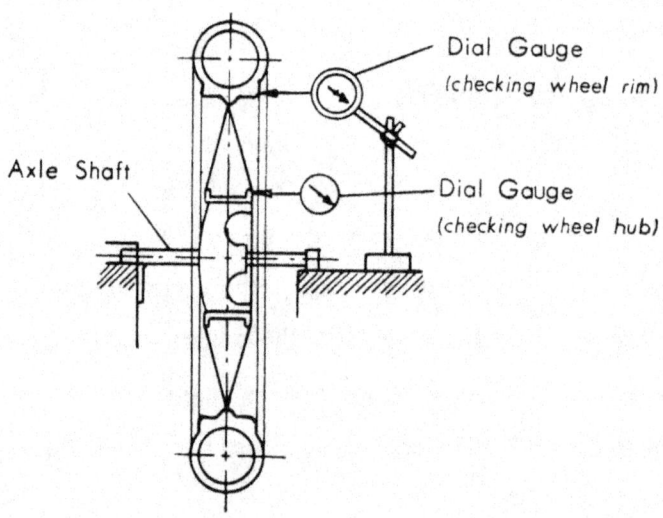

Fig. II-26. Checking nun-out of wheel at rim and drum

(5) Tightening spokes

Retighten and adjust the spokes evenly so that run-out of the rim will be within 3.0 mm (0.12"), and if it is found that, this cannot be a quite remedy, the rim may be warped which should be replaced.

(6) Brakes

Measure outside diameter for wear and replace if it is out of specification p. 161 Replace the brake shoe complete if the lining exceeds the wear limit.

Insert the brake cam into the brake panel and fix the cleated end with brake arm. Install the brake shoes on the panel and fix with brake shoe springs, (C92STD) Check tolerance between brake shoes bore and the anchor pin for excessive wear and if it is deemed unserviceable replace the brake panel and/or brake shoe (CB92) Install the brake shoes on the panel and set the clip rings on the end of anchor pins. (CB92)

(7) Install the rear wheel hub onto the rear flange, the panel and the collar, insert the rear axle and tighten the nut after adjusting the graduation of wheel adjuster.

11-6. FRONT WHEEL AND BRAKE

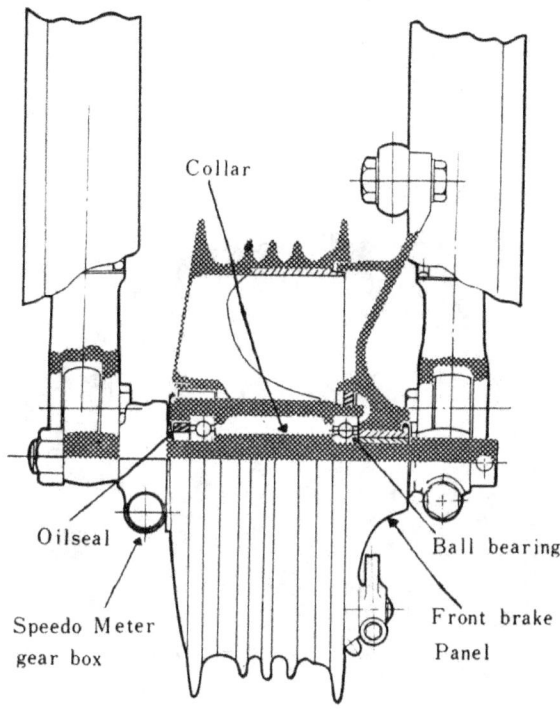

Fig. II-27 Construction of front wheel support.

1. Disassembly of front wheel

Place a stand of suitable height under the engine to lift the front wheel from the ground. Remove the brake adjusting nut, front arm lock bolt on left side for C92STD. and CA95 and both front pannel stopper bolt and axle nut. Withdraw the axle and raise the front fender up enough while the wheel is taken out from under the fender. (Fig. II-29)

Fig. II-28 Removing front wheel (C92 & CA95)

The front fender of the CB92 is attached on the front brake panel and it is removed from the front fork as unit with front wheel. To take out from the front fork turn the fender to where the dents of the fender meet with the both side torque link supports and draw out through them. (Fig. II-29)

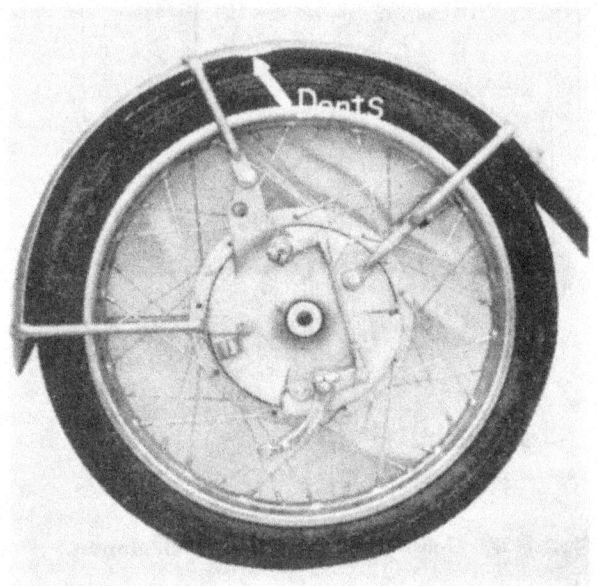

Fig. II-29. Removal of front wheel and fender

The brake shoes are easily removed when the shoe springs are removed for C92STD and CA95, but for CB92 remove each anchor pin set ring with set ring remover, and remove after the springs have been removed.

Fig. II-29. Removal of front wheel and fender

II. Inspection rnd reassembly

Inspection and reassembly of the front wheel is refered to the procedure as described in the paragraph of rear wheel and brake: Check the front panel spacer for excessive tolerance to the panel and replace if necessary. (Fig. II-30)

For CB92, as double cams are applied on the front brake, adjustment of the brake rod is required as referred to p. 132 after reassembly.

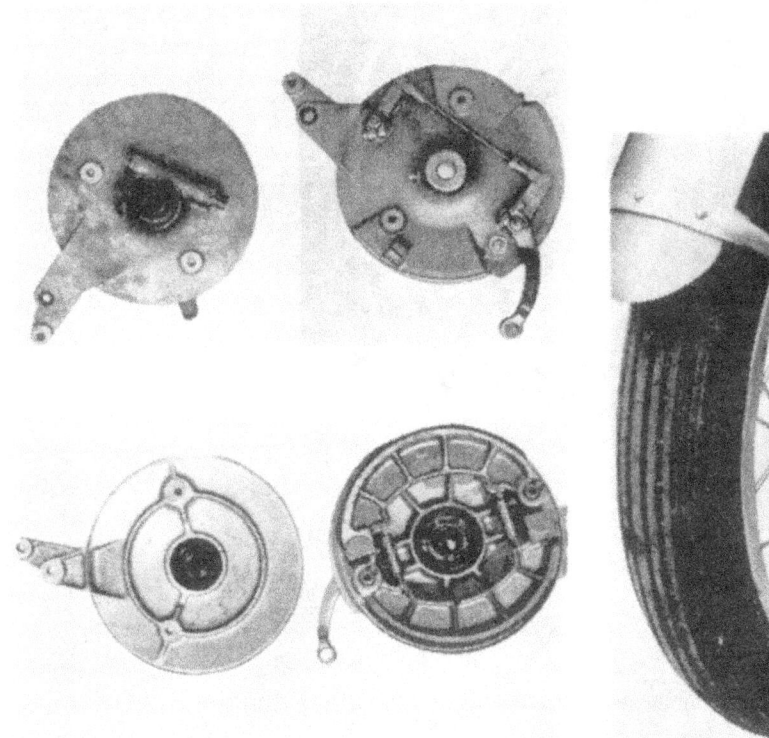
Fig. II-31. Front brake shoes and right and left side panels.

Fig. II-32. Removing panel air guide cap (CB92)

All the nuts should be tightened to the specified torque, and the front tyre must be inflated to 28 lbs./in.

(Note) Front and rear brake panel air guide cap is provided on CB92 so that they can be removed for cooling of brakes at entry of races. (Fig II-32)

II-7. DRIVE CHAIN AND DRIVE FLANGE

A special size of drive chain (No. 428) is applied on all models, and the transmission of power to the rear wheel is made by a flange interlocking with the rubber couplings in the rear wheel.

The chain is sealed completely with the chain cases for C92STD and CA95, and for CB92 is not sealed completely. (Fig. II-33)

Fig. II-33. Removal of rear wheel (C92, CA95)

1. Disassembly.

Remove the chain case or chain cover and disconnect the drive chain. Remove the axle sleeve nut and remove the rear flange. (Fig. 34, 35)

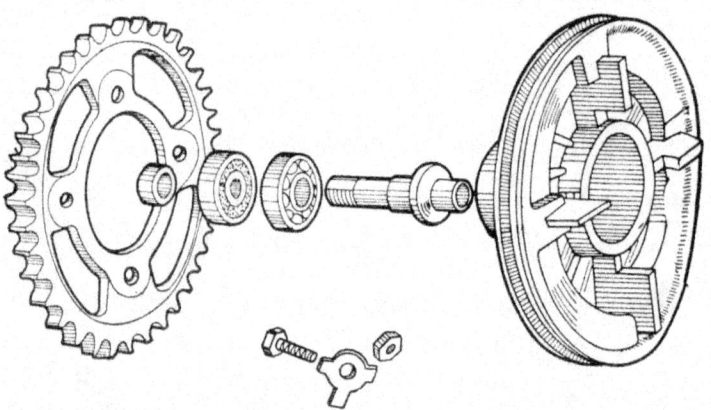

Fig. II-34. Rear drive flange and sprocket (C92 & CA95)

Straighten the folding washers using chisel and hammer and remove the nuts. (C92STD and CA95). Remove the cotter pins on the lock nuts then remove the rear sprocket. Withdraw the sleeve shaft and take out the oil seal and bearing.

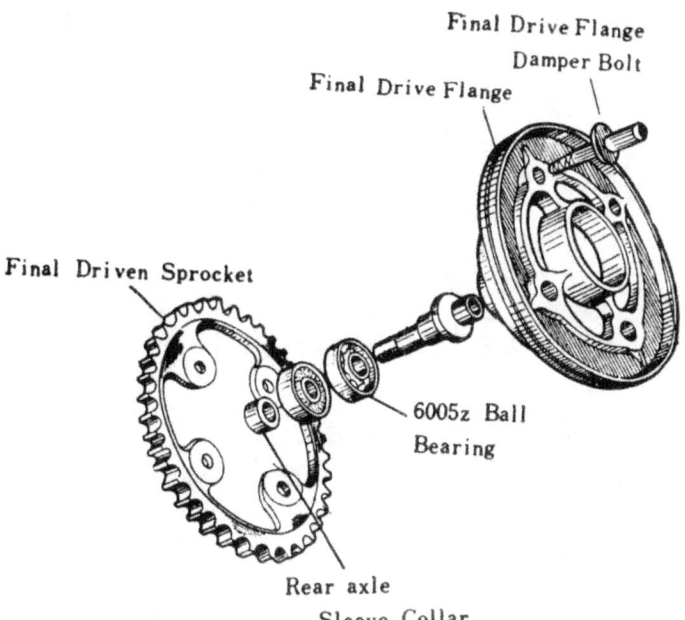

Fig. II-35. Rear drive flange and sprocket (CB92)

II. Inspection and reassembly.

(1) Cleanse all the parts with solvents and check for wear of the bearing, sprocket and oil seal whether to be disposed or not.

Repack grease,, reassemble the complete parts and install to the wheel hub.

(2) Drive chain

Wash the chain thoroughly with petrol and dry it.

Interlock the chain with the driven sprocket about 2/3 way of the circumference and check looseness by pulling the chain at the middle portion, then if distortion exceeds more than 5 mm replace the chain.

To grease the chain, melt some amount of chain grease in a vessel with a slow fire, dip the clean chain in the grease for a while and take it out from the grease. Wipe off extra grease stuck around the chain.

In the connection of the chain, a caution is to be paid that the opening of the connecting link clip faces opposite direction of chain rotation.

(3) Visually inspect the bearing and oil seal, and replace if excessively worn.

(4) If the damper rubbers are deteriorated, replace them.

(5) In the event where the spocket is replaced, fold up the washer of the binding nuts securely.

II-8. FUEL TANK AND FUEL COCK

The fuel tank is supported to the frame through the vibration insulating rubber cushions. Under the left side of the frame, the fuel cock whose tap is operated at three positions; "Stop",

"Reserve" and "on", is located. At the position of "RES" the tank reserves about two liters of petrol.

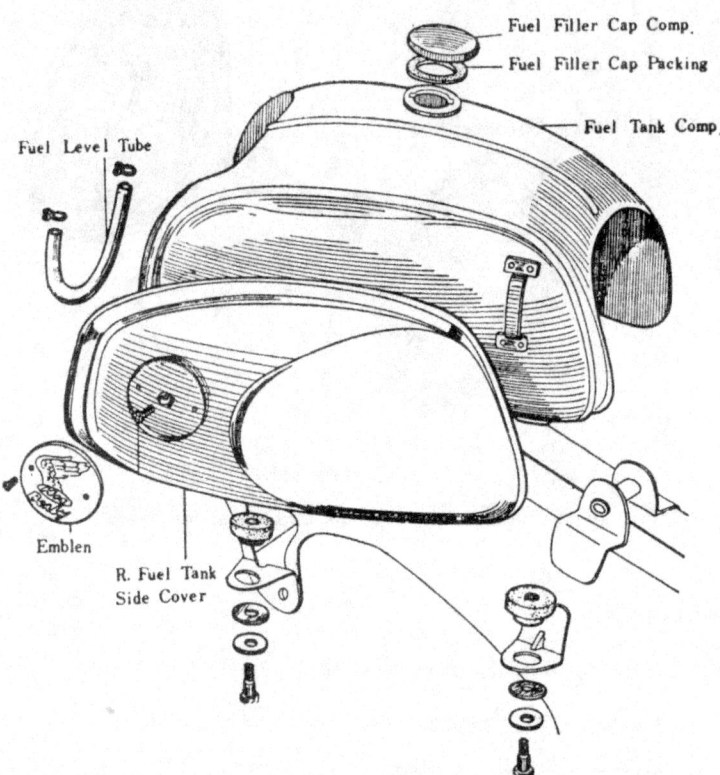

Fig. II-36. Fuel tank support (C92 & CA95)

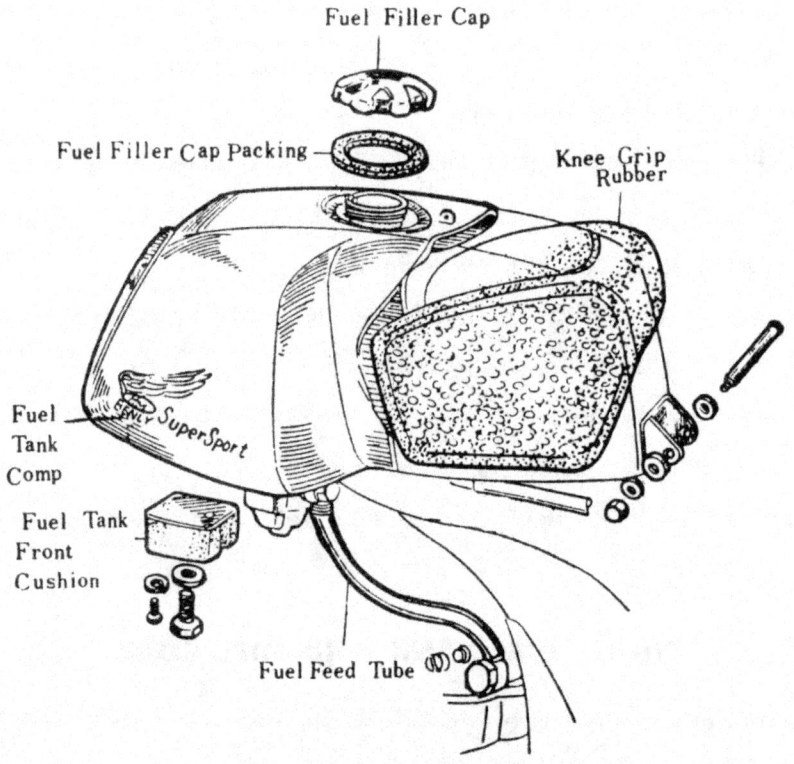

Fig. II-37. Fuel tank, support (BC92)

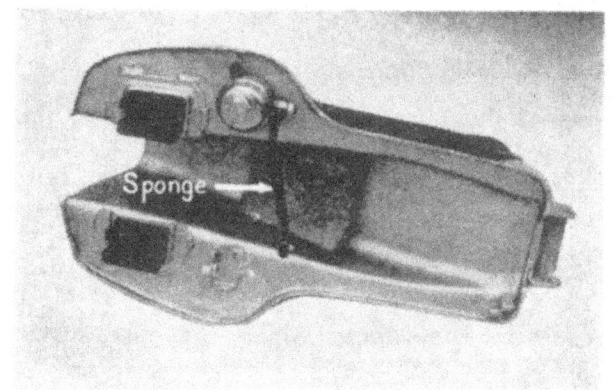

Fig. II-36 Support and sponge (CB92)

1. **Disassembly**

    (1) Remove four mounting bolts.

    (2) Set the tap of the fuel cock to "stop" and disconnect the tube leading to the carburetter. Then disconnect the front level tube and plug the holes so that the petrol does not flow out. Remove the fuel tank four mounting bolts (92 STD), and two mountings front and one hinge bolt at rear end on the frame (CB92) Then the fuel tank can be dismounted from the frame. Remove the fuel tank. (fig. 36, 37)

    (3) Replacing the fuel cock

    Remove the fuel bowl and take out the rubber gasket, then unscrew the three screws retaining the cock to the tank. Before removing, fuel should be drained. (fig. 38)

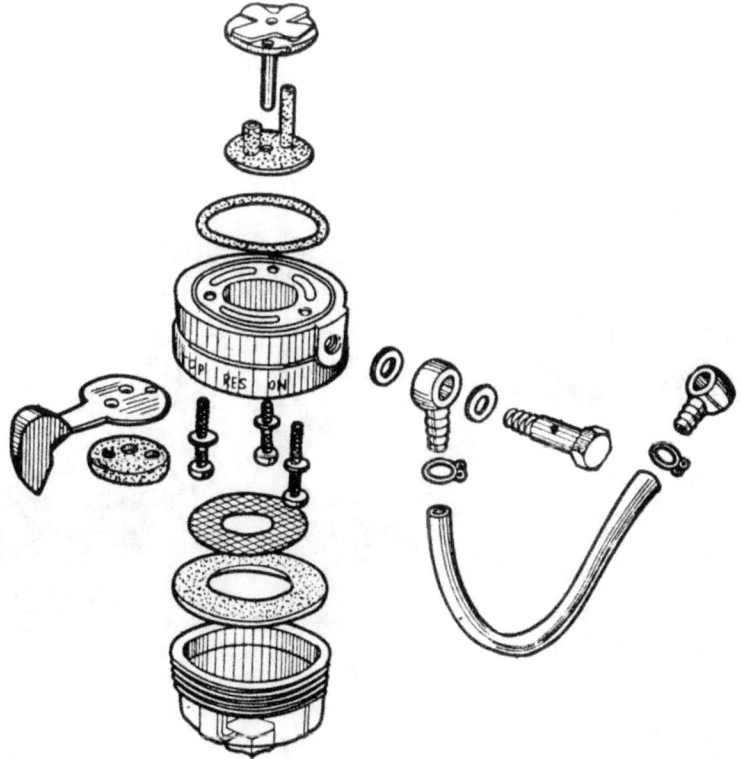

Fig. II-38. Fuel cock

2. Replacement of side cover

If it is required to replace the fuel tank side cover, remove the tank emblem and unscrew the screw behind and remove the chromium plated side cover thrusting backwards.

11-9 AIR INTAKE

The air cleaner element is made of filter paper which prevents dust from entering sufficiently. The air cleaner is located in the middle part of the frame and connected with the rubber tube to the carburetter. (fig. II-39)

I. Disassembly

Remove the carburetter covers, and then insert the hand under the carburetter and disconnect the connecting rubber tube at the end of the air cleaner removing the clamp on it. Remove tool box cover on the left side and tool tray board with the air cleaner as fixed on. (fig. II-40)

II. Installation

After servicing the air cleaner as referred in p. 135., be carefull to insert the connecting tube, air vent plastic tube and power air jet tube (for CB92, CA95) to their respective holes.

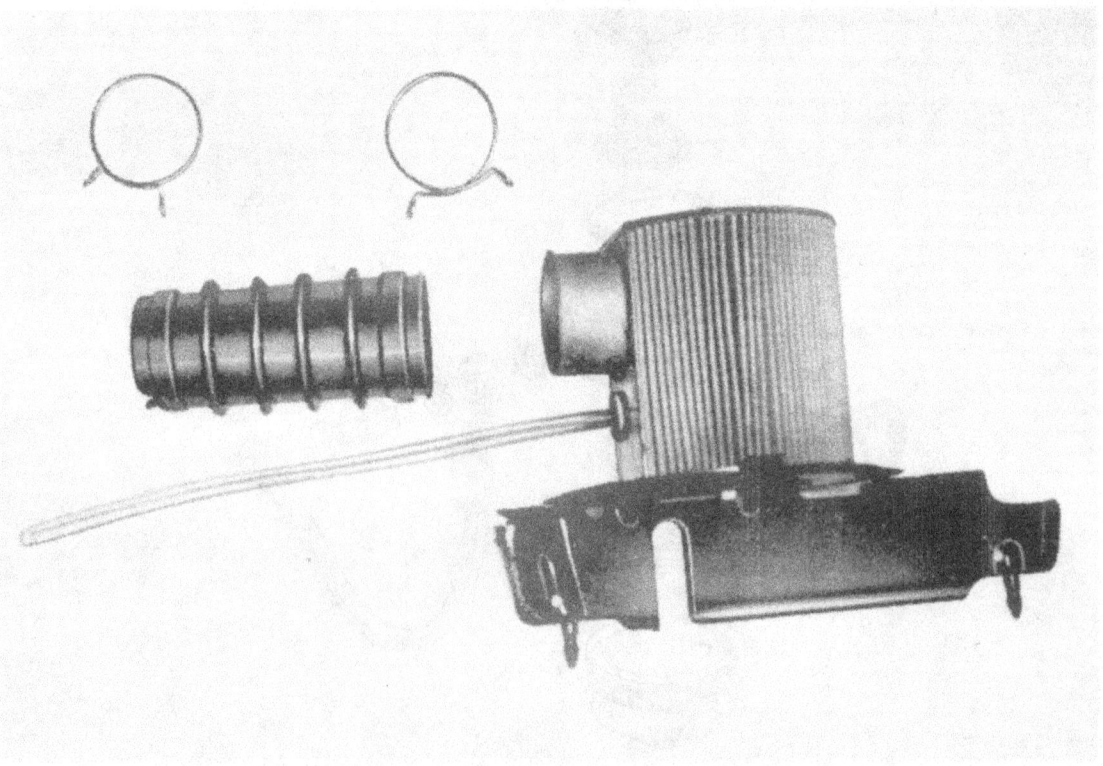

Fig. II-39. Air cleaner (C92. & CA95)

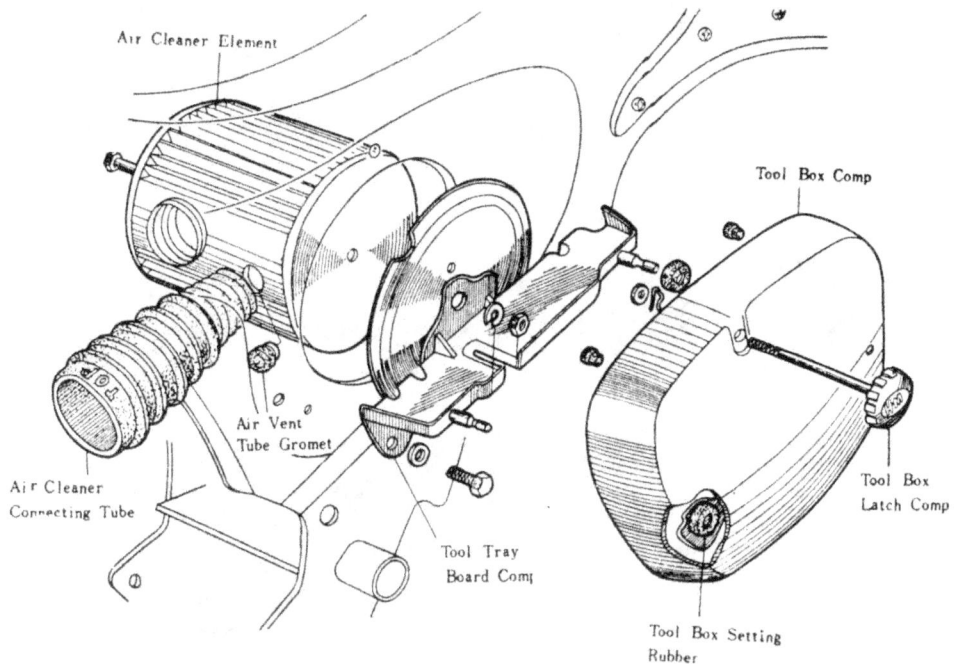

Fig. II-40. Location of tool tray board

II-10 EXHAUSTS

As to C95, up swept exhust and mufflers are provided for use connected with their attachments and tool and battery box.

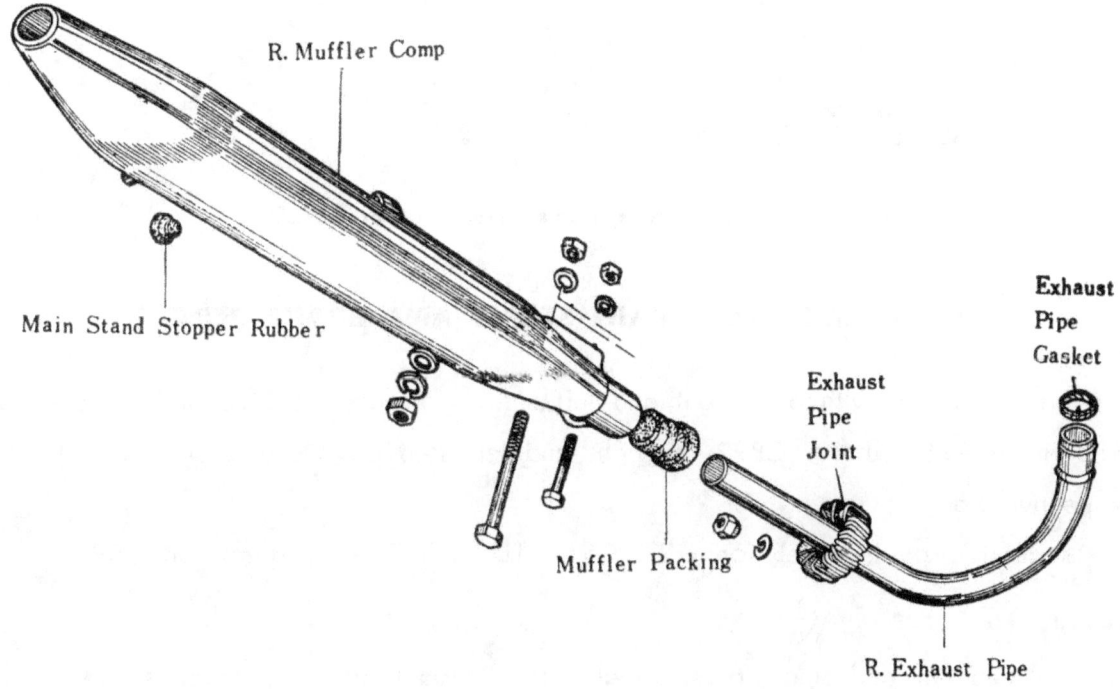

Fig. II-41. Exhaust pipe and muffler (C92 & CA95)

For the purpose of entering races with CB92, a set of megaphone pipe which do not contain silencers are provided.

The standard type muffer provides the detachable inner diffuser to be removed for cleaning. It can be removed when removing the bolt at the end.

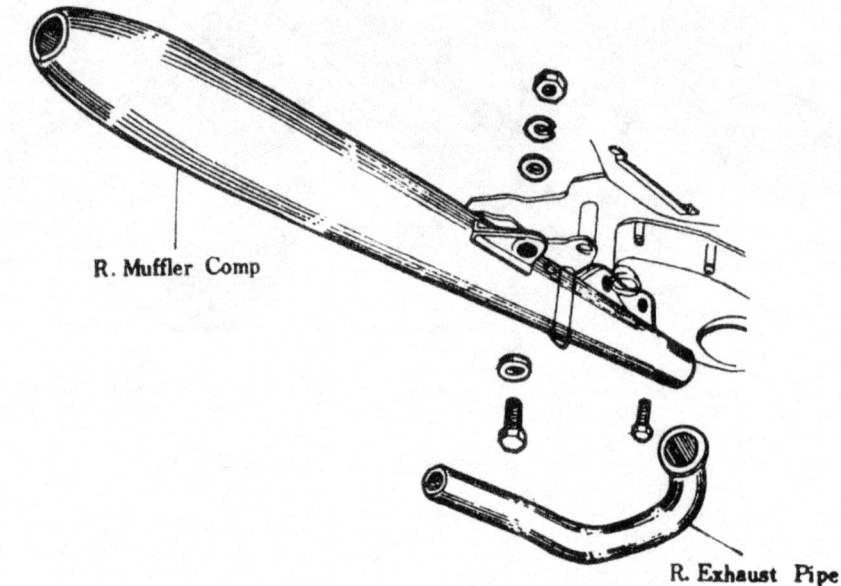

Fig. II-42. Exhust pipe and muffler (CB92)

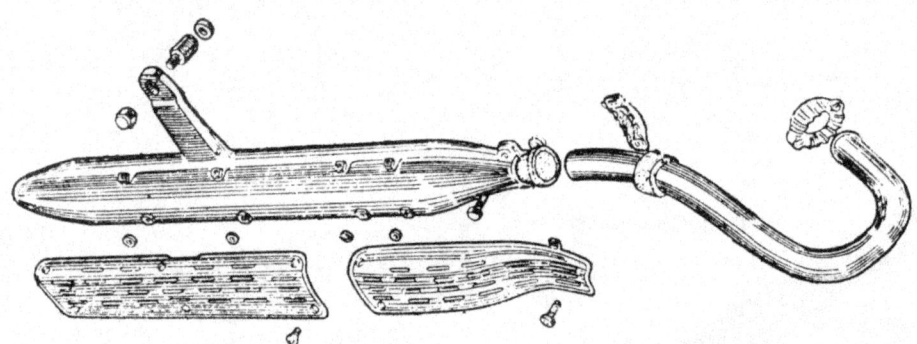

Fig. II-43. Exhanst pipe, muffler and protector for CS92.

II-11 STEP BAR, MAIN STAND AND BRAKE PEDAL

The step bar integrated with both right and left side is attached on the under crank case for C92 STD and CA95, but for CB92 the right and left step plate are seperately attached to their respective side.

The side stand is provide merely on C92, C95 STD and CA95 and not on CB92.

Disassembly

(1) The step bar and step plates are able to dismount after the mufflers were removed. (fig. II-44, II-45)

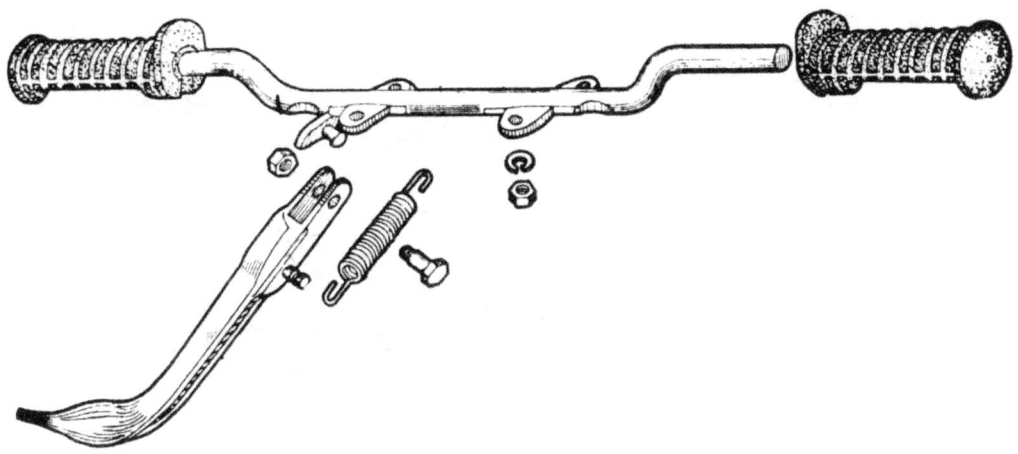

Fig. II-44. Step bar (C92 & CA95)

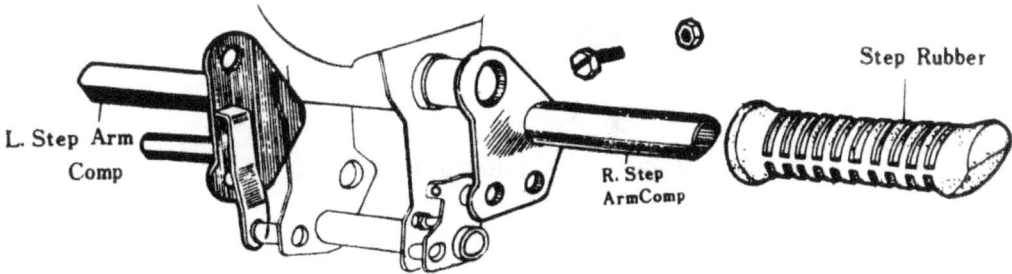

Fig. II-45. Step plates (CB92)

(2) The brake pedal can be removed when the cotter pins on the brake rod and brake pivot pipe were removed (C9, C95 STD).

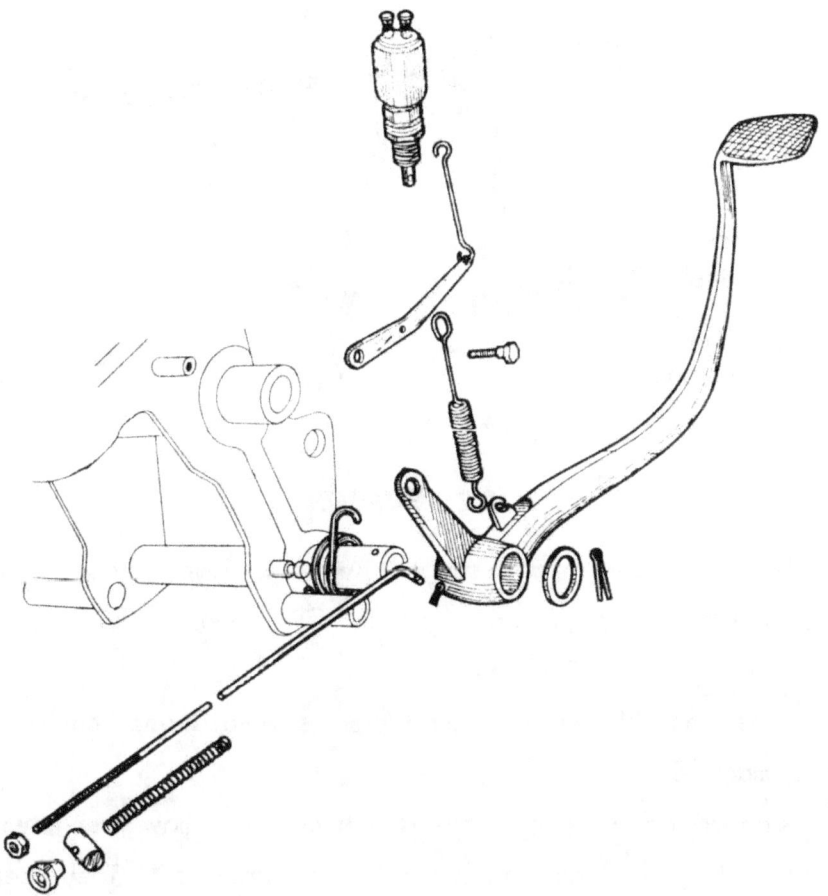

Fig. II-46. Brake pedal and link (C92 & CA95)

Remove the brake pedal pivot bolt of CB92. (Fig. II-47)

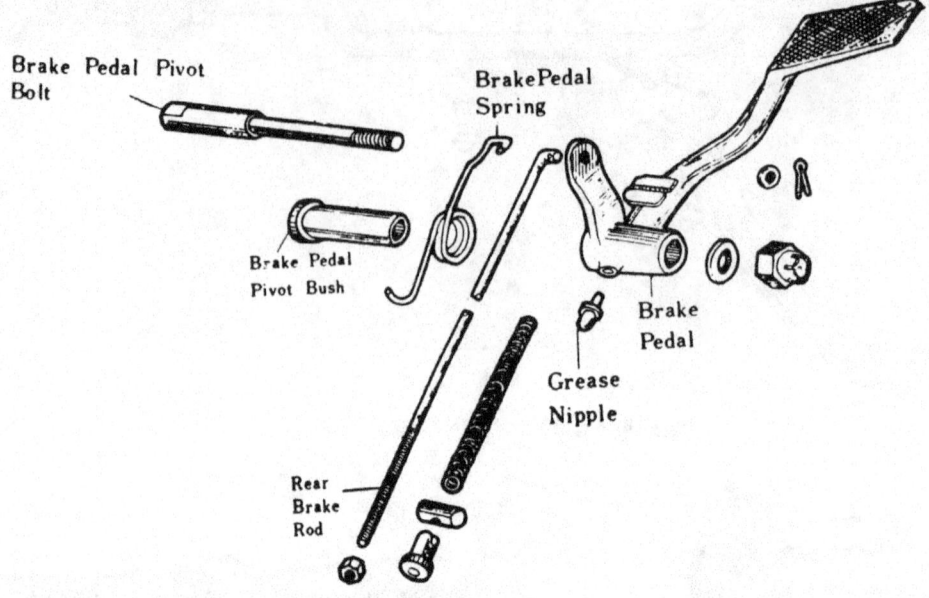

Fig. II-47. Brake pedal and link (CB92)

(3) Remove main stand anchor bolt and remove the main stand spring hook.

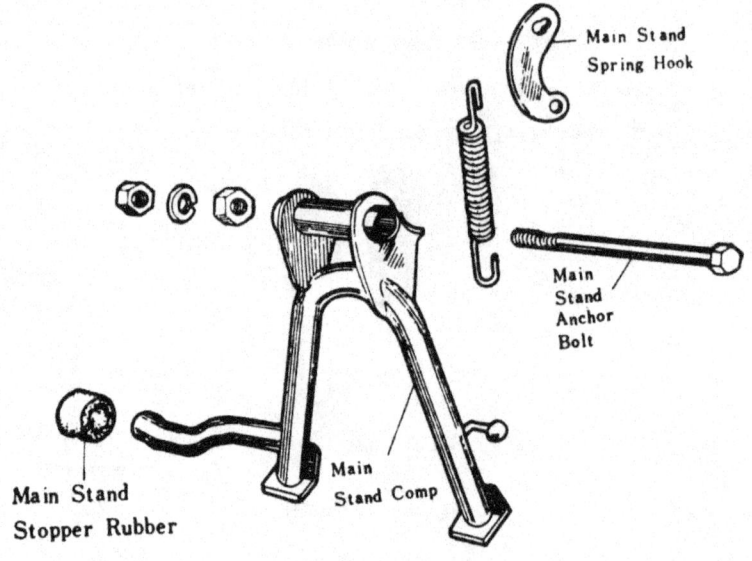

Fig. II-48. Main stand

II-12 FRAME

The frame and rear fender is made in a single unit which is welded together both side halves. The frame for CB92 is shorter than the one used in C92 and CA95 and the flat rubber mud guard is attached to the end. (Fig. II-49)

On the front part of the frame the steering head pipe is welded and the steering ball races are fitted by pressing machine.

The frame could be stripped off when all parts and accessories have been removed.

Replace the ball races if they are damaged, worn out or streaked. They can be driven out by tapping with a driver and hammer.

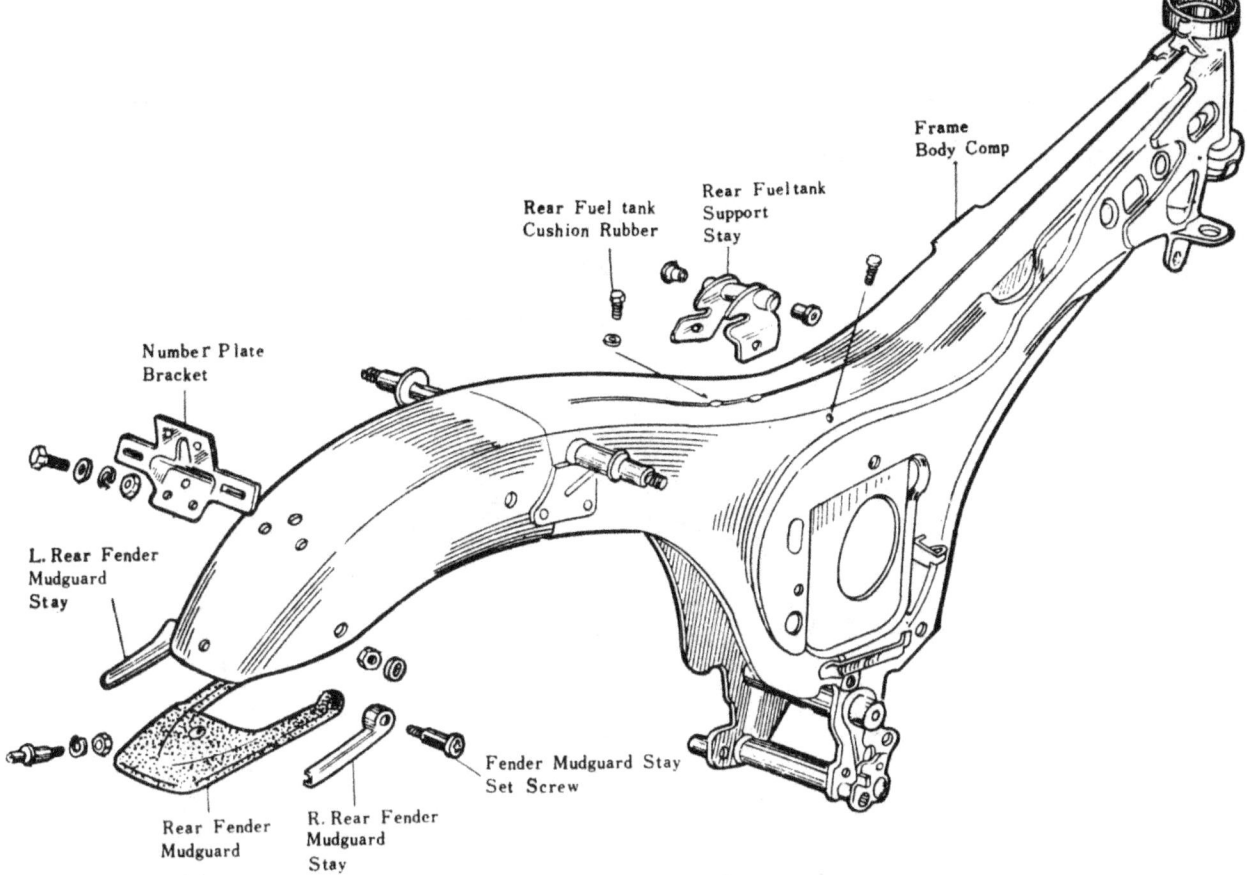

Fig. II-49. Frame (CB92)

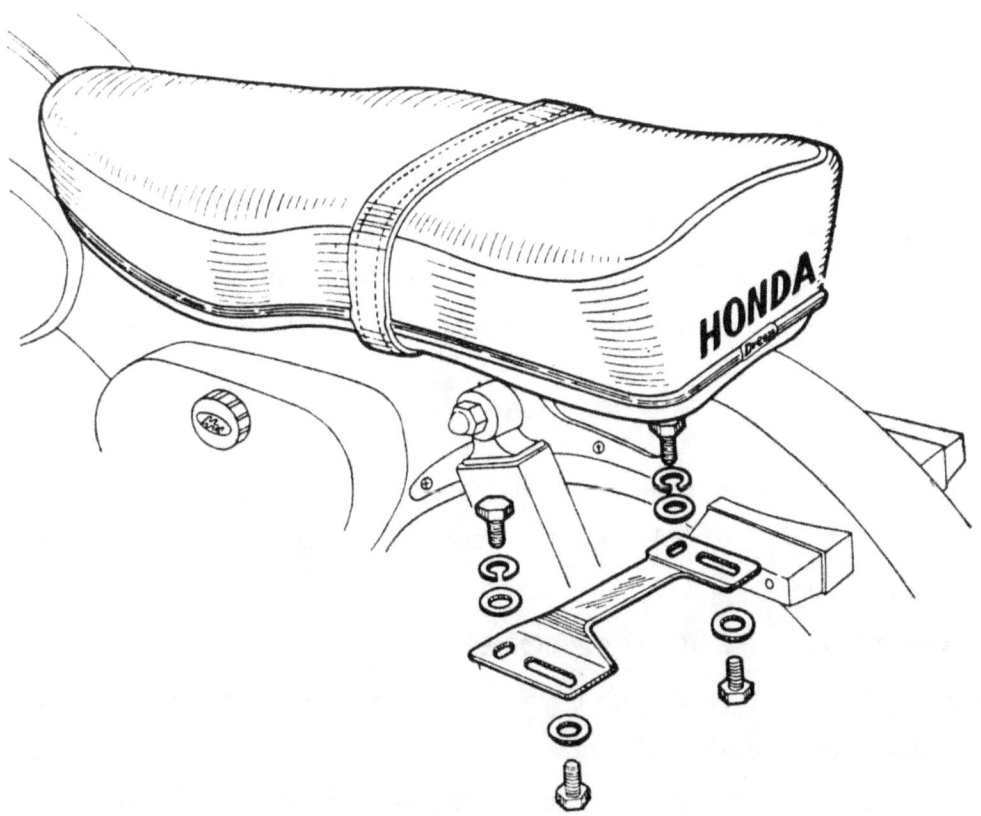

Fig. II-50. Tandem seat and bracket (C92 & CA95)

II-13 SEAT

For C92 and CA95 two kinds of seats are attachable, one of which is single seat with luggage carrier and the other is a tandem seat. The seat is to be replaced only after the fuel tank has been removed. For CB92 a special tandem seat is used and there is provided a racing seat with a hump on the rear end.

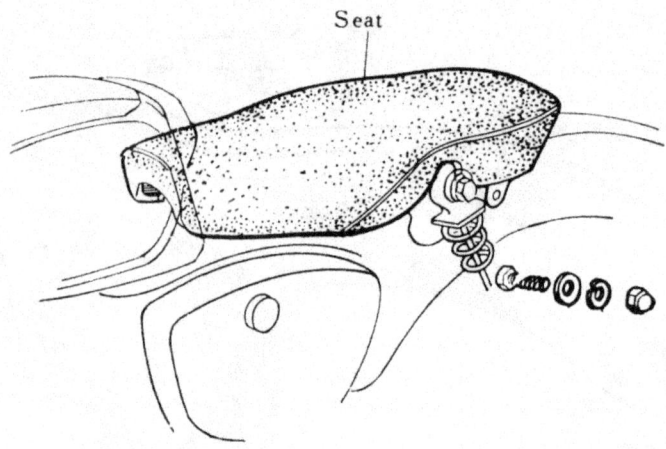

Fig. II-51 Seat (CB92)

They are replaced by removing the fuel tank.

II-14 SPEEDOMETER, HANDLE LOCK AND AUXILIARY TOOL KIT.

A. SPEEDOMETER

The magnetic eddy current type speedometer is located on the top of head light case and driven by the speedometer cable introduced from the gear box attched to the front brake panel. This is of same for the models C92, C95 as well as CB92 and CA95, but for the CB92 and CA95 the same shape tachometer is provided to be replaced with it. The speedometer glass is sealed tightly so that it cannot replace by itself.

The speedometer can be removed when the head light has been removed, and the speedometer cable should be replaced by removing the front fender, while disconnecting the other end at the gear box.

B. HANDLE LOCK

The handle lock is located on the right side of the frame head pipe. And it is inserted in the casing and merely held by the cover, it is replaced by unscrewing the retaining screw of the cover. (Fig. II-52)

C. AUXILIARY TOOL KIT AND ACCESSORIES

The tool kit which is contained in the tool bag listed as follows are provided in the tool box for owners use.

A small tin can of touch up paint, auxilliary fuse for electrical circuits, an air pump for inflating tyres and a piece of rubber and paste are provided for aid of touring. (Fig. II-53)

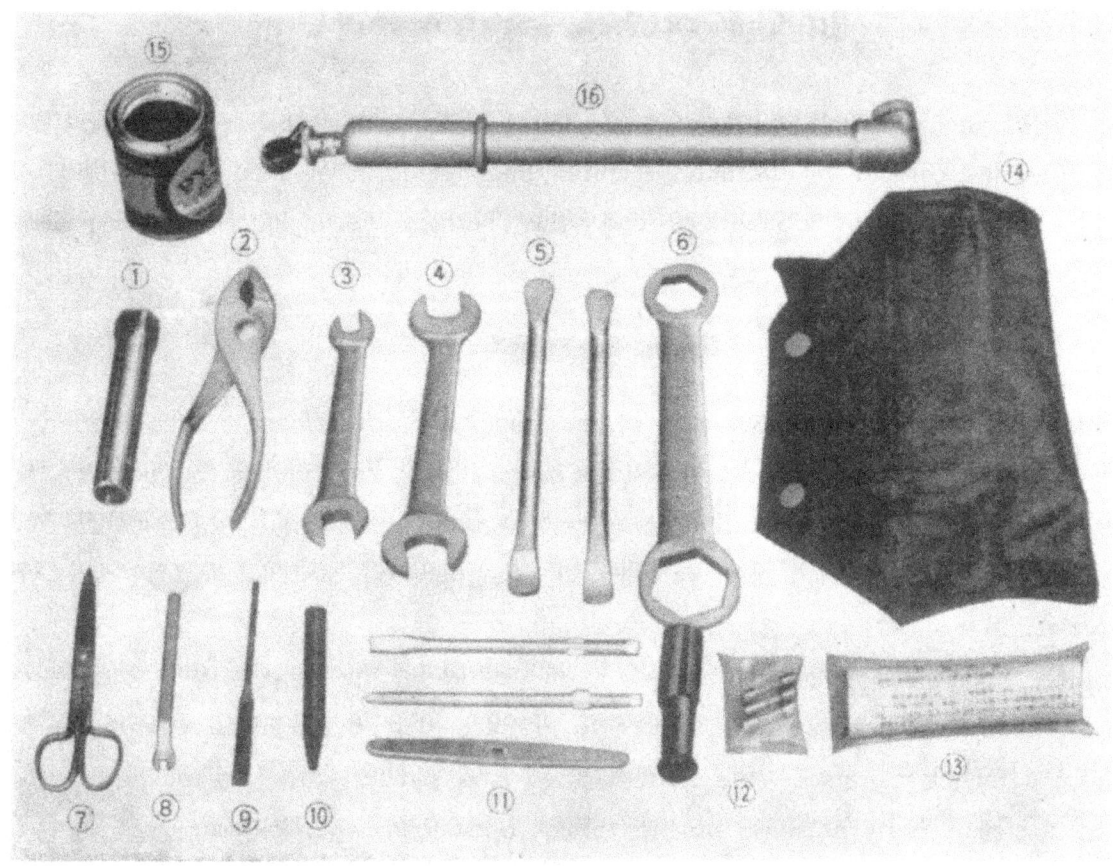

Fig. II-53 Auxiliarly tool kit

MEMO

III ELECTRICAL EQUIPMENT

The electrical equipment may be divided into five groups. These groups include the storage battery, and the generating, starting, ignition and lighting equipment. In addition winker equipment, horn, neutral indicating lamp and cable "harness" are included in the miscellaneous equipment.

III-1. BATTERY

The Battery is mounted on te left side of the frame and contained in the battery box. It is held by the battery clamp to the frame side. With the engine running at normal speeds the current generated by the A.C. dynamo and rectified by the celenium rectifler should satisfy the electrical requirements of the ignition system, lamps and various accessories.

When the engine is switched off, or when starting the engine with starter motor, or when the demand for current is otherwise greater than the dynamo output, the battery supplies the reqired current. The battery used is a plastic case containing three cells each of which consists of seven positive plates and eight negative plats.

Plates are insulated from each other by "separators" and are immersed in an electrolyte which is a solution of sulphuric acid and water.

Capacity of the battery is 11 Ampere hours at 6 Volts. This is connected from the selenium rectifler through a fuse. The negative terminal is grounded to the fame with a ground strap.

1. **Removal and installation of battery**

    Remove the battery box cover, then remove the battery clamp unscrewing 6 mm bolts.

Fig. III-1

Disconnect both end terminals at the poles of the battery and take out the battery. When installing the battery, wipe the battery clean and firmly tighten both poles to their terminals. (fig. III-1)

Care should be taken not to obstruct the vent pipe of the battery.

II. Maintenance

Batteries to be supplied overseas are not charged and do not contain "electrolyte". When charging the battery for the first time, it is necessary to perform the instructions attached to the battery, which read as follows —

Keeping the electrolyte level to the specified amount is sufficient for battery maintenance. But if it is noticed that the level decreases exceptionally rapid, check the A.C. dynamo for over-charging.

In cases where discharging is apparent in the use of electric equipment, charge the battery on the bench.

Relations between specific gravity and the amount of charge is as follows.—

Specific gravity	Capacity of charge
1,130—1,500	0%
1,200—1,210	50%
1,260	100%

The above are standard figures at 20°C and for approximate calculations at different temperatures use the following formula.

Specific gravity at $20°C = (t°C$ Spec. grav.$) + 0.007\ (t° - 20°)$

In the above formula, $t°$ stands for electrolyte temperature in centigrade.

If the specific gravity falls below 1.210 when it is converted to 20°C, it requires charging.

Dry-Battery

Type	Capacity	Initial charging curent (A)	Normal charging current (A)	Volume of electrolyte (liter)	Density of filling electrolyte (at 20C°)
MBK 76	6V. 11 Amph	1.1	1.1	0.4	1.260

(1) Precaution Before use

This battery contains dry and charged plates but no electrolyte. When the battery is needed to be used immediately, or where lack of time or charging equipment does not permit an initial charge to be given, the battery can be placed in service. However, an initial charge is recommended before placing in service when time and equipment permit so that its characteristic performance is secured.

(2) Filling Electrolyte

For filling, use the dilute sulfuric acid of proper-specific gravity (see table above) cooled below 30°C beforehand. Fill it up to the electrolyte level line (upper line).

(3) Standing

Battery must stand for two or three hours after electrolyte has been filled before starting charge.

After standing period, if level has fallen, add electrolyte with the same specific gravity to restore level.

(4) Charging

After the temperature of electrolyte has fallen below 30°C, charge the battery at the rate given above for approximately 15 to 20 hours. If the cell temperature during charge rises higher than 45°C, discontinue charging temporarily or reduce current to half and continue charge.

If necessary to restore the electrolyte level during charge, use only distilled water.

(5) Completion of Charging

At the final period of charging, adjust the specific gravity of electrolyte to between 1.250 to 1.270 at 20°C, and again continue charging for two or three hours. After completion of charge, wash off acid spillage by clean water and dry.

(6) Attention for handling
1. Never open sealing of a vent plug and an exhausting pipe.
2. Before use remove the sealing tope and tube affixed on a vent plug and an exhansting pipe and at the time of placing the battery on the machine be sure to replace with the vinyl-pipe provided.

Sulphation

If the battery discharges excessively, sulphation, a phenomenon where white powder forms on the surface of the positive plates, will occur, and after a long time white powder deposits at the bottom of the cells.

Where such sulphation has occurred, remove the top caps of the battery empty all electrolyte and wash out inside. Repeat washing thoroughly with drinking water.

Refill the battery with new electrolyte and fully charge.

Hydrometer

For checking specific gravity, a hydrometer should be used. (fig.)

For this purpose, a specific gravity tester is provided. (fig. III-2)

This tester reads the condition of specific gravity by means of the balls floating or or sinking as follows :-

Bed ball	float	float	sink
White ball	float	sink	sink
Specific gravity	over 1,240	1,240—1,180	under 1.180
Capacity of charge	100%	50%	0%

III-2 CHARGING SYSTEM

The charging system, includes the A.C. dynamo and celenium rectifier. A.C. current induced by the A.C. dynamo is altered by the rectifier into D.C. current for charging the battery.

A. A.C. DYNAMO

The six pole permanent magneto is attached to the left end of the crankshaft and rotates at the center of the six coil stator base.

This type of dynamo is a special design which regulates the maximum output automatically so that current output does not directly correspond to the RPM of engine. (fig. III-3) Therefore no special voltage regulator is required.

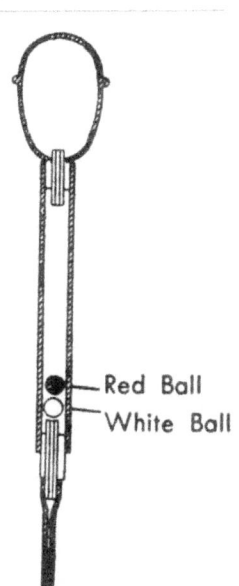

Fig. III-2 Specific Gravity Tester

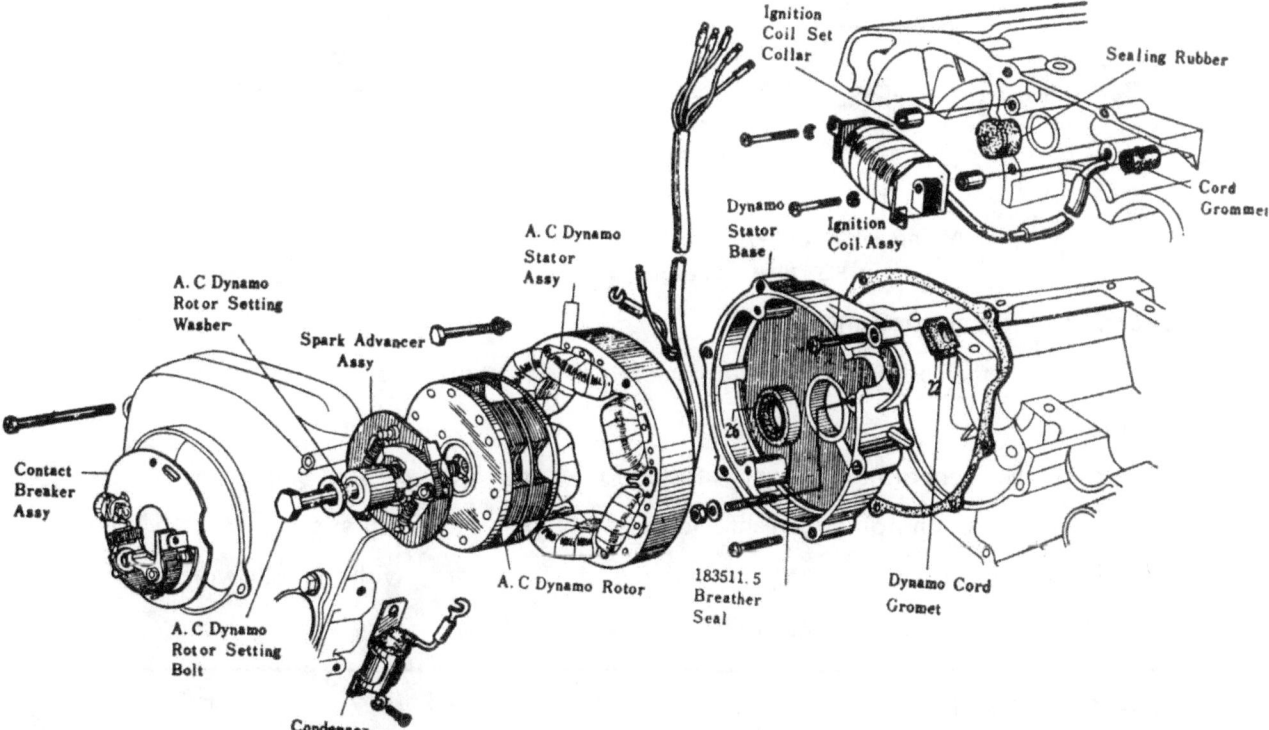

Fig. III-3 Display of A.C. dynamo system.

While using lights during night operation all coils are in use, but for daytime running, portion only of the coils are utilised. (fig. III-4)

1. Disassembly and assembly

Disconnect the wiring, and remove R. crank case cover and chain case cover. Remove the screws retaining the A.C. Dynamo. Remove screws for clamping wire on the crank case and disconnect the neutral switch terminal.

Remove the spark advancer, and the dynamo rotor with the extractor.

Assembly is done by following the whole disassambly procedure in reverse.

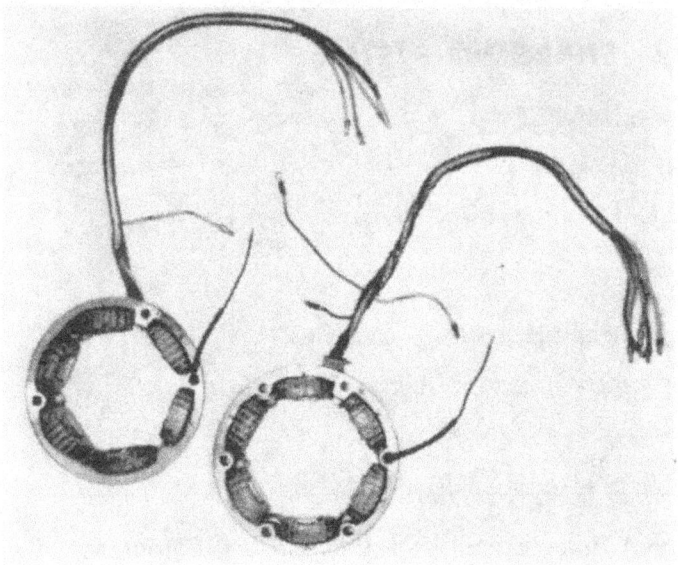

Fig. III-4. A.C. Dynamo stator base

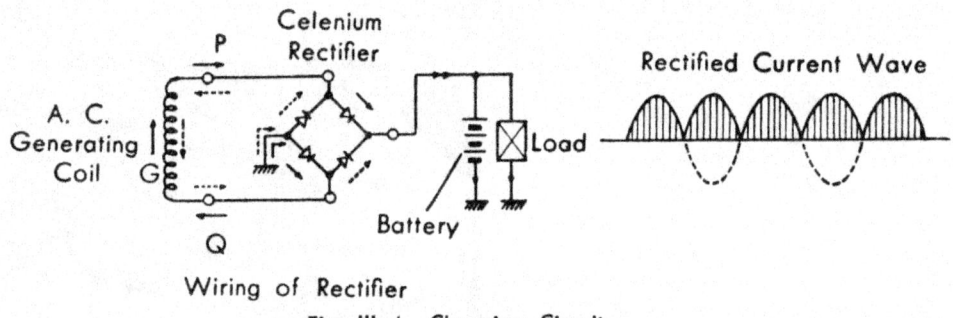

Wiring of Rectifier
Fig. III-4 Charging Circuit

II. Inspection and maintenance.

(1) To check the output of the dynamo, use a service tester or an ammeter.
p. 122

Check the generating current according to the RPM of the engine.

The standard charging current measuring under 6~8 Volts is shown as follows, and the results of checking must meet the standard with an allowance of + 0.2 Amp. at each R.P.M. rating.

Speed at top gear		30 km/h	50 km/h
Craft shaft + RPM	1000 rpm	2200 rpm	3700 rpm
Generating current, (day time)	+1.0	+4.5	+6.5
Genating current (night time)	−3.0	−1.0	+2.3

(2) When the magnetic power of the rotor is found to be weakened, have it remagnetized by a specialist for this work.

B. CELENIUM RECTIFIER

The celenium rectifier is used for rectifying the A.C. current from the A.C. dynamo. It consists of 8 sheets of celenium plate (50 mm square) and operates by full wave rectification of A.C. current. To avoid any contact with other wire or cables all edges of the plates are covered with rubber.

I. Dismounting

As the celenium rectifier is attached by one nut to the left side of the frame immediately below the center of fuel tank, it should be removed using a long spanner. Dismount the carburetter and remove the celenium rectifier out from the opening behind it. Disconect the terminals of wiring, with cross headed type screw driver.

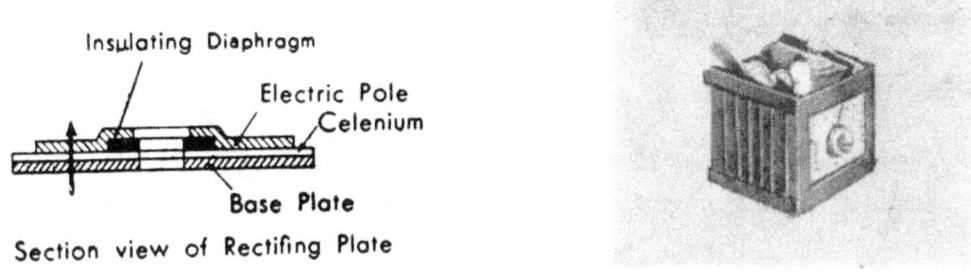

Fig. III-11. Celenium rectifire

II. Installation

Connect the wiring to agree with the colour code of wiring and of celenium rectifier terminals.

Take care not to interfere with other wiring or cables of the installation. As it is grounded to the frame at the portion of mounting, secure the tightening without insulation.

The celenium rectifier will not burn if the plates are not shorted.

III-3. IGNITION SYSTEM

Ignition system is provided for the purpose of delivering a high-voltage, 15000-2000 Volts to each spark plug at the correct time to fire the compressed charge of fuel and air in the cylinder. Included are seven elements: ignition switch, ignition coil, distributor, breaker points including condenser, spark plug and battery.

The distributor is abolished from engines after serial numbers of C92E-937065 (C95-915183) and a simultaneous ignition system is applied so that the both plugs are fired at the same, time, ie, firing twice in one cycle of the engine.

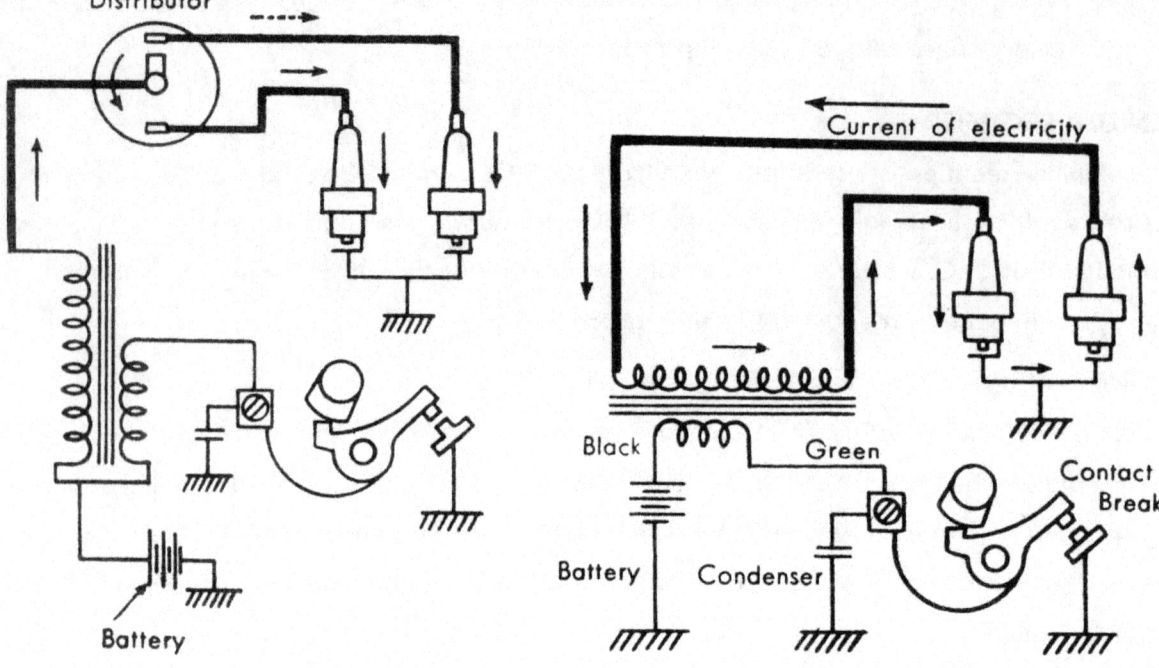

Fig. III-7 Ignition System Wiring (Distributor Method)

Fig. III-8 Ignition System Wiring (Simultaneous Method)

A. IGNITION COILS.

From the same engine serial numbers, the ignition coil is located on the inside of the frame instead of being located on the left side of crank case as previously. The ignition coil has a great influence on the engine performance.

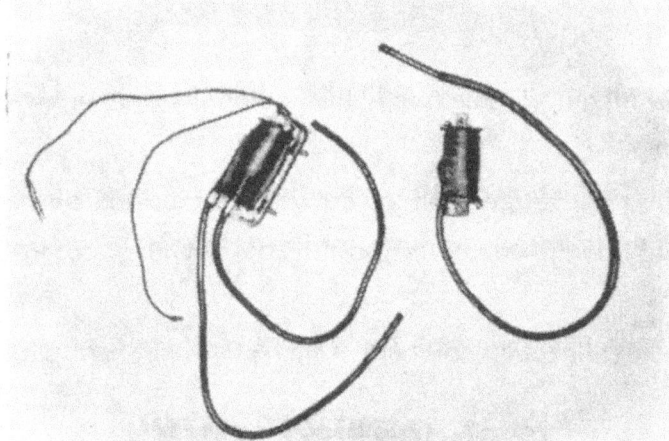

Fig. III-9 Two kinds of ignition coil
(left is the one attached to frame)

1. Replacing ignition coils

   Remove right crank case cover and chain cover.
   Remove the screws retaining the coil.
   Remove the primary wire terminal and secondary wire from the distributor cap, then take off the distributor cap.

Remove battery box cover and battery. Take off the tool tray board attached with the air cleaner.

Unscrew the nuts retaining the coils from the outside of the frame. Remove the primary wire terminal and spark plug cap from the secondary wire. (for simultaneous ignition type)

As there is no diffence in the efficiency between the coil of the distributor type and the non distributor type, the coil for the distributor type is replaceable with the other type. In this case the distributor cap should be attached on the cylinder head side cover for dust protection, and the secondary wires taken to spark plugs directly.

II. Coil test

(1) Power test

In inspecting the coil output, it is recommended to test with the three needles tester. (fig. III-10)

This tester is provided in the "Service Tester".

Connect the + wire of an tester to the end of the secondary wire and ground − terminal to the frame of engine and on the end of other side of secondary wire, attach the spark plug which is submitted sparking in air.

Rotate the crankshaft using starter motor. Then read the maximum sparking distance between the two main pointers, which is found by moving one pointer when the sparks discontinues to occur with the corresponding constant frequency according ot the crank revolutions. The minimum gap should be 8 mm at crank revolution of 300 to 3000 RPM.

(2) Conduction test

In order to check whether there is a disconnected wire or short circuit in the

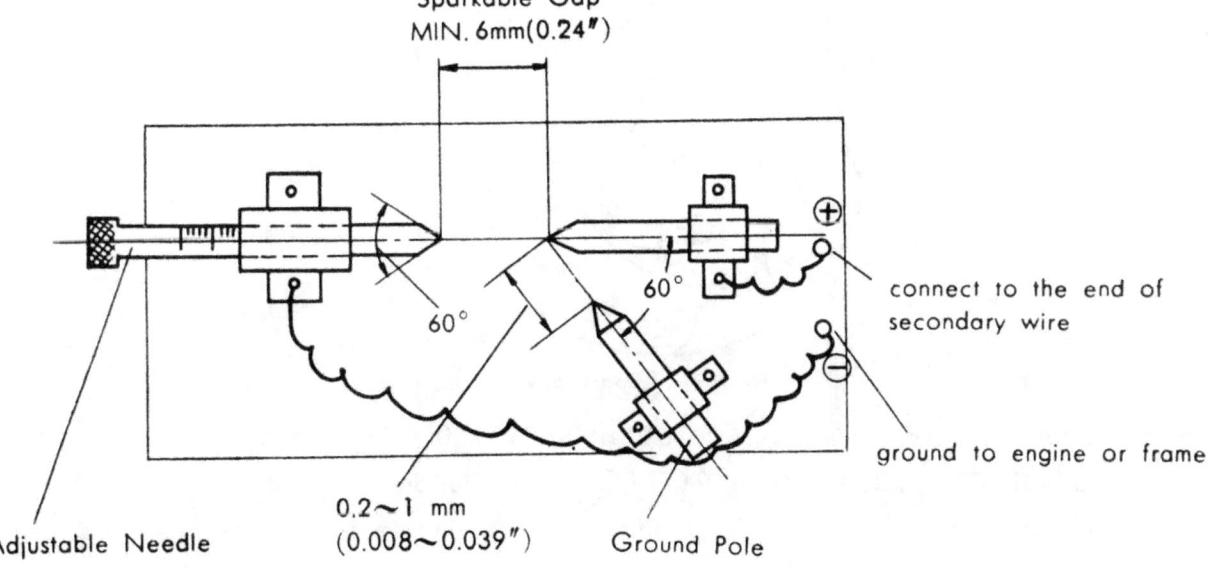

Fig. III-10 Three Needles Spark Tester

ignition coil, a conduction test is available.

Use a tester connecting one lead wire to the terminal and the other to the earth or core of the coil. The service tester (p. 122) is in use.

The earth conduction check should show no resistance, but connection to the coil core must be open circuit.

If either test shows as a failure, replace the coil.

B. BREAKER POINTS

The breaker points are located at the left end of the crankshaft where the contact breaker cover is attached. The condenser is located on the left side crank case.

I. Replacement of breaker points.

Remove the breaker cover on the L. crank-case cover and remove the screws holding the breaker arm and point. After replacing the breaker points set the ignition timing correctly referring p. 126.

II. Repair of breaker points.

Check the points for contamination, pitting or burning. Contamination with oil may result in the ill-performance of the engine, therefore wipe off with clean cloth. In cases where they are badly pitted so that the surfaces cannot be smoothed with a point file, replace the points assemby as a set.

C. SPARK ADVANCER

The spark advancer is attached on the dynamo rotor behind the contact breaker base plate.

The spark advancer regulates the ignition timing at high speed. As mentioned in the

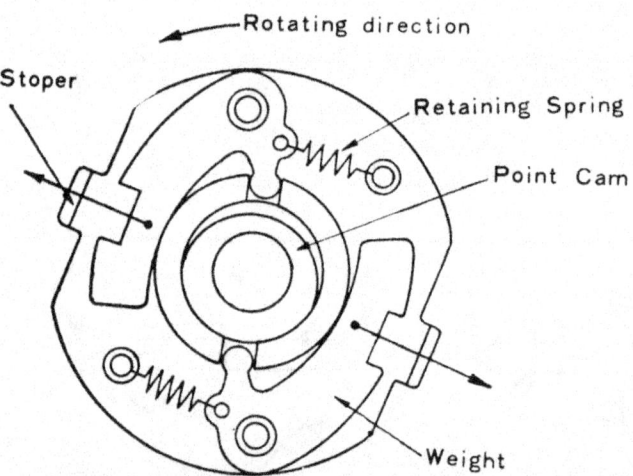

Fig. II-11 Spark advancer

specification the advancer stays 5° BTDC at 900-1200 RPM. and then starts to advance up to 45° BTDC at 2300-2700 RPM. of crank revolution.

The advancing angle and the state of advancing referring to the crank revolutions can be checked by service tester. (p. 122)

If it is not stable at any RPM or exceeds or less advance than above, it should be replaced.

Replacement of the spark advancer

Remove the breaker points cover and breaker points base plate.

Remove an 8 mm bolt at the end of the spark advancer and take off the advancer.

Check whether the springs are in good condition, and that the point cam is moving with sufficient grease between the shaft.

D. CONDENSER

The condenser is fixed in parallel with the breaker points so as to absorb excess current and so assist the function of the breaker points.

The capacity should be $0.2\,\mu$ Farrad.

A faulty condenser is sometimes indicated by badly burned breaker points, weak sparks, or difficulty in starting the engine.

Use the service tester to check the insulating resistance between the terminal and outer tube.

Judgement should be made in accordance with the data given below.

over 50MΩ	Good
50~10MΩ	rather good ⎫ replace
below 10MΩ	faulty ⎭

It is necessary to tighten fully the condencer terminal to the primary circuit of breaker points.

E. DISTRIBUTOR

The distributor is used to deliver the high tension current to each spark plug. The rotor located inside of the cap switches this current to the cables leading to the different spark plugs.

Replacement of distributor cap or rotor.

Routine service for cleaning the inside of the cap and the rotor is required.

Fig. III-12. **Removing distributor cap and rotor**

In case of cracks or traces of carbon deposit being found within the poles, replace the parts.

Excessively defaced contact plate of the rotor and or the center electrode of the cap should be replaced.

To replace the cap, unfasten the clamp and unscrew the screws holding the high tension wires.

F. SPARK PLUG

The Spark Plug used on the engine 125cc and 150cc are identified as follows.

	C92 & C95	CB92	CA95	YB
For normal use	C7H	C10H	C10H	C12H
For heavy stressed operation	C8H	C12H	C12H	

The Spark Plug should be wholly dry and have a thin accumulation of gray or brownish coating and the insulator scorched golden brown color under the condition of normal usage.

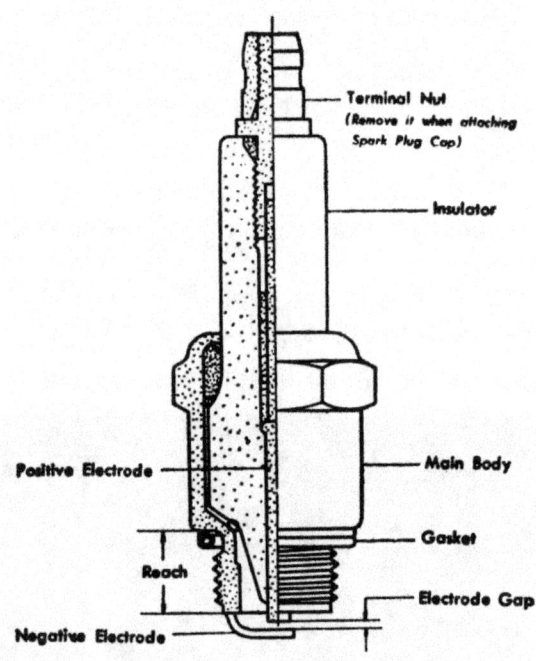

Fig. III-13 Cutting view of spark plug.

1. Maintenance of spark plug

Clean the Spark Plug if found sooty or wet or with excess carbon deposit, using Spark Plug Cleaner or wire brush. After cleaning, set electrode gap to 0.6-0.7 mm (0.0024-0.0028"). Replace the Spark Plug if damaged or Showing excessive wear.

If the Spark Plug tester is available, check the spark plug under 7-10 Atmospheric pressure. Replace the Spark Plug if the tester rejects.

To install, first tighten the Spark Plug to "finger tight" then tighen 1/4 turn further with Spark Plug wrench. Do not forget to position the Spark Plug washer.

II. Trouble shooting of spark plug.

Symptoms	Cause	Remedy
Insulator cracked or damaged,	Over heating	Use a colder type spark plug
	Over heating due to loose tightening	Tighten it firmy
Insulator and electrodes are sooty or wet,	Plug is too cold,	Change to hot type plug
	Carburetter fuel air mixture is too rich or excessive use of choke shutter,	Adjust carburetter mixture correctly.
	Burning oil due to worn piston rings or comming down into cylinder,	Repair the trouble in the engine.
	Weak sparks at spark plugs,	Check and repair high tension circuit.
		Check and clean the contact point surfaces and correct the gap.
		Recharge the battery if discharged.
Unusual wear of electrods or granular substance growing at the insulator	Excessive heating,	Replace with a colder spark plug.
	Over heating due to loose tightening of the spark plug,	Tighten it firmly.
	Fuel/Air mixture is too lean	Adjust the carburetter.
	Too advanced or too retard ignition timing.	Adjust the timing.

III-4 ELECTRIC STARTER

Pushing a button fixed in a case on the right handle bar, 100 Amp current flows into the Self Starter Motor giving it force to revolve. This force is conveyed to the engine by chain and the engine starts. After the engine has started, an automatic clutch which is called the "Over-running Clutch" intercepts the connection.

Wiring is as below:

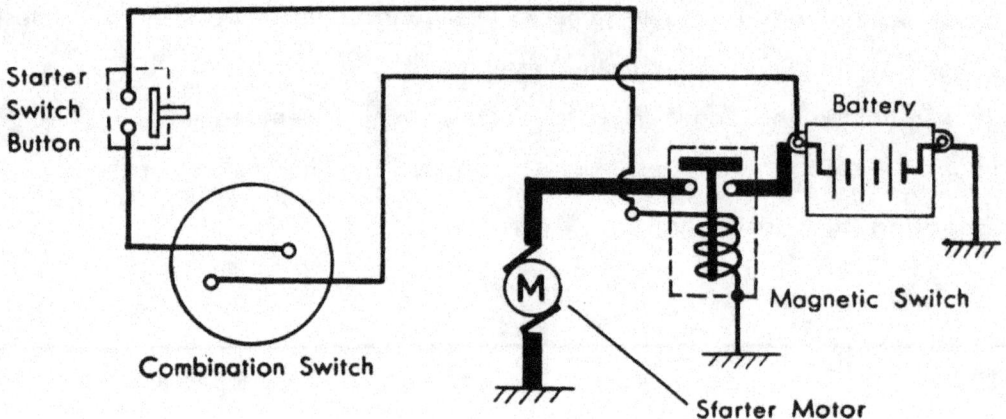

Fig. III-14 Wiring diagram for electric starter

A. STARTING MOTOR

Capacity of the motor at the time of cranking is:

    2.3 V,   200 Amp.   Torque 1.8 Kg-m,   0.3 HP.

Two reductions are actuated between the motor and the crank, namely:

    Primary.................Shaft-Sprocket (Planetary gear) 7.33 : 1

    Secondary............Sprocket-Crank Sprocket   2.77 : 1

                                        Total..................20.3 : 1

Number of the crank rotation at the starting stage under cold weather will become 250-300 rpm.

1. Disassembly and Assembly

As shown in the exploded view (Fig. III-16) remove the covers on both sides of the starting motor, unscrew one long and 3 short 6 mm bolts fixed on the crank and disconnect the motor from the chain

As the sprocket is fixed on the motor shaft by means of serrations, a set ring, must be removed and then the sprocket is pulled off. Then unscrew bolts on the gear case and disassemble the front part of the motor. Here, three planetary gears are fixed by pins on a plate. On the side of the main body is fixed a ring gear. Then the Commutator cover and screws on the rear part of the motor, are removed. The bearing may then be detached and the commutator and armature coils which are located further inside may be taken out.

As the brushes contact armature at this time loosen screws for each brush, and remove them by pulling the springs.

To reassemble, the above steps will be carried out in reverse order. However, it would be better to fix the sprocket on the shaft first and then attach the planetary gears.

II. Checking and Maintenance

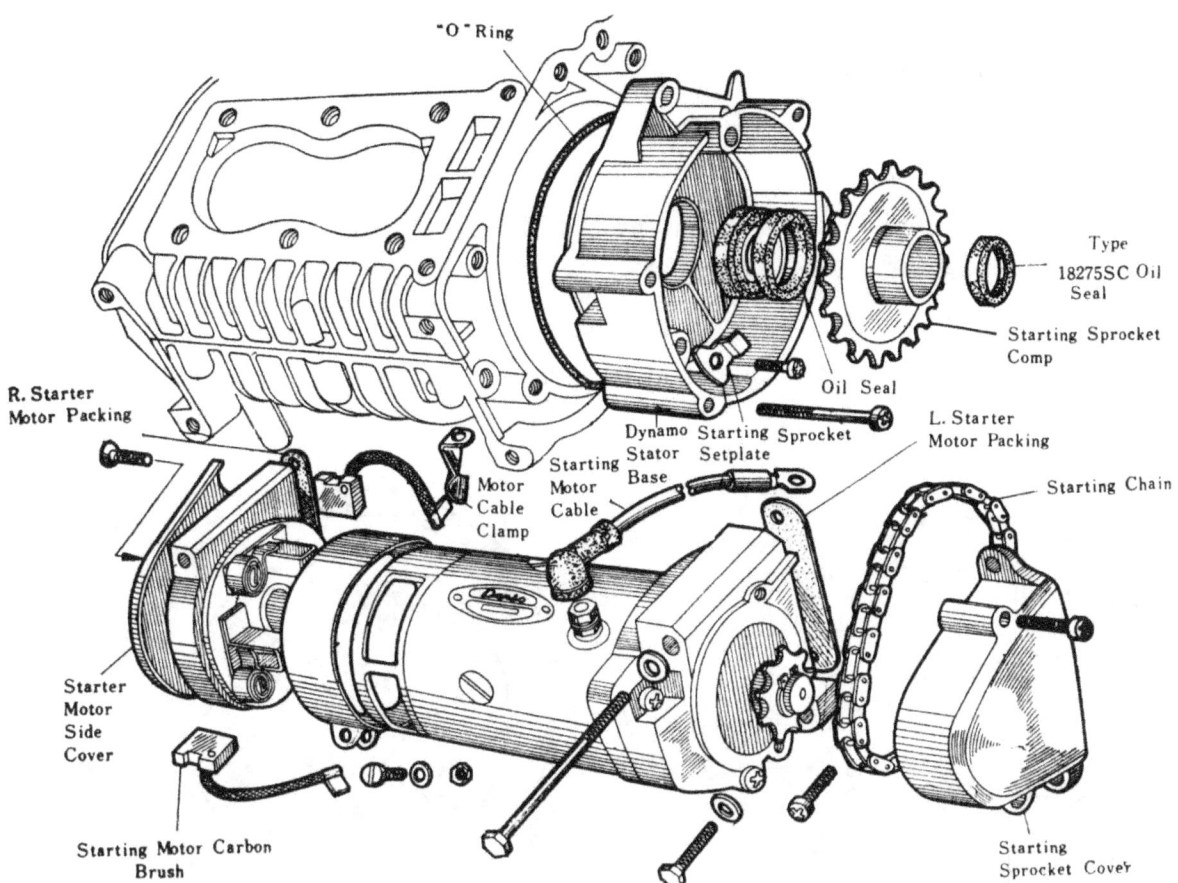

Fig. III-16 Exploded view of starting system

Defects of gears are seldom encountered. Should a tooth be chipped, remove the gear holding pin and replace the chipped gear.

When the copper segments of the Commutator are worn out and its efficiency is decreased, it is advisable to have the specialist's shop undercut insulating micas If the brush is worn out or the spring faulty, a replacement will easily be done by removing the bearing cover.

If the starting motor is immersed in water, disassemble the motor and dry the interior parts as soon as possible.

B. STARTER MAGNETIC SWITCH

As the current for the starter motor is approximately 100 Amp. use of a thick cable and special connector is necessitated. The Magnetic Switch especially is provided for this reason. (III-14)

When a Magnetic Switch is used for long period of time, the contacting plate is burnt by high current, resistance increases, and finally the flow of current will be stopped. Such is the case when the self-starter button is pushed in, a click is heard, but the motor does not start. In this instance, take out the switch, unscrew its two screws, and break up the parts and file the contact plates with a fine mesh file or sandpaper.

C. OVER-RUUNING CLUTCH

An Over-running Clutch is such a device that at starting the engine, rotation of the self-starter motor is transmitted to the crank but when the crank begins to turn by itself its rotation is not reversely conveyed to the self-starter motor. Its construction is as shown in the Diagram (Fig. III-15)

When the chain is moved in the direction as shown in the (Fig. III-15 (6)) by the starter motor the sprocket is rotated in the arrow direction and the three rollers are

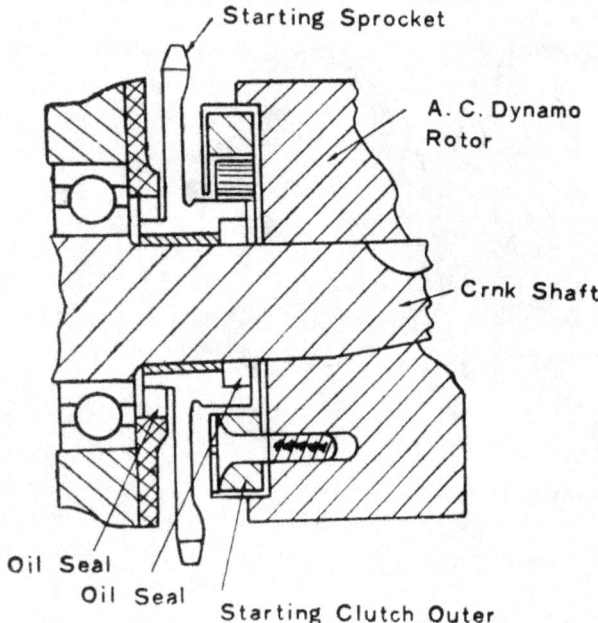
Fig. III-15 (a) Section of Over-running Clutch

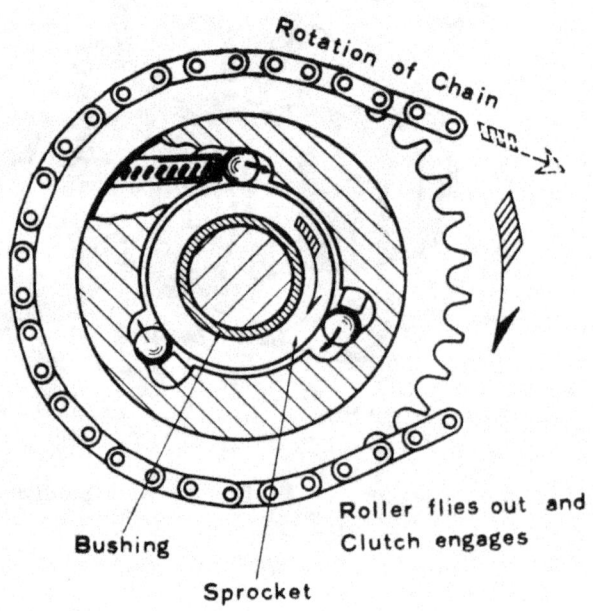
Fig. III-15 (b) Side view of Over-running Clutch

pushed out by respective springs in the arrowed direction along the taper of clutch outer. Thus the sprocket and the outer wedge rotate together. As this outer is fixed on the A.C. dynamo rotor with three screws the crank shaft is rotated.

Then, when the engine starts operating, the crank shaft rotation becomes faster than the rotation of the motor. As the cluth outer rotates, the three rollers are thrust by the centrifugal force toward the deeper part of the groove and remain there becoming separated from the sprocket and thus the rotation is not transmitted to the sprocket.

1. Disassembly and Check.

Remove the right side cover and then the stator base of the A.C. dynamo. Remove the starter motor chain sprocket and disconnect the starter motor Dynamo rotor and starting sprocket are pulled off the crankshaft at the same time.

(1) Check the oil-seal in the crank-case and the oil-seal of the starting sprocket.

(2) Change the starting spocket bushing if the inner diameter is excessively worn.

To judge the degree of defacement follow the Specification.

(3) Check the part that the starting sprocket roller repeatedly hits and pressure mark and wears on clutch outer. If these are excessive, replace the defective part.

(4) Check whether the Roller Spring is correct or not.

II. Assembly

Set three springs, spring caps and roller on the clutch; install the clutch onto the A.C. dynamo rotor with three screws tightened firmly.

Set the sprocket on the crankshaft and interlock the chain on it.

Wedge the woodruff key into the slit of the crank shaft, coincide with the A.C. dynamo rotor, and thrust the rotor against the sprocket rotating in the direction of crankshaft revolution while holding the chain stationary, When the clutch will be set in.

Then complete asembling with installation of spark advancer and A.C. dynamo base. At the time of assembling, thinly apply on the roller, grease of less than sticky nature (For instance, Silicon Grease DC 44).

III-5. MISCELLANEOUS EQUIPMENT.

Horn and light systems belong to the miscellaneous equipment. The starting motor belongs to this system, but it is specially described in the previous chapters

A. HORN

A.C. coil type Horn is used, and by applying the trumpet principle the volume and quality of sound are improved. Cross-Section is shown below. The horn sounds by vibrating the diaphragm magnetically and is amplified by a coiled trumpet. A regular horn has a volume of **90-115 Phons** when measured by a phon-meter at two meters in front of the horn. When a horn is used for a long period of time, the contact point surfaces become uneven and current decreases, resulting in weak and inferior sound. So, when the sound has become weak remove the horn cover, loosen the lock nut, and adjust by the adjusting nut. Slowly turn the adjusting nut clockwise (paying attention to the change of tone and volume), and the volume will increase and the quality will improve. Stop turning the nut when the sound is best and tighten the lock nut.

The diaphragm is made from very thin hard metal. When this has been damaged the quality of sound becomes inferior. It must then be replaced.

For causes of failure of sound, consideration should be given to defective contact of horn-button or defective connection of the terminals before checking horn itself.

By directly connecting the horn to the battery it may ascertained whether or not the cause of failure lies in the horn.

When the horn fails to recover after checking and adjustment it must be renewed.

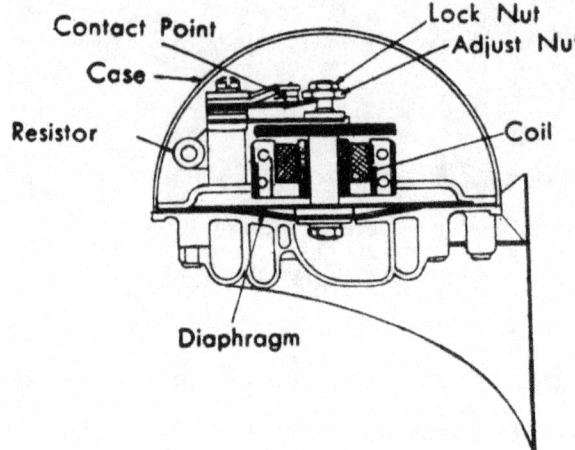

Fig. III-17 Cross-section of Horn

B. WINKER

The Winker Relay is fastened on the inside of the frame together with the saddle mounting bracket by common bolts.

The construction of the Relay is, as shown in the Fig. III-18, being made so as to blink by the balancing between the magnetic force of the relay and the spring.

The standard wink frequency is **70-110 times per minute.**

If one side of the winker does not blink but remains lit when switched on, it means that one of two lamps (either the front or the rear one) of the same side is burnt out. If both front or both rear lamps blink at the same time when the switch is changed to either side, it means faulty wiring. On the other hand, if one side

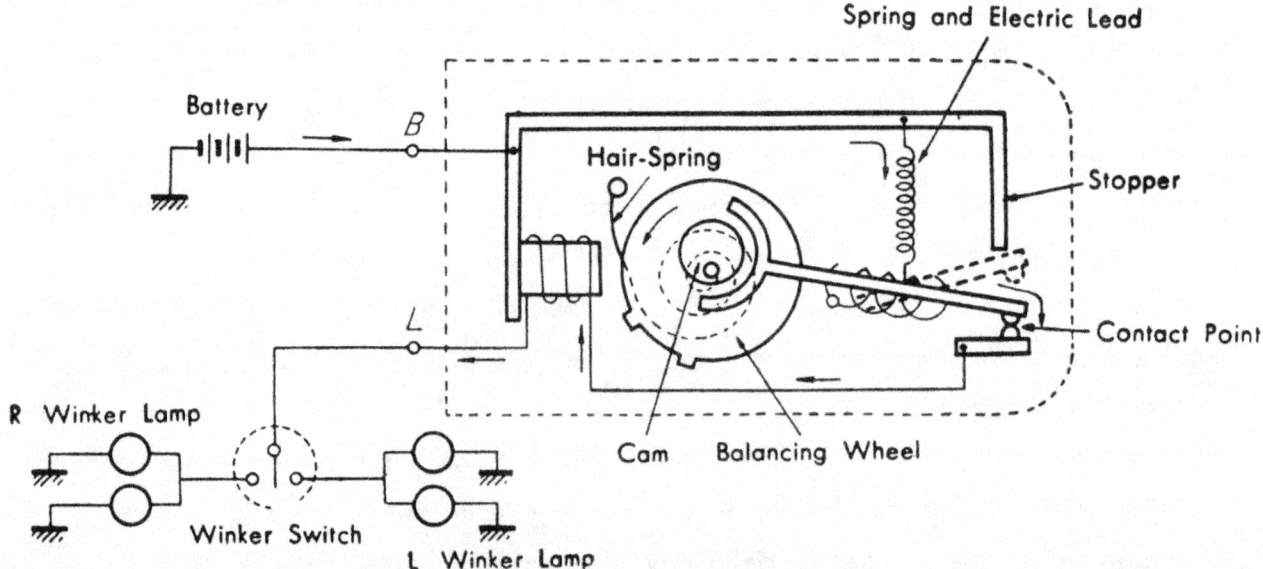

Fig. III-18 Structure of Winker Relay

remains lit or the blinking is unstable, or if it does not light at all, it may be safely assumed that the relay is defective. In this instance, replace the relay completely.

C. HEAD LIGHT

Two different types of head lamp are used but are completely interchangeable. One is of the semishielded beam type and the other the fully-shielded beam type.

Details of the semishielded and fully shielded beam types are as shown in (fig III-19) The semi-shielded beam Lamp is shown in the (Fig. III-19 (a) with the lens and reflector fixed on one body, made to push into a socket with the head light bulb. To change the bulb when it is burnt out, the socket must be removed.

Contrarily, as shown in the Fig. III-19 (b) the fully shielded beam lamp is so made that the light bulb is fully shielded by the lens and reflector, and naturally, it is impossible to removed only the bulb. When the bulb is burnt out, the whole lamp body must replaced. The advantage of this type is that a much larger light bulb can be used to obtain a higher brightness and because the bulb is bigger, a longer filament can be utilized which enables the bulb to bear less heat load with the same capacity power resulting in longer life of the bulb.

Those two types are available in accordance with destinations where the motorcycles are supplied. The bulb for semisealed beam is twin filament and screened under the dimmed filament.

The output of either lamp is **6-8 V, 35 W (when dimmed 25 W)**. The illuminating power is over 20,000 candle power at the central part of the beam projected on a screen at 10 m from the head lamp for cruising beam, and over 5,000 candle power at the central part for dimmer beam as in the diagram (fig. III-21).

The illuminating angle is adjusted by the Head Lamp Adjusting Screw. screwed in the beam is directed upwards, and when unscrewed, downwards. Adjustment is made

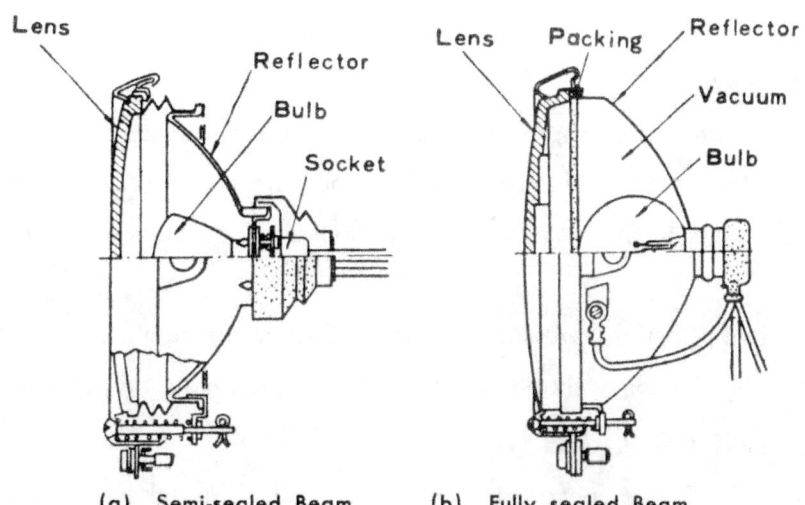

(a) Semi-sealed Beam   (b) Fully sealed Beam
Fig. III-19 Difference between head lights.

when the motorcycle is loaded with a normal adult with the beam projecting to a vertical wall as shown in Fig. III-21.

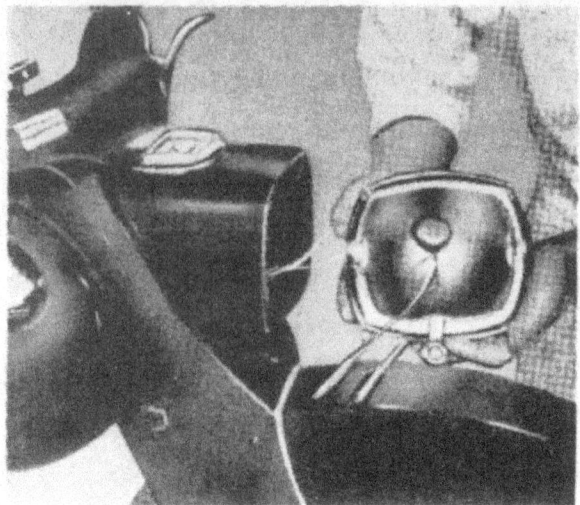

Fig. III-20 Removing head light

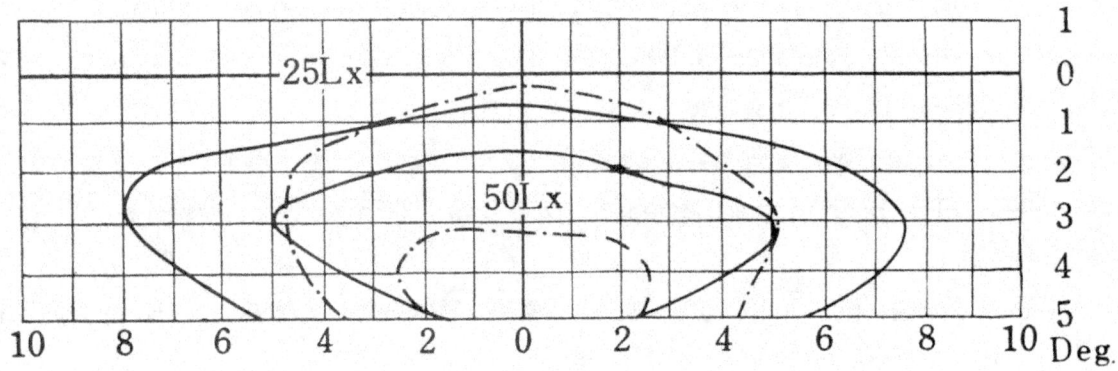

Fig. III-21 Illuminating power projected from 10m a head
———— main beam, ———·——— dimmed beam.

D. WINKER LAMP

Special shaped bulbs (cylinder type) are fitted in the winker lamp bodies fixed at the front and rear, under the amber colored lenses, as shown in Fig. 3-35.

E. TAIL AND STOP LAMP

The Tail and Stop Lamp are respectively covered with a red and a white plastic lens. The light bulb contains double filaments whose outputs are **3 W ((6-8 V) for tail and 6 W (6-8 V) for stop light** When the stop switch is operated the stop lamp will be lit.

To take out the bulb, loosen two screws which fasten the light lens. After the lens is removed, the bulb of same shape as the winker light, may be removed.

F. METER-LAMP & NEUTRAL LAMP

As shown in Fig. III-22, the meter lamp is fixed in the Speedometer and the Neutral lamp inside the head light Case. Both bulbs are of **6-8 V, 3 W.** Either bulb can be taken out from their sockets by turning to the left after the head light is removed. The neutral lamp socket is held by the rubber tube.

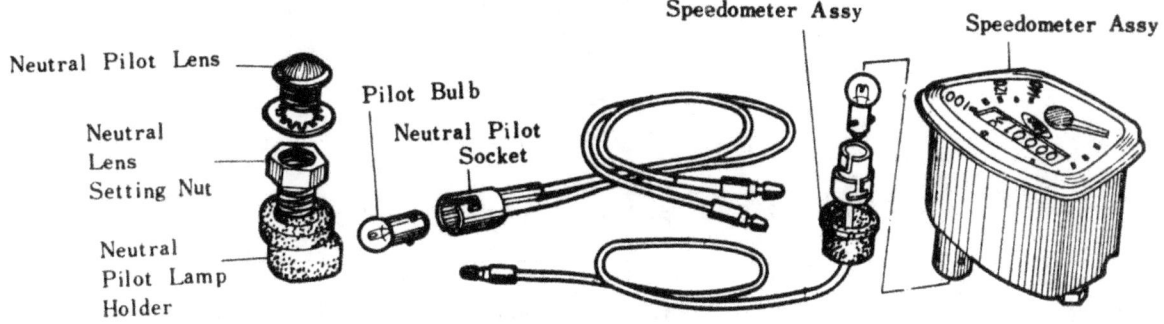

G. WIRE HARNESS

The Wire Harness is a bundle of wires running from the battery to the Head Light case clamped on the left side of the frame, running in the recess of the tank and alongside the frame, entering by the first opening on the side of the frame.

Connectors pertaining to the head light wiring are stored in the head light case and several connectors are bundled together with a cube-shaped polyethylene coupler. Other connectors are bundled together with a cube-shaped polyethylene coupler, covered with a rubber tube and clamped above the peep-hole on the rightside of the frame. The lead wires on the rear side from the battery run through the channel of the reinforcing plate inside the frame to protect them from damages by dirt, moisture, and flying pebbles.

When connecting wires, care must be taken that they are respectively of the same color and pattern, otherwise a fire may be caused. Be sure to refer to the wiring diagram when connecting wires.

III-6 SWITCHES

A. COMBINATION SWITCH

Switches for lights and engine system are combined in one switch case and fixed on the left side of the head light. The switch is in four steps. Three (3) identical keys are supplied with each motorcycle. (If the dealer keeps one, this will be found convenient in case the owner should lose his own keys).

To dismantle, take the head light apart, Unscrew binding nuts on the outside of the switch with a special pin spanner. Then take out the Switch body. When attaching be sure to coincide the slot on the Head Light case and the knotch of the switch. When the switch is operated but any one of the said four steps is not actuated properly, chek the concerned line of wiring. If the wiring is found correct, the failure lies in the switch. Separate conduction tests may be applied for checking. Each conduction test may be carried out by following the wiring diagram.

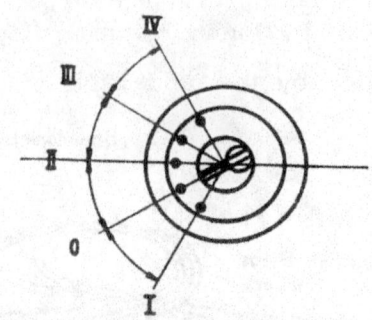

Fig. III-23 Key position of combination switch

SIGNS written on the back of Switch			BAT	ST	IG	HE	TL	SE	DY
COLOR of wire leads			Red	Black & Red	Black	Green	Black & White	Yellow	White
POSITION of KEY Insert	Object for using	Whether the key is pulled out / Circuit leading to	Battery	Starting Switch	Ignition Coil, Neutral Lamp, Horn, Winker, Stop Lamp	Head Lamp, SpeedoMeter Lamp	Tail Lamp	Celenium Rectifier	A.C. Dynamo
0	Daytime Parking	Can							
I	Preparation for starting	No	O—O						
II	Daytime Riding	No	O—O—O						
III	Nighttime Riding	No	O	O	O	O	O	O—O	
IV	Nighttime Parking	Can	O			O			

Note: O—O shows an closed circuit

B. WINKER, HEAD LIGHT CHANGE SWITCH, HORN BUTTON, AND STARTER-MOTOR BUTTON

On the left handle bar are fixed a headlight dimmer switch and horn button, and on the right, winker lamp right-left switch and starter motor Switch button. They are contained in respective switch cases.

In the case of faulty operation of knobs, failure of switch work, defective contact or wrong wiring, repair or replacement is required.

For defective contact, and faulty operation of knob, unscrew two bolts on the handle switch case, break up the parts and correct the defect. If replacement of parts connected with the harness is required, undo the nuts for fixing the handle bar, remove the headlight lens, uncouple the terminal connector in the headlight case, and remove the harness from the handle-bar. At assembling, care must be taken the way the harness passes through the frame.

C. NEUTRAL SWITCH

On the shift drum shaft in the upper crank case under the kick cover, a bakelite rotor contact point is fixed with 6 mm screws. The stator is fixed on the case and it is made so that the lead wire may be inserted.

If the gear position is in neutral, the lamp will light as the key is turned. In the case of failure of this lamp to operate due to defective switch contacts, replace the switch or repair or replace the contact points.   A conduction Test is advised to check in this instance.

Fig III-24. Neutral switch

D. STOP SWITCH

The Stop Switch, fixed in a small case in front of the battery under the left cover

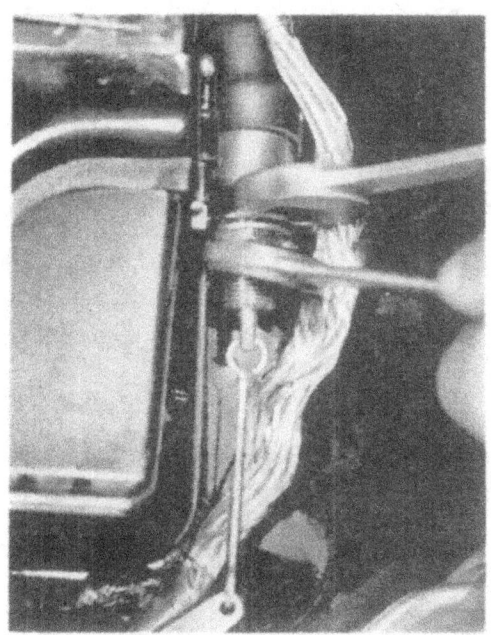

Fig. III-25 Adjusting stop switch

is designed to operate relative to the action of the brake arm.   See the chapter for brake pedal (Fig. III-25) for construction.   It is constructed similar to the ordinary contact switch except that two nuts are provided by which the height of the automatic action is changed so as to adjust the timing of switch actuation against the timing of break actuation, that is the tail-light lighting time is made possible,

Time of lighting is so adjusted that the switch will actuate at about one third of the brake pedal.

III-7 SERVICE TESTER

For the convenience of checking and adjusting the electrical parts and systems, here is is the set of testers provided in one case. Testing capacities are as shown below:

Purposes of Test	Indication	Contents
Current check	Red lamp is lit (when current is available	Check for presence of current
Conduction	Red lamp	Disconnection of the wiring and switches check
Resistance	Meter	Measuring the resistance of secondary coil and celenium rectifier.
Insulation	Meter	Investigation of the insulation of the condenser, and also measurement
Condenser Capacity	Meter	Judging condenser Capacity (0—0.6 or under)
A.C. Voltage	Meter	Battery and load system investigation (0—15V)
A.C. Current	Meter	Load current, charge current investigation (−15—−15 Amp.)
Speed of Rotation	Meter	Speed of revolution at the crank and other rotary parts. (0—6,000 rpm)
Dynamo Output	Meter	Testing the output of Dynamo 1 and 2. (0—15V)
Coil Test	Spark distance measured by Three points Tester	Testing the sparking faculty of the ignition coil
Timing Tests	Indicate by Timing Light (Using 6 V Battery	Spark Timing and advance angle of governor investigation

Detailed directions for the use of respective testers are supplied with the set. Testing is done by simply connecting respective leads to the required part of the electric equipment accorrding to its purpose.

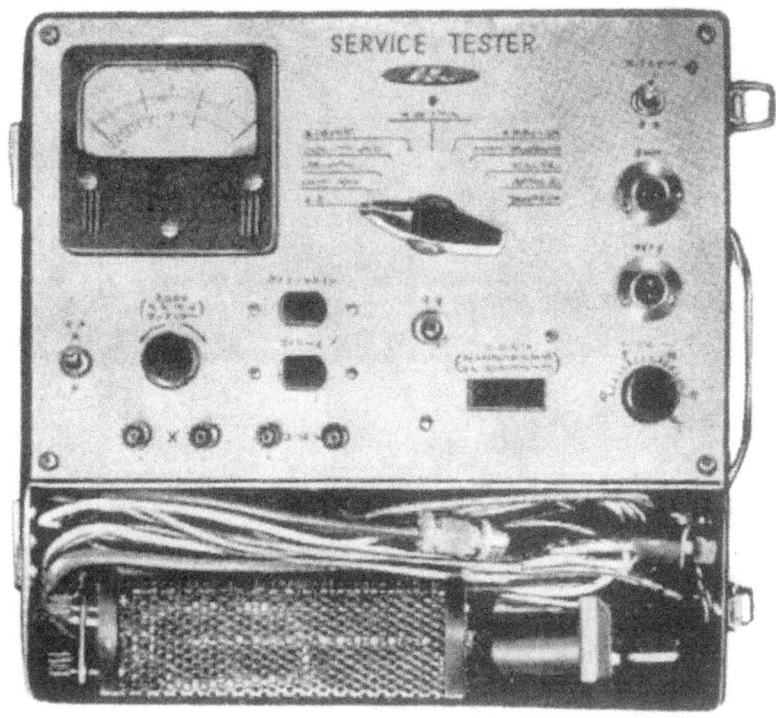

Fig. III-26. Service Tester

MEMO

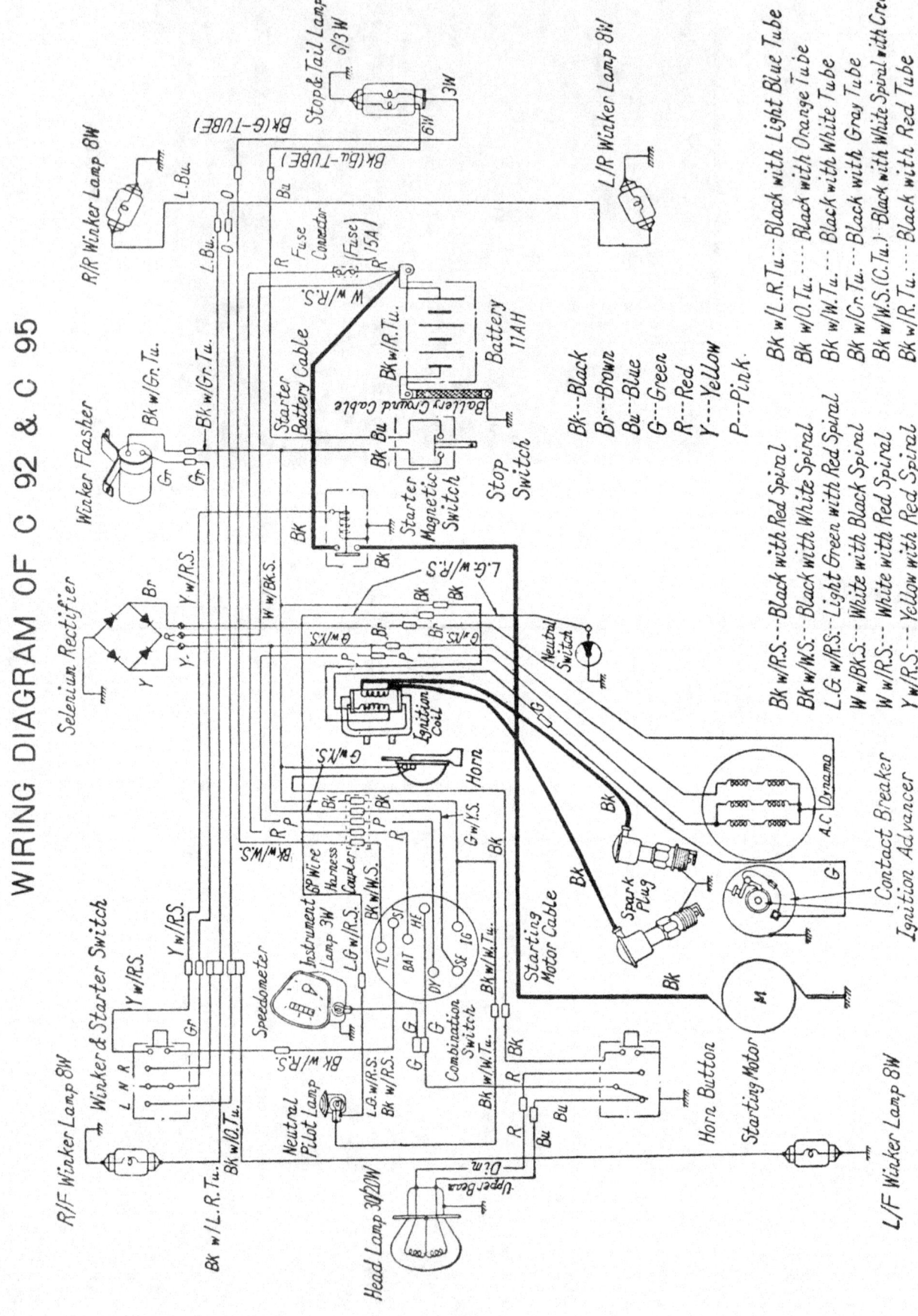

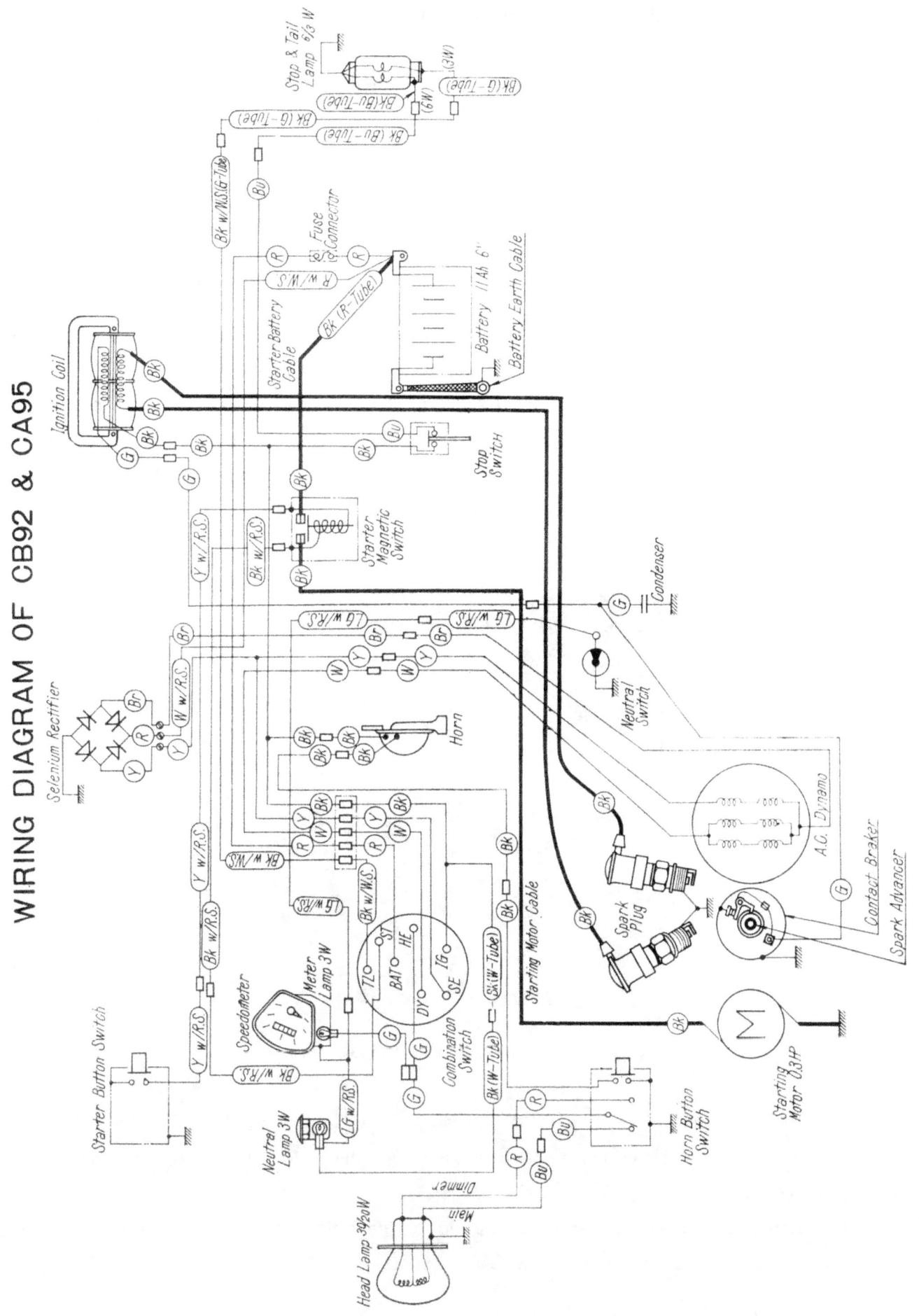

IV. ADJUSTMENT AND SERVICE

IV-1. IGNITION TIMING ADJUSTMENT

Check ignition timing and contact breaker point surfaces for contamination periodically every two or three months. Faulty timing or point surfaces may result in the poor performance and erratic revolution of the engine. The timing at idling speeds of 800–900 RPM is 5 degrees BTDC, at the moment when the mark "F" aligns with the indicator. Start advancing at 1200 RPM. The full advance of 45 degrees BTDC is obtained at 2300 RPM. The procedure of adjusting is as follows:—

(1) Remove the contact breaker cover, rotate the crankshaft until B rests on the peak of the cam C, and adjust the point gap to 0.3–0.4 mm. (0.012~0.016")

(2) To adjust the point gap, first loosen the screw D, and move the screw E to the left or right. The point gap is decreased by turning in and is increased by turning out.

(3) To adjust the ignition timing, rotate the crankshaft until the mark F (red) on the rotor aligns with the mark J on the generator stator.

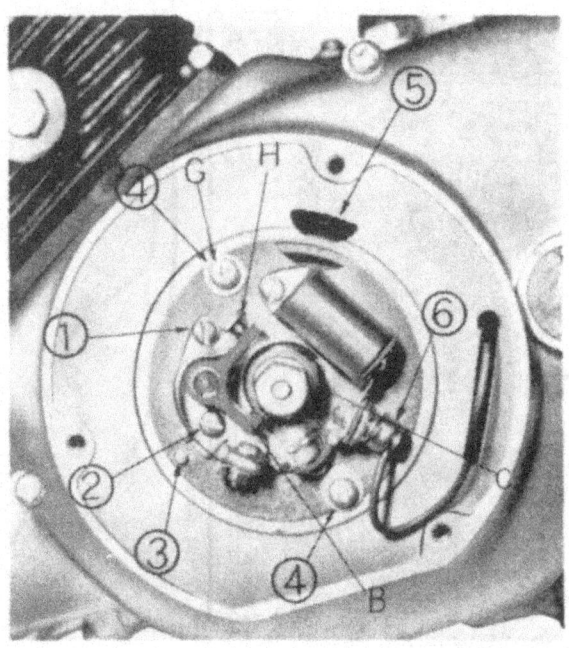

Fig. IV-1 Whole view of contact breaker point

Loosen the 2 screws G (one is at the top of the plate and other is at the bottom), rotate the plate assembly to the position where the points just close, and tighten the screws G.

(4) In order to confirm the instant of closing of the points, a tester or miniature lamp is available to check contact between them. (Fig. IV-2)

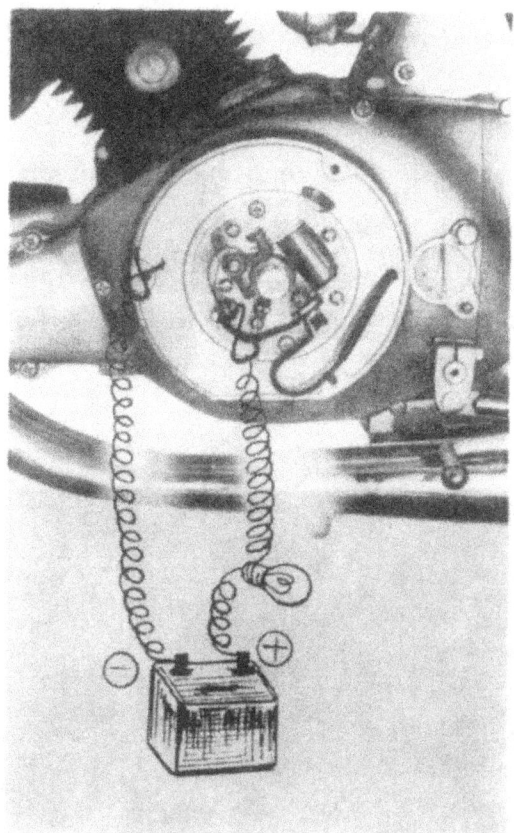

Fig. IV-2 Using miniature lamp 60 V checking timing

(5) For checking the timing dynamically while the engine is revolving the timing light provided in service tester (P. 122) is useful. This light is also effective for checking the state of timing advance relative to RPM. (p. 108)

(6) When adjustment has been made recheck the ignition timing after a few turns of the crankshaft.

(7) The burned or pitted points should be filed with a suitable pointfile, and if it is found that the surfaces are wet with oil, wipe off with dry cloth.

(8) Apply a slight quantity of good grease to the oil-slipper in the regular maintenace service.

(9) In cases only concerning power at higher R. P. M., using diffuser megaphone pipes and special jets of racing kits, on CB92 it is advisable to set the timing at 10 degrees BTDC. To set the timing the same amount, mark a point on the A. C. dynamo rotor at 10 degrees from the mark " T " counter-clockwise or at the same distance from " T " to " F " on the circumference.

IV-2. VALVE TAPPET CLEARANCE ADJUSTMENT

Tappet clearance has a great deal to do with the correct operation of the valves.
It exerts an influence upon the actual valve timing, therefore, in cases where the clearances

are too small, the engine will not run smoothly. On the contrary if they are too large the tappet noise becomes too loud.

Adjustment is done by the following steps:—

(1) Remove the contact breaker cover and align the pointer on the generator with the mark "T" (black) on the rotor. (10)

(2) Remove four caps using axle wrench or open end spanner loosen the lock nuts and turn the adjusting screw with special wrench provided to obtain the specified clearance. (Fig. IV-3)

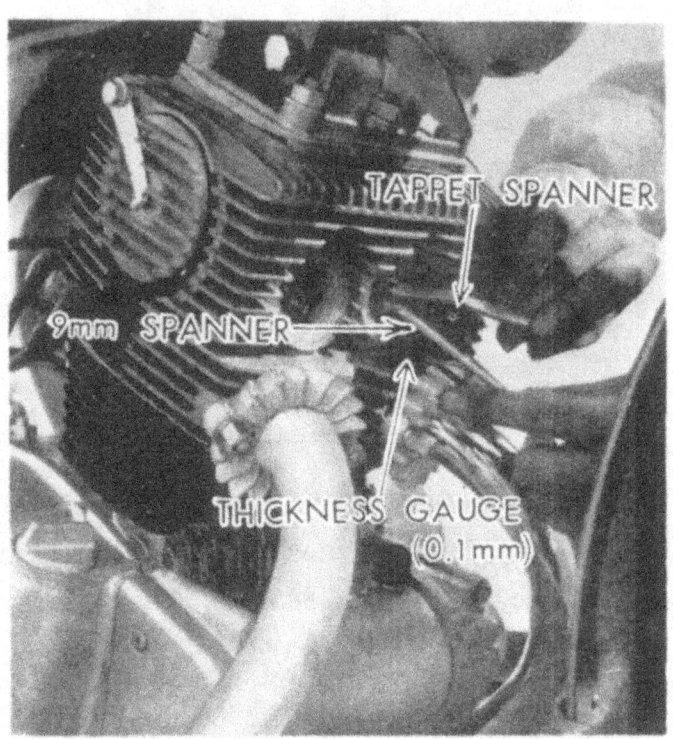

Fig. IV-3 Adjusting tappet clearance

Turn "the adjusting screw" "in" to decrease the clearance and "out" to increase the clearance.

The specified clearance is 0.1 mm for both intake and exhaust valve tappets when the engine is cold. This valve tappet clearance adjustment should be made with the specified thickness gauge. (which is supplied in the accessory tools)

(3) With the adjusting screw held ie the required position, tighten the lock nut Then, rotate the crankshaft one revolution and make the same adjustment on the opposite side.

(4) After the adjustment has been completed, it is necessary to kick the kick starter a few times and recheck the clearance.

IV-3. CARBURETTOR ADJUSTMENT

Adjustment of carburettor is mentioned on p. 67

But the condition of carburettor is apt to change during the use of the engine. Therefore, it requires minor adjustment, especially with respect to the idling condition, and cleaning at regular intervals.

Finally the desired idling speed (about 800-900 rpm) is obtained by adjusting the throttle stop screw B. (Fig. IV-4)

When the adjustment is correct, the engine runs evenly while idling and should neither stall nor stop when the throttle is slowly opened.

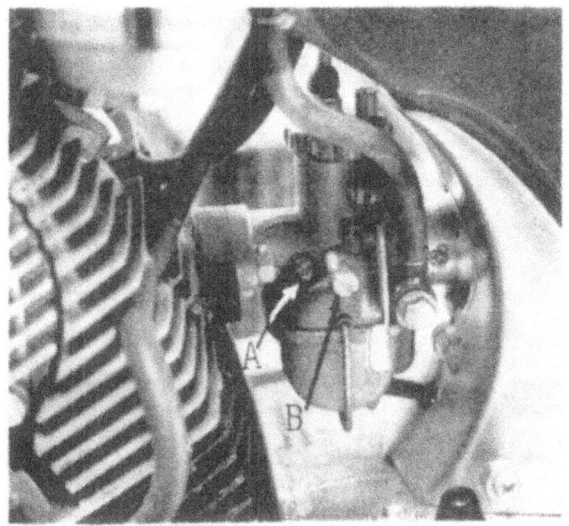

Fig. IV-4 Idling adjusting screws. of carburettor

IV-4. CLUTCH ADJUSTMENT

If the clutch adjustment is insufficient, no matter how excellent the engine performance is, it cannot exert its power fully and the vehicle cannot be driven at the highest efficiency.

In the event where the vehicle jumps or the engine stalls while running, with the gears being shifted from neutral to low position, the clutch will not release satisfactorily.

Otherwise, in the case where the vehicle speed does not agree with the revolution of the engine when accelerating or runing at high RPM, the clutch is slipping.

Adjustment of the clutch is done by the following procedure to give 10-15mm free play in the lever.

(1) Loosen the bolt A and adjust the clutch by turning the clutch adjuster. The clutch may slip when the clutch adjuster B is tightened excessively and the clutch may not disengage easily when the clutch adjuster is loosened excessively. (Fig. IV-5)

(2) While pulling the clutch lever in or out, kick the kick starter down and check the clutch for engagement and slip.

(3) The clutch should have 10-15mm of "play" at the end of the lever.

Fig. IV-5 Adjusting clutch

(4) Main adjustment is completed through items 1 to 3, but in order to facilitate the adjustment of free play, a cable adjuster is especially provided on the clutch cable for CB92. (Fig. IV-6)

Fig. IV-6

IV-5. DRIVE CHAIN ADJUSTMENT

Adjustment of drive chain greatly effects the power output at the rear wheel and also the duarability of the chain.

When the chain tension is too tight, it may result in the excessive resistance for power transmission, and on the contrary, when too loose, it may be a cause of excessive wear.

(1) Remove the rubber cap on the chain case and adjust the drive chain in order that about 10~20mm (0.4~0.8″() of deflection is obtained. (Fig. IV-7)

(2) To adjust the drive chain deflection, loosen the medium size axle nut and large size axle sleeve nut and turn the adjuster nut in thenecessary direction. Turn the nut "in" to tighten the drive chain. Turn the nut "out" to loosen the drive chain. (fig. IV-8)

Fig. IV-7 Max. deflection of drive chain

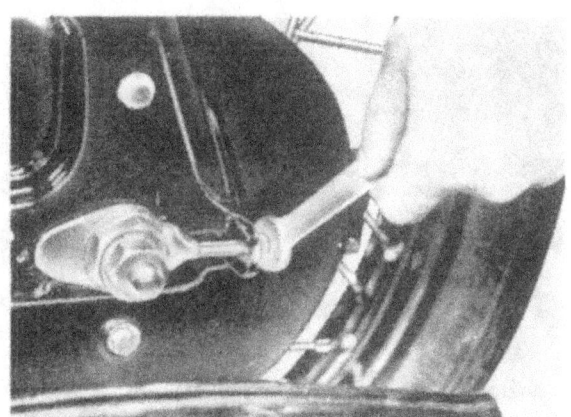

Fig. IV-8 Adjusting drive chain adjuster

(3) Gradually adjust both side adjusters while checking the deflection and note that the notch mark on the adjuster should rest at the same graduation of notches on the rear fork at both left and right hand sides.

Failing to do this results in the rear wheel inclining at an angle, and so produces unstable running.

IV-6. CAM CHAIN ADJUSTMENT

Faulty abjustment of cam chain may cause the occurrence of cam chain noise, and a routine adjustment is advisable.

(1) Loosen the cam chain adjusting lock nut and the cam chain adjusting screw (Rubber cap is installed)

(2) Rotate the crankshaft in the reverse direction, and then rotate it in the regular revolving direction until the rocker arm for the exhaust valve starts to operate. (This is noticed by removing the exhaust side tappet hole cap and observing the movement of the rocker arm)

(3) Turn the loosened cam chain adjusting screw in far enough until the tip of the screw just touches against the cam chain tensioner spring guide. As this is not visible determine it by the tightness of the adjusting screw.

(4) Hold the adjusting screw stationary with the screw driver and tighten the cam chain adjusting lock nut. (fiig. IV-9)

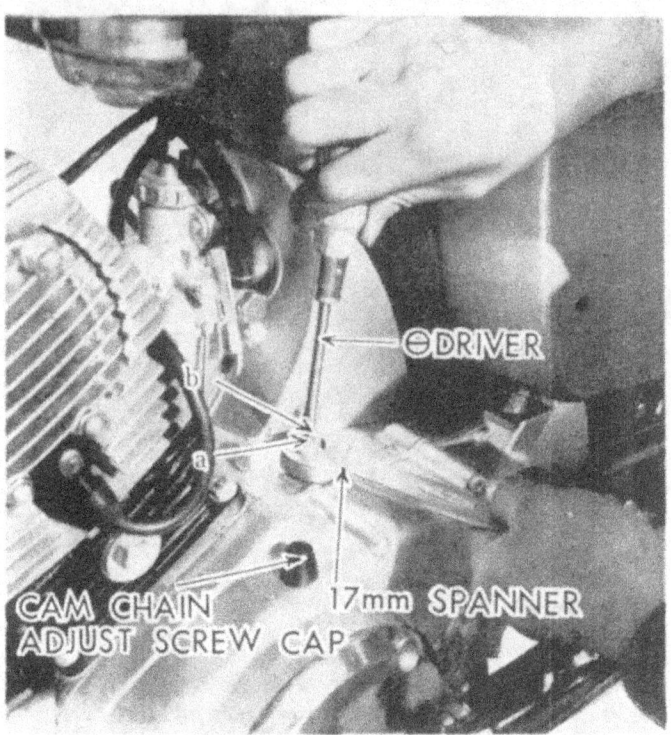

Fig. IV Adjusting cam chain

IV-7. BRAKE ADJUSTMENT

Rear brake pedal adjustment is made by correcting the amount of free play in the brake pedal. Take care that the brake should not drag or be too loose.

A. REAR BRAKE

(1) Adjust the rear brake pedal reserve movement to obtain about 30-40mm (1.2~1.6") of pedal free travel which is the distance between the position where the pedal is depressed and the position where the brake starts to operate. (fig. IV-10)

(2) To adjust, turn the rear brake adjusting nut in the necessary direction. Turn the nut in to reduce the pedal reserve and out to increase the pedal reserve.

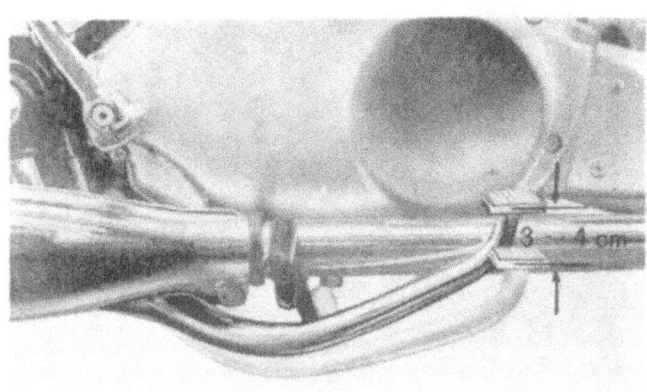

Fig. IV-10 Adjustmont of rear brake

B. FRONT BRAKE

(1) Adjust the handle lever to obtain about 30-40mm (1.2~1.6") of free travel which is the distance between the position where the lever rests and the position where the brake starts to operate measured at the end. (Fig. IV-11)

(2) To adjust turn the front brake adjusting nut in the necessary direction. Turn the nut in to decrease the lever free travel and out to increase the lever free travel. (Fig. IV-11)

(3) For CB92, the adjustment will be performed as follows :-

3-1. To enable the minor adjustment of front brake lever free play, an adjuster is provided on the brake cable.

3-2. When the brake shoes are newly replaced, the brake rod should be connected so that the two cams equally work at the same time.

In this case, adjust the brake rod at the joint to the length required to suit the distance between the upper brake arm and the under brake arm.

After attaching the joint pins and cotter pins, check that the brake rod has side play. If the brake rod is too tight between the arms, adjust the rod to shorten.

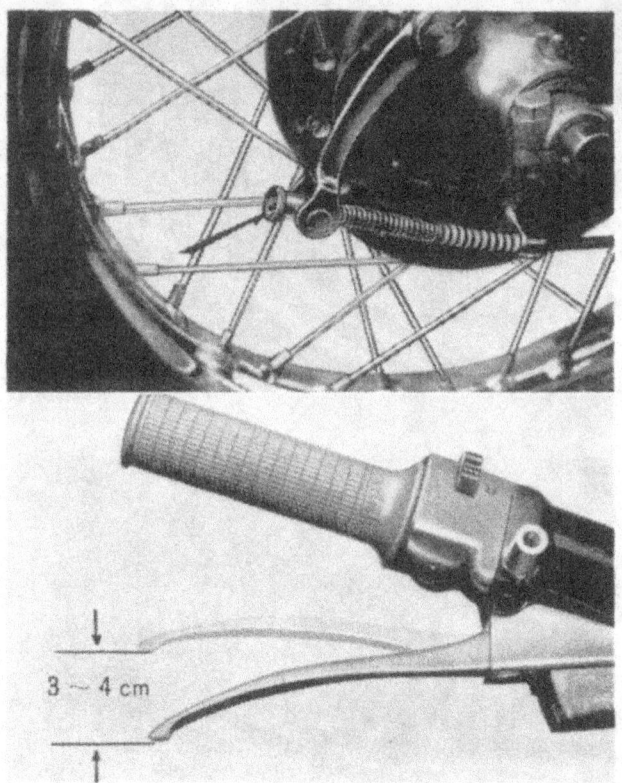

Fig. IV-11 Adjustment of front brake

Fig. IV-12 Front brake (CB 92)

3-3. The major adjustment is done at the cable adjuster at the end of the brake arm, as like as the standard model.

3-4. In instances where the brake is used much more often such as in when partaking in races, the air guide caps (front) and (rear) may be removed for better cooling of the brake drum. For normal use, they should be attached to prevent sand from gaining admittance.

IV-8. CLEANING AIR CLEANER

The air cleaner should kept clean, also avoid damaging or wetting. In case of dust accumulating, air intake meets extreme resistance and this may result in poor efficiency of performance. Also damage may be caused by dust invading the cylinder and increasing wear. Therefore periodical cleaning is advisable.

The procedure is as follows :-

(1) Remove the air cleaner element as refered in P. 92
(2) Clean the dirty element by tapping gently and blowing with compressed air or brushing outside with soft brush.
(3) An element wetted with oil or water cannot filter the incoming air properly. Be careful that the element is not fouled by oil or grease. In the case of such fouling or if broken, replace the element.

IV-9. CLEANING OIL FILTER

Oil filter is cleaned as follows :-

(1) Remove the oil filter cover and pull out the oil cleaner.
(2) Remove the oil filter cap and wash the dirty oil cleaner inside thoroughly with petrol

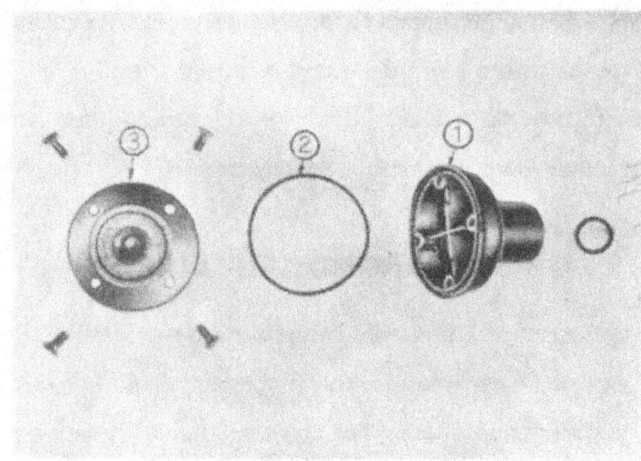

Fig. IV-13 Removal of oil filter

IV-10. CLEANING FUEL STRAINER

Dirt accumulation is observed from outside through the plastic strainer cup.
Remove the strainer cup using a suitable wrench and clean the strainer cup inside and the screen (Fig. IV-14)

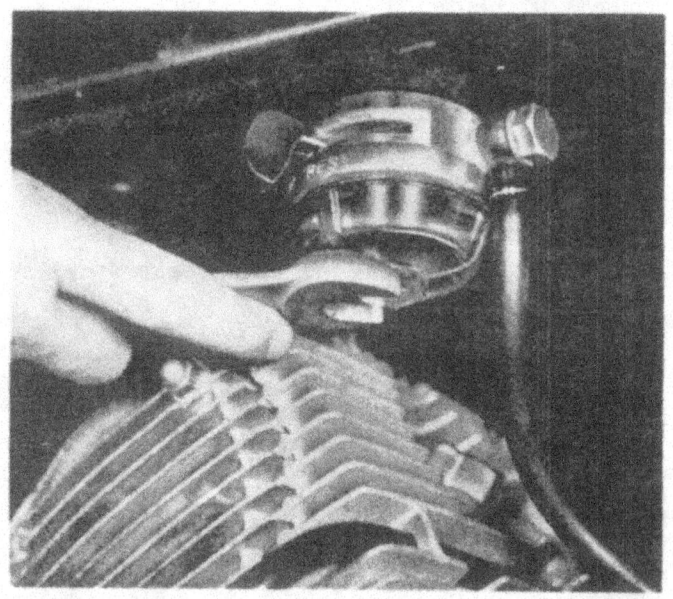

Fig. IV-14 Removing fuel cock strainer

IV-11. THROTTLE CABLE AND GRIP ADJUSTMENT

(1) To adjust the throttle grip free travel, loosen the nut ② and turn the adjuster ③ in the necessary direction. The free play of the throttle grip is preferable for the amount of 5 mm (0.2") on the circumference.

(2) Stiffness of twisting the throttle grip is adjusted by the adjusting screw ① with screw

driver after the nut is loosened. After adjusting secure the nut firmly.
(Fig. IV-15) (Fig. IV-16)

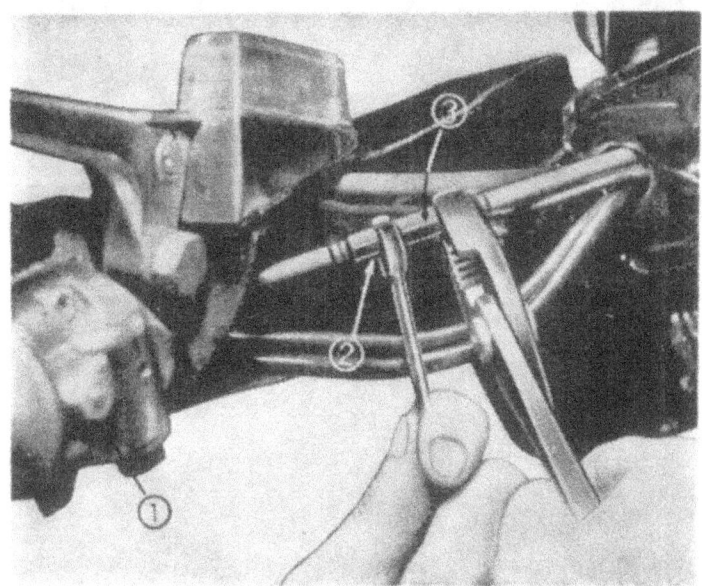

IV-15 Throttle adjustment (C92)

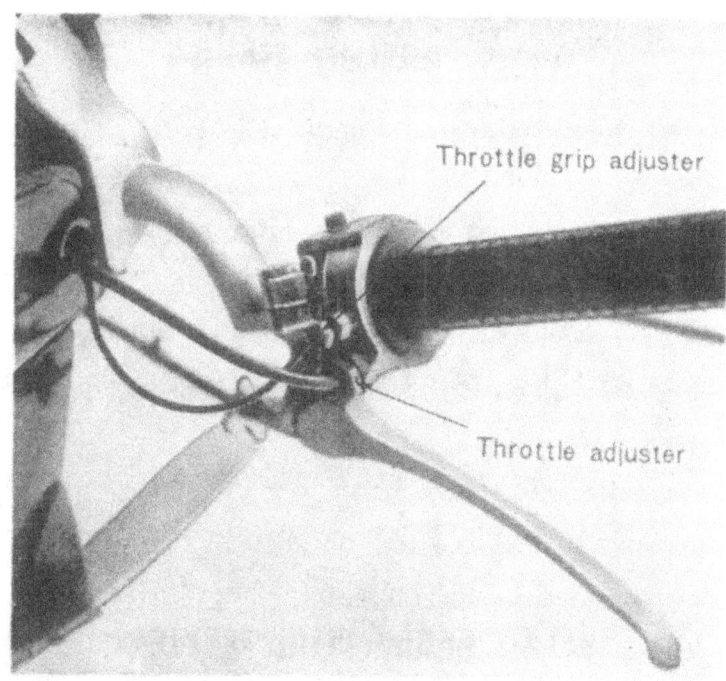

IV-16 Throttle adjustment (CB92)

IV-12. ADJUSTMENT OF CHANGE PEDAL

For the standard model the position of the change pedal is unadjustable, but for the CB92 the angle of the pedal may be adjusted to suit owner's foot.
Unscrew the lock-nut with a 10mm spaner and turn the change rod with a hand or plier. Tighten lock nut after adjustment. (Fig. IV-17)

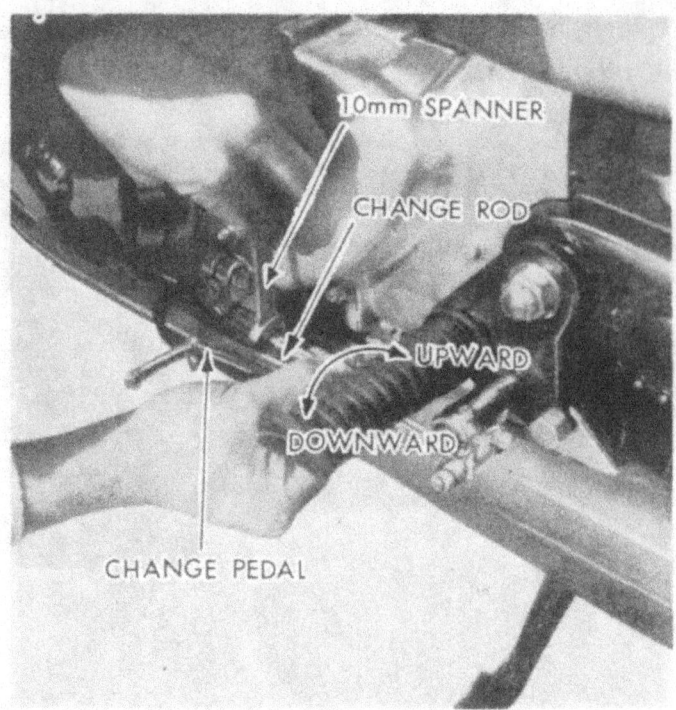

Fig. IV-17 Adjusting change pedal

IV-13. BATTERY SERVICE

As the maintenance of the battery has been mentioned in P. 100 the routine service only is described in this section.

(1) The level of electrolyte should always be above the lower-most level line on the side of battery case.

(2) When the level of electrolyte has lowered, add distilled water or drinking water to the upper-most level Do not attempt to use sulphuric acid for this purpose. (Fig. 32)

(3) Do not over-fill above upper level

(4) Ensure the vent pipe is not obstructed.

IV-14. SPARK PLUG SERVICE

The spark plug condition may greately effect the performance of the engine, therefore it should be checked periodcally.

The process of cleaning the electrodes and adjusting the gap to 0.6-0.7mm (0.24∼0.28″) is recommended. Details are described in p. 110.

IV-15. ADJUSTMENT OF HEAD LAM AND STOP LIGHT TIMING

These items are detailed in their respective paragraph p. 117 and p. 121.

IV-16. LUBRICATION

I. Engine Oil

As the engine oil is absolutely essential to the engine life and its satisfactory operation, extreme caution should be taken tn its checking and changing. More frequent oil changes are recommended under severe service conditions.

(1) Stand the machine on the main stand, remove the threaded plug A from under crank case and drain the oil from the engine throughly.

Performing this operation at the normal operating temperature of engine (oil warm) will aid the complete drainage of the used oil.

Replace plug A after complete drainage.

(2) Remove the cap B and pour new oil into the engine to the level of the mark C on the dip stick (usually it needs about 0.8 liters but when oil is drained throughly from oil passages and the filter, it needs 1.2 liters). When checking the level, do not screw in the oil dip stick, just insert it. (Fig. IV-18)

After the engine has been running, stop and check the level of oil again. (Fig. IV-18)

Fig. IV-18 checking oil level

(3) Oil recommended is always heavy duty oil, and the brands to be recommended are,

SHELL ——————— RETINAX

PENNSYLVANIA ——— PENDRAKE / PENZOIL

CASTROL ──────── MOBIL OIL

and the "HONDA ULTRA OIL" which is specially produced for Honda machines.
(4) The grade which should be used:
        over 15°C (59°F)   #30 SAE
        below 15°C (59°F)   #20W SAE

2. Replenishing of Grease

(1) Grease Nipples

Periodically replenish grease in all the nipples with grease gun referring to the routine maintenance chart. Fiber grease is advisable.

The places where the grease nipples are attached are as follows.

    Front brake arm
    Front brake panel
    Front arm pivot bushing (R. & L)
    Clutch adjuster
    Rear brake arm
    Speedometer gear box
    (Extra portions for CB92)
    Front brake arm (upper)
    Change pedal pivot
    Brake pedal pivot
    Brake and clutch cable

(2) Front and rear axle bearings

Replace grease for front and rear wheel bearings every 5000 miles. Procedure for removal and installation of wheel bearings are mentioned on p. 81

Pack grease between balls and coat some on inside of the wheel hub.

(3) Drive chain

As mentioned on p. 89, the chain should be thoroughly cleaned and let permeate grease into the rollers of chain.

V. PERIODICAL MAINTENANCE

The items which have to be done as routine maintenance are described on the drivers manual. Some of which are under an obligation to be performed by servicing dealers for a year after the motorcycle has been sold to customers.

Items \ Duration	1st time after 200 miles	2nd 2nd month	3rd 5th month	4th 8th month	5th 11th month
Adjust and/or service drive chain	O	O	O	O	O
Check and/or service battery		O	O	O	O
Change oil	O	O	O	O	O
Clean oil cleaner		O	O	O	O
Adjust tappet clearance	O	O	O	O	O
Grease all nipples		O		O	
Check tightening of bolts and spokes		O		O	
Adjust ignition timing	O		O		O
Adjust cam chain		O		O	
Clean carburetter			O		
Clean fuel strainer			O		
Grease wheel bearings			O		

VI. RACING KIT FOR CB92

To comply with the desire for entering races a special racing kit is provided. Using this kit enables an improvement to some extent, to be made in performance, or to provide racing equipment on the motorcycle according to the type of race.

The parts and their use and application are described as follows:

VI-1 RELEVANT PARTS FOR ENGINE

1. Piston and piston ring

    High compression pistons and thin piston rings for raising compression pressure and decreasing friction between the piston rings and the cylinder wall. (Refer to p. 25)

YB 921360	Piston	1 pcs
YB 921361	Piston	1
YB 921364	Piston ring set	2

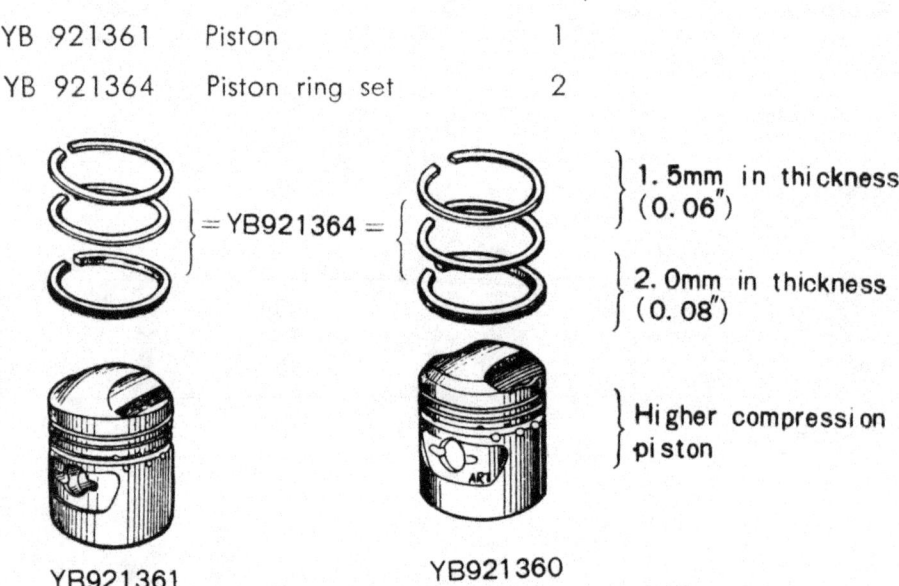

YB921361 (left)   YB921360 (right)

2. Removing starter motor and A.C. dynamo

    For decreasing the weight, the starter motor, A.C. dynamo and rotor are removeable. After removing the A.C. dynamo, ignition coils of higher efficiency should replace the standard coil to keep the battery life long enough to finish the races. In this event, at entry to a race the battery should be replaced with a fully charged one.

YB 921119	Front crank case cover	covering space of starter motor
YB 921163	〃　〃　〃　〃	packing
YB 921807	Governor shaft	Substitution for the rotor to keep the spark advancer in position
YB 921808	Stator base cover	Substitution for A.C. dynamo starter
YB 921806A	Ignition coil	Higher efficiency at high R.P.M.

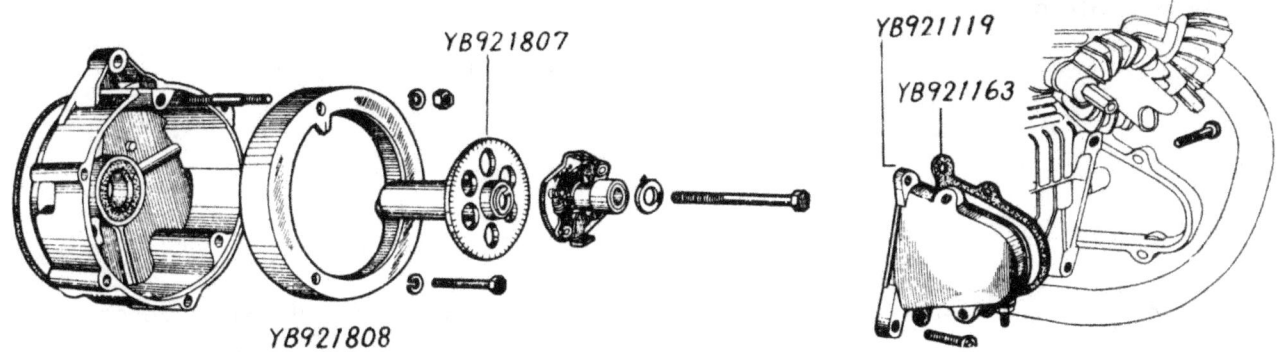

3. Spark plug

Colder type spark plugs are available. On these spark plugs, sparking gap should be set as 0.014–0.016" (0.35–0.40 mm).

    YB 921817A   Spark plug   C10H, C12H   2 pcs

3. Cylinder head gasket

Increasing compression pressure.

    YB 921227   Cylinder head gasket   1 pc

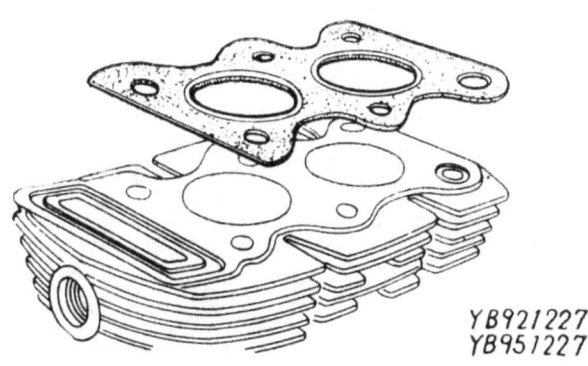

5. Drive sprocket

To be selected gear ratio in accordance with racing condition.

    YB 922317   Drive sprocket :   14 teeth   1 pc

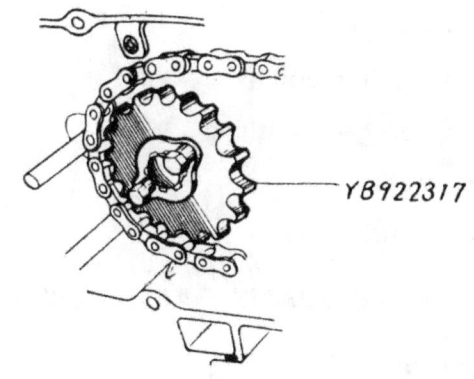

6. Cam shaft and exhaust valve

The exhaust valve is reinforced with stellite welding for the prevention of wear. The cam shaft is for high revolution valve timing.

YB 921416	Cam shaft	1 pcs
YB 921416B		1
YB 921547	Exhaust valve	2

YB 921416 is superseded by YB 921416B which is made integral with tachometer drive worm gear. The later is adopted for complete engines from CB92E-010511 and CA95E-010139

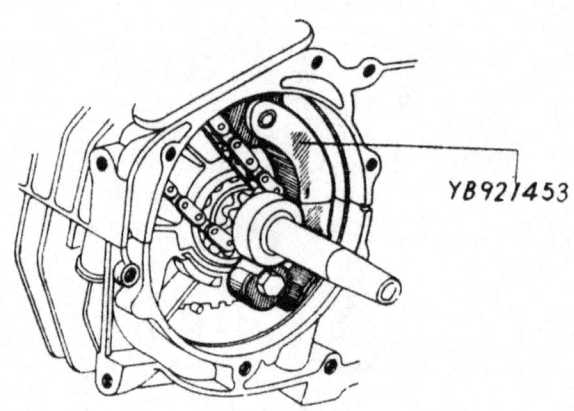

7. Carburettor setting jets

To improve performance use together with the megaphone diffuser pipe.

YCZPW22/15	Main jet	1 pc
YCZPW20A/04	Power jet	1

8. Tachometer gear box

For engines without the tachometer gear box devices, numbered up to CB92E-010510, & CA95E-010138, the following parts are required to attach the tachometer. (Refer to p. 15)

B921206C	Cylinder head complete.	1 pc
B921212B	R cylinder head side cover	1
B921216B	Cam shaft complete	1
B921465	Tachometer gear	1
B921467	12 m/m sealing bolt	1
B921470	Tachometer gear bushing	1
B921472	20 mm sealing nut	1
B922883	12 mm sealing washer	1

VI-2 RELEVANT PARTS FOR FRAME

1. Megaphone type diffuser pipe

Diffuser pipes without the silencers to increase the efficiency.

    YB 923961A   R. Exhaust diffuser   1 pc
    YB 923962A   L.   //   //   1

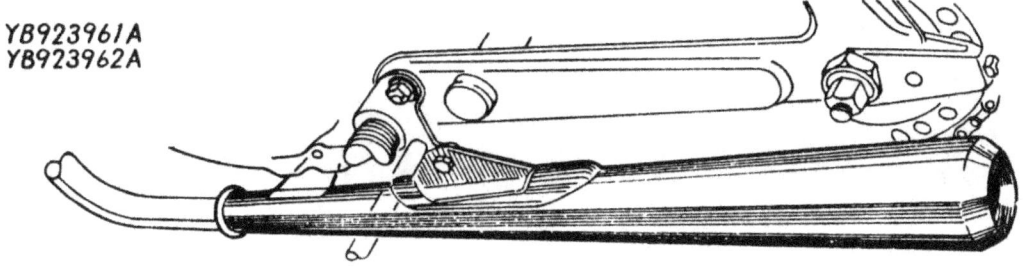

2. Saddle seat

Saddle with a hump at the back end to improve riding position.

    YB 924926   Saddle seat   1 pc

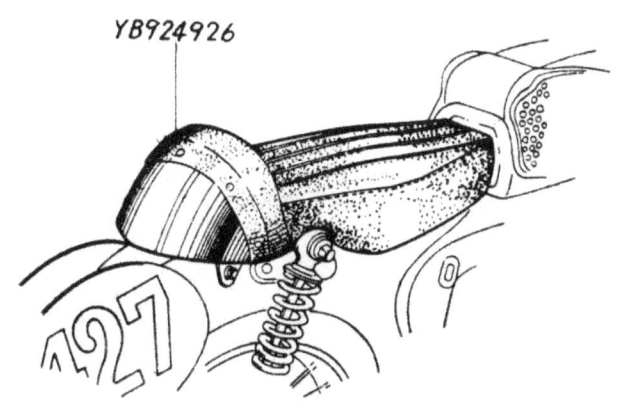

3. Front and rear cushion

Heavy load springs with stiffer dampers to decrease surging of chassis and improve steering ability at high speed.

    YB 925166   Front cushion ass'y.   1 pc
    YB 926116   Rear   //   //   1   Spring tension 177-1kg
                                                                               at displacement of 102.4mm

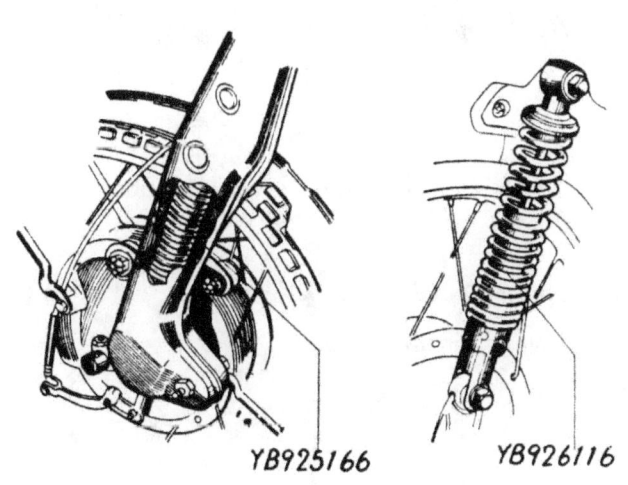

4. Steering handle

Down swept handle bar for road racing.   The round tip handle levers are provided.

YB 925201A	Steering handle pipe	1
YB 925205	R. Steering handle lever	1
YB 925206	L. ″ ″ ″	1
YB 925207	R. Steering handle bracket	1
YB 925208	L. ″ ″ ″	1

5. Tyres

Deep block type for cinder track, scramble and trial race.

YB 925401.6	Front tyre	2.50-18	1 pc
YB 926401.6	Rear ″	2.75-18	1

6. Final drive sprockets

To enable free choice of gear ratio at final driving in accordance with the condition of races.

YB 926226	Drive chain DK428 (120R)	1 pc
YB 926433	Final driven sprocket 38T	1
YB ″ B	″ ″ ″ 42T	1
YB 926433C	″ ″ ″ 48T	1
YB ″ D	″ ″ ″ 43T	1

7. Tachometer

For reading RPM of the engine when running

YB 924828	Tachometer	1
YB 924829	″ cable ass'y.	1

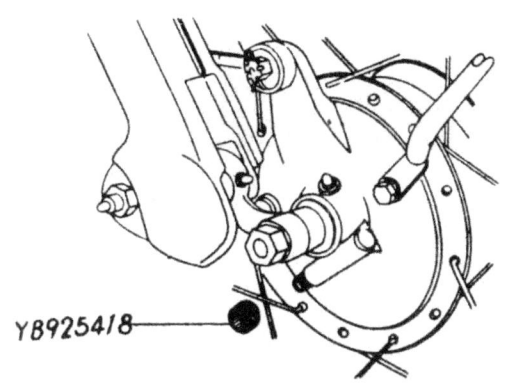

8. Others

For replacement of the cover of the front brake panel ventilator, the grilled guide is provided.

A cap for speedometer gear box unit for protection after removal of the speedometer cable, and side stoppers for both step arms to prevent feet slipping aside, are provided.

YB 925418	Gear box cap	1 pc
YB 924221	R Step arm complete	1
YB 924222	L ″ ″ ″	1
R 714226	Step end piece	2
R 714224	Step rubber	2
BH 645	6×45 bolt	2

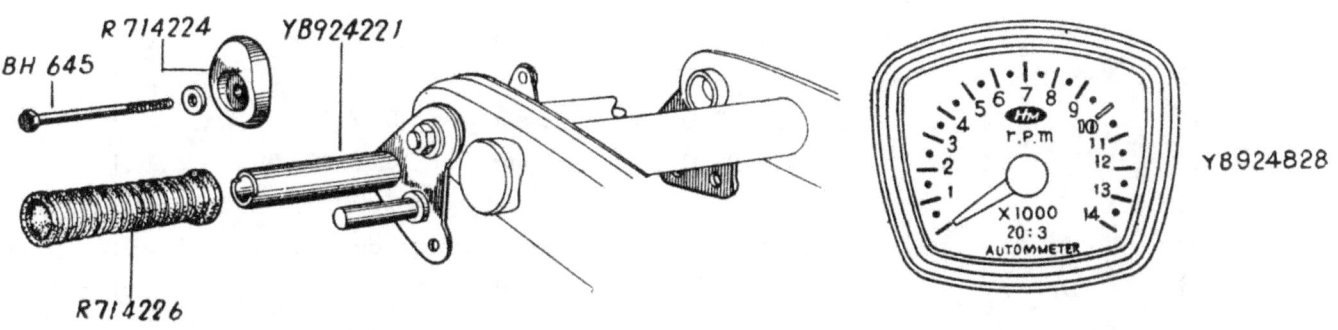

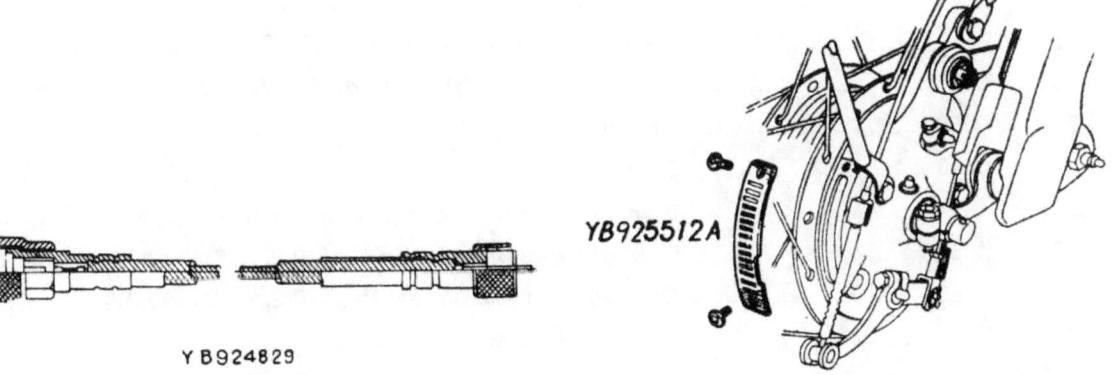

VII SERVICE TOOL

Necessary tools for disassembling, reconditioning and reassembling the Honda 125 and 150 are listed hereunder.

They are containing in two tool sets, one of which is so called common tool that is available to all kinds of motorcycle and the other is the special tool for use of Honda 125 and 150 exclusively.

1. Common tool

(Ref No.)	(Tool No.)	(description)	(qty)
1	K-1	T-Handle fore head driver (#2).	1
2	K-2	T-Handle cross head driver (#2)	1
3	K-3	T-Handle fore head driver (#3)	1
4	K-4	T-Handle cross head driver (#3)	1
5	K-5	T-Handle cross head driver (#4)	1
6	K-6	$8^{m}/_{m}$ T-Handle socket wrench (0.32)	1
7	K-7	$9^{m}/_{m}$ T-Handle socket wrench (0.35)	1
8	K-8	$10^{m}/_{m}$ T-Handle socket wrench (0.39)	1
9	K-11	$14^{m}/_{m}$ T-Handle socket wrench (0.55)	1
10	K-13	$17^{m}/_{m}$ T-Handle socket wrench (0.67)	1
11	K-14	$19^{m}/_{m}$ T-Handle socket wrench (0.75)	1
12	K-15	$21^{m}/_{m}$ T-Handle socket wrench (0.83)	1
13	K-17	$26^{m}/_{m}$ T-Handle socket wrench (1.02)	1
14	K-21	Socket wrench for inserting, $6^{m}/_{m}$ stud bolt (0.24)	1
15	K-22	Socket wrench for inserting, $8^{m}/_{m}$ stud bolt (0.32)	1
16	K-33	8×9 Double head spanner (0.32×0.35)	1
17	K-34	10×14 Double head spanner (0.39×0.55)	1
18	K-35	17×19 Double head spanner (0.67×0.75)	1
19	K-36	21×23 Double head spanner (0.83×0.90)	1
20	K-37	Fore head driver with wooden handle $100^{m}/_{m}$, $150^{m}/_{m}$	1
21	K-38	Fore head driver with wooden handle $100^{m}/_{m}$, $150^{m}/_{m}$	1
22	K-39	Fore head driver with plastic handle	1
23	K-48	Pliers	1
24	K-49	Thin nose pliers	1
25	R-50	Feeler gauge (0.04, 0.06, 0.10, 0.12)	1
26	K-51	Feeler gauge (0.35, 0.4, 0.65, 0.07, 0.75)	1
27	K-52	Rubber hammer	1
28	K-53	Snap ring remover	1
29	K-54	Nipple spanner for tightening spoke	2
30	K-55	Tap with handle, 5·6·8$^{m}/_{m}$ (0.2, 0.24, 0.32)	1 set
31	K-56	Dies with handle, 5·6·8$^{m}/_{m}$ (0.2, 0.24, 0.32)	1 set
32	K-57	Tool box	1

Common Tool

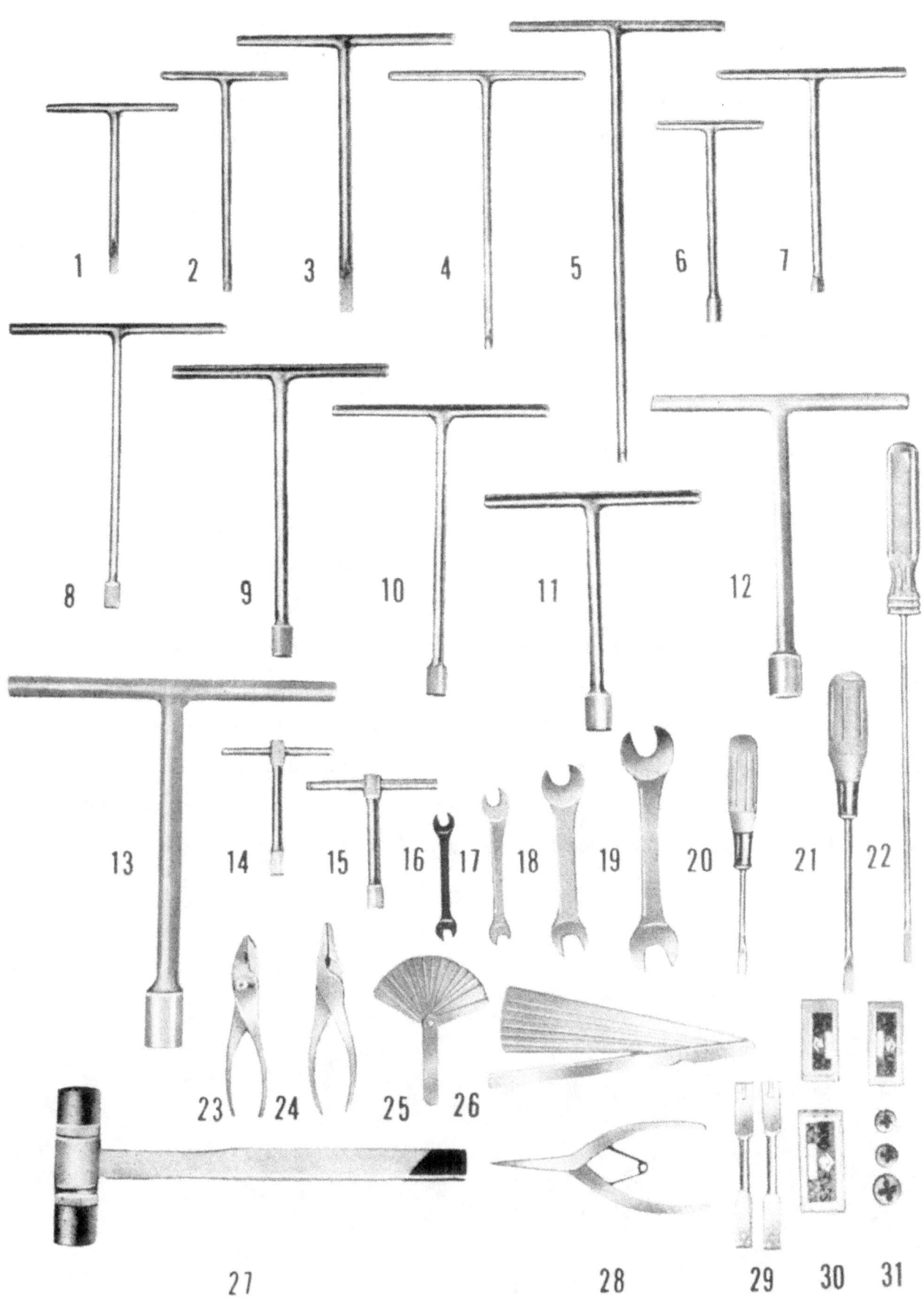

2. Special tool

(Ref. No.)	(Tool No.)	(Description)	(qty)	(Comments)
1	C-903	Piston ring compressor	2	installing cylinder onto piston
2	C-904	Dynamo rotor puller	1	for removing dynamo rotor
3	C-905	Valve lifter	1	for removing value cotters.
4	C-908	Main switch pin spanner	1	for removing main switch
5	C-909	$4^{m}/_{m}$ pin spanner	1	for adjusting steering top ball race.
6	C-910	Timing gear puller	1	for removing timing gear
7	C-911	Valve seat cutter; 120 angle	1	for repairing valve seat (for exhaust valve seat.)
8	C-922	Valve seat cutter; 120 angle	1	for repairing valve seat (for inlet valve seat.)
9	C-912	Valve seat cutter; 90 angle	1	for repairing valve seat
10	C-913	Valve seat cutter; 20 angle	1	″ (for inlet valve seat)
11	C-923	Valve seat cutter; 20 angle	1	for repairing valve seat (for exhaust valve seat.)
12	C-915	Valve guide reamer	1	for reaming valve guide
13	C-914	Valve seat refacer bar	1	available with cutters
14	C-916	Drive sprocket holder	1	for holding drive sprocket
15	C-917	Driver; for timing gear	1	for fitting timing gear
16	C-919	Tappet wrench	1	for adjusting tappets
17	C-921	Crank shaft bearing puller	1	for removing crank shaft main bearing
18	A-7034	Wood block	1	for holding onto piston
19	K-51	Tool box	1	

Special Tool

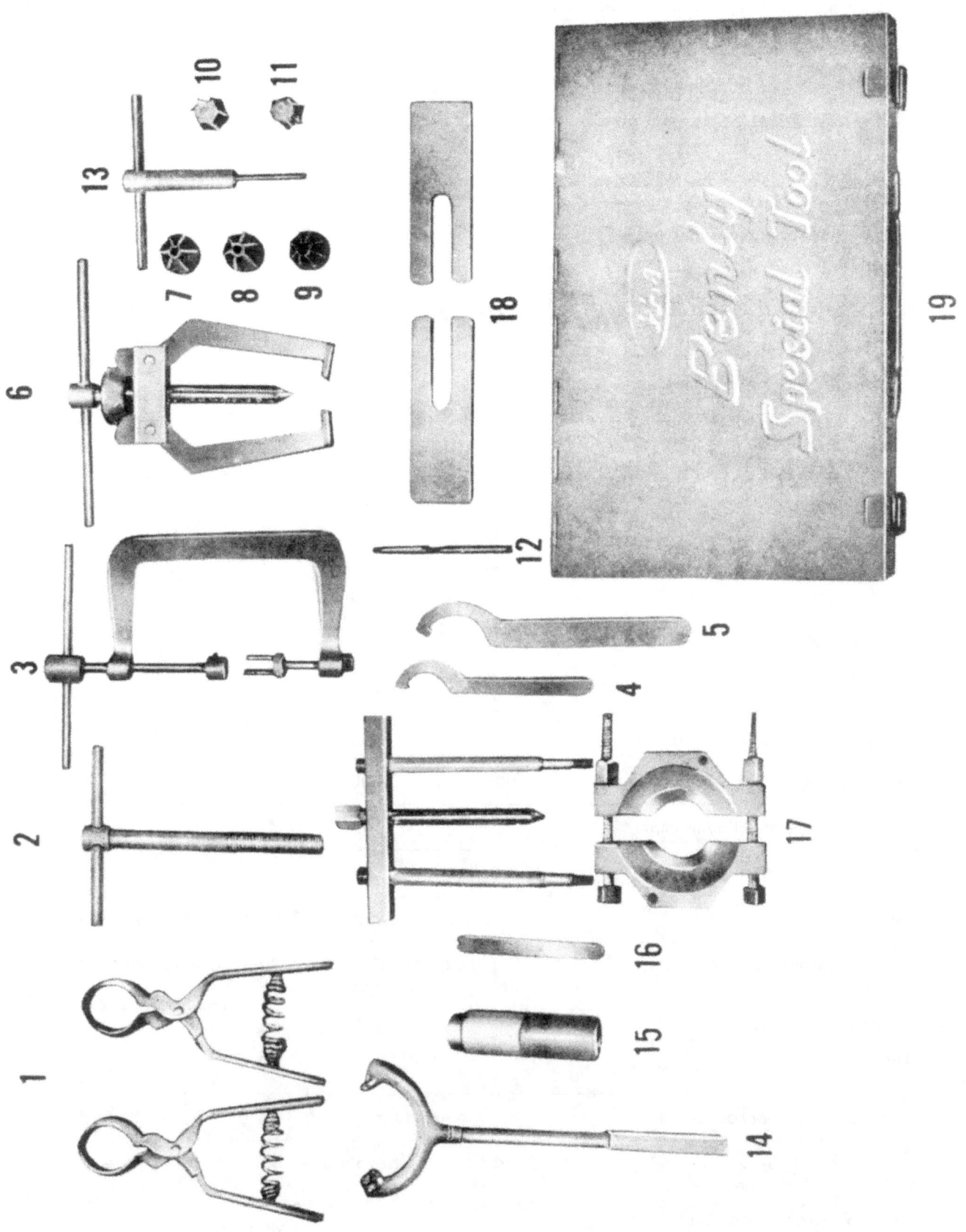

VIII TECHNICAL DATA

Important data for maintenance is listed in this chapter which is divided into three sections. The section of "General data" includes the general features of performance of the complete motor cycle, the "dimensions and limits" section includes dimensions of component parts with tolerances for standard and repairing limits, and the last section is "torque specification" listing the specific torque for tightening bolts and nuts.

Representation of signs is as follows.
　　* for C92, (*) for CB92 and (**) for CA95.
　　The numbers without the above signs are common for all models.

VIII-1. GENERAL DATA

1. **Dimensions and Performance**

Dimension: mm (in)	*	(*)	(**)
Overall length	1,900	1,875	1,900
Overall width	640	595	720
Overall height	955	930	1,007
Wheel base	1,245	1,260	1,250
Min. ground clearance	130	140	135
Weight: Kg (lbs)			
Total dry weight	120	110	124
Weight distribution, front	55	52	58
Weight distribution, rear	65	58	56
Min. turning radius: mm (in)	1,700	2,000	1,700
Max. top speed: Km/hr (mph)	*115	(*) 130	(**) 125
Climbing gradient: degrees	18° 26'		
Stopping distance: m (ft)	8; braking at speed of 35 Km/hr on flat level road.		
Fuel consumption: Km/l (mpg)	*65; (*)60; (**)55; constant cruising speed of 35 Km/h on a flat and paved road.		

2. **Engine**

Stroke & Number of cylinder	4 st. twin cylinder
Location of valve	Overhead cam & valves
Bore x Stroke: mm (in)	* (*) 44×41　　　　(**) 49×41 (1.73×1.62)　　　(1.93×1.62)

2. **Engine** (Cont'd)

Total displacement: cc	*(*) 124; (**) 154
Compression ratio	*8.3 : 1; (*) 10 : 1; (**) 9.7 : 1
Max. output: HP/rpm	*11.5/9,500; (*) 15/10,500; (**) 16.5/10,000
Max. torque: Kg. m/rpm	*0.9/8,200; (*) 1.06/9,000; (**) 1.24/9,000
Engine weight: Kg(lbs)	*36 (79.2); (*) (**) 37 (81.4)
Compression pressure: lb/in^2	*120; (*) (**) 130
Carburettor Bore size	*PW18 HOV18A; (*) (**) PW20HOV20A

Battery
  Type
  Capacity: V, Amp-h
	
	MBK 7-6
	6-12Ah

Spark plug
  Type
  Size: mm
  Spark gap: mm (in)
	
	*C7H; (*) (**) C10H
	10 × 12.7
	0.6-0.7 (0.024-0.028)

Ignition timing
  Initial setting: degrees
  Advance angle: degrees
  Contact point gap: mm (in)
	
	5 BTDC
	40 BTDC
	0.3-0.5 (0.012-0.02)

Timing drive	Cam chain (78 links)
Tappet clearance: mm (in) (in & ex. when cold)	0.1 (0.039)
Lubricant capacity: l. (pt)	1.2 (2.1)
Starting device	Electric starting motor (provided with kick starter)
Type of air cleaner	Filter paper
Lubricating system	Wet sump and plunger pump.
Type of oil filter	Centrifugal oil filter
Type of clutch	Wet and multi-plate
Type of transmission	Constant mesh forward 4 speeds
Type of changing	Foot control

Gear ratio	
Gear ratio of gear box	
First	*2.61; (*) (**) 2.36
Second	1.61; 1.47
Third	1.19; 1.04
Top	0.88; 0.84
Primary transmission	
Type	Gear drive
Gear ratio	*3.88; (*) 3.88; (**) 3.88
Final transmission	
Type	Chain drive
Gear ratio	*2.67; (*) 2.93; (**) 2.40
Total gear ratio	
First	*27.04; (*) 26.83; (**) 21.98
Second	16.68; 15.76; 13.69
Third	12.33; 11.12; 9.68
Top	9.12; 8.98; 7.82

3. Chassis

Max. steering angle	45°
Handle bar size: mm (in)	*640 (25.2); (*) 595.(23.44); (**) 700; (28.00)
Caster: degrees	*61; (*) 60; (**) 61
Trail: mm (in)	*(**) 95 (3.74); (*) 100 (3.94)
Tyire	
Size front	*(**) 3.00-16-4 ply (*) 2.50-18-4 Ply
Rear	*(**) 3.00-16-4 ply (*) 2.75-18-4 Ply
Air pressure	
Front	25 lb/in^2
Rear	30 lb/in^2 (for solo)
"	40 lb/in^2 (for pillion occupied or racing)
Frame	Single unit, made of pressed steel.
Suspension	Pivot link with coil spring and oil damper (front & rear)
Brake	
Type	Internal expanding band brake

3. Chassis (Cont'd)

Brake pedal free play: mm (in)	30–40 (1.2–1.6)
Handle lever free play: mm (in)	30–40 (1.2–1.6)
Fuel tank capacity	*(**) 9.1 (2.4) (*) 10.5 (2.8)

4. Electric Apparatus

Generator type Charging current: Amp	daytime 51.6 night time 51.8 at 3,000 RPM.

Bulb: V-W
  Head lamp
  Tail and stop lamp
	
	6-30/20
	6-3 (tail) ; 6-6 (stop)

Winker lamp: V-W	6-8×4
Meter lamp: V-W	6-2
Neutral lamp: V-W	6-2
Celenium rectifier Output voltage: V	 15

Horn
  Type
  Sound volume: phon
	
	Diaphragm
	100-110

Winker relay blinking frequency: times/min	50-120
Fuse: V-Amp	6-15
Condenser capacity: μF	0.24-0.34

VIII-2. DIMENSION AND LIMITS

Standard value indicates the manufacturers standard size or standard size for reassembling or adjusting.

The repairing limit represents the limit of the part required to be replaced or repaired.

In this list the number without units indicate mm and (in), and others according to the unit indicated.

Item	Standard	Repairing Limit	Remarks

Cylinder
  bore
	*(*) 44.00~44.01
	      (1.7336~1.7339)
	(**) 49.00~49.01
		44.1
		(17.1~1.74)
		49.1	

Wall thickness	4 (0.16)	3 (0.12)	

—155—

Item	Standard	Repairing Limit	Remarks
Out-of-round	0.01 (0.0004)	0.05 (0.002)	
Bore taper	0.01 (0.0004)	0.05 (0.002)	
Oversize available	0.20, 0.50, 0.75		
Height of cylinder barrel	63.55–63.65	63.0	
Cylinder head			
Valve seat angle	45°		
Valve seat width	1.0 (0.04)	2.0 (0.08)	
Tightening tolerance of valve guide	0.07–0.11		shrink fit at temp 250°C
Flatness of gasket surface	max. 0.03	0.05	
Cam shaft bearing			
Inside dia	30.00–30.02 (1.182–1.183)	30.1 (1.186)	
Cylinder gasket thickness	1.1–1.2 (0.043–0.049)		
Valve guide inside dia	5.5–5.51 (0.17–0.2171)	5.45	both in. ex.
Valve guide outside dia	10.04–10.05 (3.956–3.960)		shrink fit at temp 250°C
Piston			
Top land diameter	*(*) 43.75–43.80 (1.72–1.726)		
	(**) 48.70–48.75 (1.919–1.921)		
Skirt max. dia (thrust side)	*(*) 43.98–44.00 (1.733–1.734)	43.9 (1.730)	
	(**) 48.98–49.00 (1.970–1.9306)	48.9 (1.927)	
Oval rate (skirt)	0.11–0.13 (0.0043–0.0051)		
Piston ring groove depth	*(*) 2.10–2.13 (0.0821–0.0839)	2.08 (0.820)	
	(**) 2.35–2.43 (0.0926 0.0957)	2.1 (0.083)	
Compression ring groove width	1.5–1.53 (0.0594–0.0603	01.6 (0.063)	Top & second

Item	Standard	Repairing Limit	Remarks
Oil ring groove width	3.01-3.03 (0.1868-0.1194)	3.1 (0.12)	
Piston min. clearance to cylinder	0.-0.03 (0-0.0012)	0.15 (0.006)	
Piston pin hole dia.	14.0-14.01 (0.551-0.552)	14.03 (0.553)	
Available oversize	0.25, 0.50, 0.75 (0.01, 0.02, 0.03)		
Piston ring			
Compression ring thickness	1.497-1.499 (0.05898-0.0590)	1.43 (0.056)	
Width	* (*) 1.9-2.1 (0.075-0.083)	1.8 (0.07)	
	(**) 2.1-2.3 (0.827-0.906)	2.0 (0.788)	
Tension	* (*) 0.56-0.68	0.4	
	(**) 0.62-0.76	0.5	
End gap in cylinder bore	0.15-0.35 (0.0059-0.014)	0.8 (0.032)	
Clearance to piston ring groove	0.02-0.06 (0.00079-0.00204	0.15 (0.0059)	
Piston ring available oversize	0.25, 0.50, 0.75 (0.01, 0.02, 0.03)		
Piston pin			
Outside dia.	13.99-14.0 (0.551-0.552)	13.98 (0.549)	
Overall length	* (**) 36.0-36.4 (1.42-1.43)		
	(**) 40.8-41.0 (1.608-1.62)		
Clearance to piston pin hole	0~0.012 (0-0.005)	0.05 (0.0019)	
Connecting rod			
Small end dia.	14.02-14.04 (0.552-0.553)	14.07 (0.554)	
Clearance between piston pin	0.016-0.049 (0.0063-0.0193)	0.07 (0.0296)	Push fit

Item	Standard	Repairing Limit	Remarks
Max. tilt at small and		3.0 (0.118)	
Large end dia.	35.055–35.015 (1.8792–1.3796)	35.05 (1.38)	
Bend and twist		0.15 (0.006)	off-set
Crank shaft			
Crank pin dia.	26.006–26.109 (1.0246–1.0287)	25.05 (0.9870	
Tightening tolerance to crank pin weight	0.05–0.07 (0.002–0.0027)		
Journal dia.	19.996–20.005 (0.7878–0.7881)	19.94 (0.7856)	
Ball bearing axial play	0.005 (0.00197)	0.1 (0.0039)	
Ball bearing radial play	0.014–0.016 (0.0055–0.0063)	0.05 (0.0197)	
Max. run out at both end	0.04 (0.0012)	0.3 (0.012)	
Center crank weight	(*) (**) 20.07–20.08 (0.7980–0.7912)		
Center crank shaft radial play	(*) (**) 0.010–0.020 (0.0055–0.0063)	0.05 (0.0197	
Exhaust valve			
Stem dia.	5.47–5.48 (0.2155–0.2159)	5.45 (0.2147)	
Length	57.1–57.3 (2.249–2.257)		
Valve head seat thickness	1.0–1.5 (0.039–0.059)	2.0 (0.0785)	same as inlet valve
Clearance to valve guide	0.02–0.04 (0.0008–0.0016)	0.08 (0.0032)	
Inlet valve			
Stem dia.	5.48–5.49 (0.2159–0.2163)		
Length	58.0–48.2 (2.285–2.293)		

Item	Standard	Repairing Limit	Remarks
Clearance to valve guide	0.01-0.03 (0.00039-0.0012)	0.07 (0.0028)	
Outer valve spring Free height Compression	28.86 (1.137) 14.2-15.8 kg (31.31-35.84 lb)	27.8 (1.09) 13.8 kg (30.43-lb)	at 20 mm (0.79) height
Inner valve spring Free height Compression	30.21 (1.189) 4.7-5.3 kg (10.36-11.69)	 4.0 kg (8.82 lbs)	at 19 mm (0.75) height
Camshaft Journal dia. Journal dia. Cam height Cam base circle	17.95-17.96 (0.706-0.708) 29.93-29.94 (1.179-1.180) 24.0 19.0 ϕ	17.0 (0.67) 29 (1.178) 23.05 18.05	
Oil pump plunger dia.	13.96-14.01	13.90	
Timing sprocket Inside dia. Teeth Valley	18.0-18.01 (0.709-0.7095) 27.56-27.66 (1.086-1.0898)	18.1 (0.718) 27.4 (1.08)	13 teeth
Cam chain total length	598.6-599.6	593.0	77 links
Rocker arm Inside diameter Clearance to clamp pin	10.0-10.015 (0.394-0.395) 0.013-0.043 (0.0051-0.017)	10.08 (0.387) 0.15 (0.006)	
Cam chain tensioner spring Compression	4.75-5.75 kg (10.48-12.68 lb)	4.0 (8.82 lb)	at length of 70 mm
Clutch outer Inside dia.	19.99-20.01 (0.7876-0.788)	20.1 (0.792)	

Item	Standard	Repairing Limit	Remarks
Friction disc thickness	3.5 (0.138)	3.0 (0.12)	
Warpage	0.2 (0.08)		
Clutch plate A thickness	1.6 (0.068)	1.4 (0.055)	
Clutch plate B thickness	3.0 (0.12)	2.7 (0.106)	
Clutch spring Free height	28.2 (1.111)		
Compression	8.0–12.0 (kg) (17.64–26.5 lb)		at length of 21 mm (0.827)
Transmission			
Main shaft dia	19.97–19.98 (0.786–0.787)	19.9 (0.784)	
	14.97–14.98 (0.589–0.590)	14.79 (0.587)	
Main shaft axial play	0.1–0.75 (0.0039–0.029)		
Rotary play between spline shaft and gear	0.032–0.096 (0.0013–0.0038)	0.2 (0.008)	
Counter shaft dia	19.97–19.98 (0.787–0.7872)	19.9 (0.784)	
	14.97–14.98 (0.5898–0.5902)	14.9 (0.587)	
Ball bearing (6204H) radial play	0.014–0.016 (0.0006–0.00063)	0.05 (0.0019)	
Counter shaft clearance to its bushing	0.016–0.045 (0.00063–0.0018)	0.1 (0.0039)	
Kick starter spindle clearance to its bushing	0.016–0.058 (0.0006–0.0020)	0.1 (0.0039)	
Contact breaker arm spring tension	500–650 gr (1.403–1.433 lbs)	400 gr (0.88 lb)	
Clearance betwn. A.C. dynamo rotor and stator	0.4 (0.016)		in radium
Change shift drum diameter big end	33.95–33.98 (0.338–1.339)	33.9 (13.36)	
small end	11.97–11.98 (0.4616–0.4720)	11.9 (0.468)	

Item	Standard	Repairing Limit	Remarks
Change shift groove width	7.1-7.2 (0.279-0.284)	7.4 (0.292)	
Shift fork inside dia.	34.00-34.03 (1.34-1.341)	34.07 (1.342)	
Clearnce between shift fork and shift drum	0.025-0075 (0.00098-0.00295)	0.15 (0.0057)	
Cushion Sring free height			
Front	262.5 kg	260	
Rear	222.1-222.3 kg (*) 199-201 kg	220 (*) 197	
Tension of spring			
Front	102 kg	90	at 146.5kmm hight
Fear	159 kg (*) 165 kg	145 (*) 150	at 75 mm displacement at 95 mm displacement
Brake drum diameter	151.8-152.2 (*) 200-200.15	149 (*) 198	
Run-out of wheel rim	2 (0.08)	3 (0.12)	

III-3. TORQUE SPECIFICATION

I. ENGINE

Part Name	Part No.	Quantity used	Torque Tightening
Clutch spring retaining plate, bolts	BH 620	4	4-5 ft-1b
Left crank case cover, cross screw	JP 660 & 640	3	3-4
Drive chain cover A, cross screw	JP 620, 630 & 650	5	3-4
Under crank case, steel nuts	NH 6	1	10-15
A. C. Dynamo stator, attaching bolts	BH 630	3	5-6
Dynamo stator base, attaching cross screw	JP 630		3-4
Ignition coil, attaching cross screw	JP 535	2	2-4
Right crank case cover, cross screw	Jp	10	3-4
Oil pump attaching stud nuts	NH 6	3	6-7
Carburettor, mounting stud nuts	NH 6	2	3-4
Left cylinder head side cover, stud nuts	NBC 6	4	5-6
Cam chain tensioner pivot	901457	1	10-13
Cam chain guide roller pin	901449	1	10-13
Cam sprocket, attaching bolts	BH 614	3	6-7
Right cylinder head side cover, cross screw	JP 617	4	4-4

Part Name	Part No.	Quantity used	Tightening Torque (Required)
Oil pump body, attaching stud nuts	NH 6	3	6-7 ft-lb
Carburetor, mounting stud nuts	NH 6	2	3-4
Left cylinder head side cover, stud nuts	NBC 6	4	5-6
Cam chain tensioner pivot	901457	1	10-13
Cam chain guide roller pin	901449	1	10-13
Cam sprocket, attaching bolts	BH 614	3	6-7
Right cylinder head side cover, cross screw	JP 617	4	3-4
Tappet adjusting hole cap	901214	4	5-7
Drain bolt	902713	1	10-13
Drive sprocket, attaching bolts	BH 610	3	6-7
Cylinder stud bolt, nuts	902756 902757	6	14-18
Spark plugs	1001818	2	3-5

2. **FRAME**

Part Name	Part No.	Quantity used	Tightening Torque (Required)
Front & rear wheel spoke, nipples	905401	36	2-3 ft-lb
Steering handle lock attaching cross screw	JO 510	2	2-3
Horn button & winker switch under case, cross screw	JP 518	4	2-3
Front & rear brake arm, bolts	BH 620	2	5-6
R. L. Luggage carrier support metal, attaching cross screw	JO 620 cr.	6	5-6
Luggage carrier support bolts	BH 817 & 828	4	12-16
Steering handle mounting steel nuts	NH 8	2	12-16
Front cushion upper bolts	907743	2	22-26
Front cushion under bolt nuts	907745	2	22-26
Front arm pivot bolt	907723	2	25-30
Fuel tank fixing bolt	707709	4	6-7
Engine hanger bolt	907705	1	25-30
Engine support bolts	BH 1040	4	25-30
Saddle cushion attaching bolts	BH 620	2	5-6
Step bar, attaching stud nuts	NC 6	4	10-13
Main stand anchor bolt, nuts	NC 10	2	12-16
Side stand pivot screw, nut	NC 10	1	22-26
Muffler mounting bolts	BH 856	2	15-20
Muffler mounting nuts	BH 10	2	25-30
Exhaust pipe joint, nuts	NC 6	4	5-6
Tool tray board, attaching bolts	BH 612	2	5-6

Part Name	Part No.	Quantity used	Tightening Torque (Required)
Rear fork pivot bolt, nuts	707770	2	32-37 ft-lb
Drive chain case, attaching bolts	BH 618 cr.	5	5-6
Rear Cushion suspension bar, nuts	NC 10 cr.	2	22-26
Rear Cushion under bolt	907707	2	22-26
Front brake drum cover, stopper bolt	907704	1	25-30
Front brake torque bolt	907724	1	24-23
Front axle nut	907767	1	35-40
Rear axle nut	907767	1	35-40
Rear axle sleeve nut	907769	1	45-50
Final driven sprocket bolt, nuts	BH 832	4	12-17
Horn Assembly mounting bolts	BS 620	2	6-7

TROUBLE SHOOTING

Procedures of diagnosis for finding out causes of trouble and their probable causes are described as follows.

1. **Engine does not start or hard to start**

    (1) Remove the carbrettor float chamber and check for fuel flow, if fuel is not supplied enough ;

    1-1.   Clogged fuel line

    1-2.   Clogged fuel tank cap vent hole

    1-3.   Clogged fuel cock

    1-4.   Clogged carburetter line or stuck needle valve

    (2) Remove the spark plugs, attach them to the spark plug caps, turn on the ignition switch and rotate the crank shaft with starter motor while the (—) electrodes are grounded. If the spark plugs do not spark well or nil ;

    2-1.   Faulty spark plug, (to make sure, check the spark plug with spark plug tester.)

    2-2.   Sooty or wet spark plug

    2-3.   Contact breaker point

    2-4.   Faulty condenser

    2-5.   Incorrect adjustment of contact breaker point

    2-6.   Short circuit or breakage in ignition coil or wiring

    2-7.   Damaged combination switch

    (3) Check compression pressure at the cylinder with a compression gauge and if lack or nil of compression is indicated in either cylinder ;

    3-1.   Incorrect tappet clearance

    3-2.   Incorrect seating of valves in valve seats

    3-3.   Excessive wear in valve

    3-4.   Excessive wear in piston ring, piston cylinder

    3-5.   Blown out cylinder head gasket

    3-6.   Seized valve in valve guide

    3-7.   Faulty valve timing

    (4) Start engine following the procedure of starting but engine seems to start but won't continue running ;

    4-1.   Too wide opened choke shutter in cold weather

    4-2.   Wide opened air screw of carburettor adjusting air-screw

    4-3.   Damaged carburettor insulator or gasket

2. Engine does not develop full power

(1) Stand the vehicle on the main stand and rotate the rear wheel by hand when the changing gear is set in neutral, if wheel does not turn easily;

   1-1. Dragging rear brake-incorrect adjustment
   1-2. Damaged wheel bearing
   1-3. Too tight drive chain tension, incorrect adjustment

(2) Check the tyre air pressure and inflate to the specified amount.

(3) Check the clutch for slip and if it is found slipping;

   3-1. Improper adjustment of clutch
   3-2. Worn clutch facing
   3-3. Weakened clutch springs

(4) Measure the highest revolutions of crankshaft with a revolution counter and if the engine does not develop full revolution;

   4-1. Clogged carburettor
   4-2. Clogged air cleaner
   4-3. Insufficient supply of fuel to the intake
   4-4. Clogged muffler
   4-5. Faulty ignition coil or contact breaker points
   4-6. Faulty seating of valve
   4-7. Incorrect ignition timing
   4-8. Weakened valve springs
   4-9. Faulty spark plug; test the spark plug with spark plug tester

(5) Check oil level in the crankcase and adjust the level to the specification, or excess amount of oil will result in trouble.

(6) Inspect for excess heating of engine and if found;

   6-1. Excess carbon deposit in combustion chamber
   6-2. Inferior grade of fuel is used
   6-3. Slippery clutch
   6-4. Lean air-fuel mixture; improper size of main jet in carburetter
   6-5. Dirty cylinder and cylinder head

(7) Check for the engine developing ping or knocking when it submit to quick acceleration or successive running at high speed and if it is so; The probable causes are same as No. (6).

3. **Engine runs erratic and/or with miss-firing.**
   (1) Adjust air screw of carburettor properly and still runs under same circumstances.
      1-1. Faulty ignition timing
      1-2. Damaged carburettor insulator or packing
      1-3. Faulty spark plug
      1-4. Faulty condenser
      1-5. Faulty ignition coil
      1-6. Faulty contact breaker point
      1-7. Incorrect tappet clearance
   (2) Check for missing at high speed
      2-1. Insufficient supply of fuel
      2-2. Incorrect valve timing
      2-3. Damaged or weak valve springs
      2-4. Other causes mentioned in No. (1)

4. **Excessive oil consumption or exhaust blue or black smoke.**
   (1) If the engine exhausts smoke while continuous running at high or low RPM.
      1-1. Worn cylinder or piston rings
      1-2. Reversely assembled rings in piston
      1-3. Excess clearance between exhaust valve and guide
   (2) If the engine exhausts smoke just after when closing throttle valve suddenly from certain opening;
      2-1. Excess clearance between inlet valve and guide
      2-2. Clogged air vent hole or plastic tube

5. **Clutch jerks or engages unsmoothly**
   (1) If the machine moves off with jerking or the engine stops at the moment when the clutch engaged.
      1-1. Uneven tensions of clutch springs
      1-2. Distorted clutch plates or facings
      1-3. Sticky movement of clutch plate in the clutch outer

6. **Gear shifting does not operate correctly.**
   (1) When the changing gear does not engage
      1-1. Worn notch on the shift drum
      1-2. Stuck shift fork to the shift drum
      1-3. Worn shift fork

(2) If the gear jumps out while running;
    2-1. Worn dogs on the gear shifter
    2-2. Worn or distorted shift fork
    2-3. Weakened shift drum stopper spring

7. **Engine runs with unusual noise when the tappet clearances assumed correctly:**

(1) If knocking noise is heard from cylinder when accererating engine.
    1-1. Excess clearance between cylinder and piston

(2) If chattering noise is heard even if the cam chain has been adjusted;
    2-1. Excess worn cam chain
    2-2. Excess worn cam chain tensioner spring or roller

(3) When knocking noise is heard from crank case
    3-1. Worn crank shaft big end
    3-2. Worn crank shaft bearing

(4) If the clutch incurs noise when operating clutch lever.
    4-1. Excess clearance between the clutch plate and clutch outer
    4-2. Excess clearance between the clutch center and clutch plate

8. **Troubles in steering**

(1) If it is felt that the steering is hard when taking a turn.
    1-1. Over-tight steering ball races
    1-2. Damaged steering
    1-3. Bent steering stem

(2) Steering wanders or pull to one side while running.
    2-1. Worn front and/or rear wheel bearing
    2-2. Distorted front and/or rear wheel rim
    2-3. Loose spokes
    2-4. Worn rear fork pivot bushing or front arm pivot bushing
    2-5. Bent front fork or frame or rear fork
    3-6. Incorrect rear wheel alignment
    2-7. Uneven strength of cushion springs on both side

9. **Troubles of brakes**

(1) The brake does not actuate properly even after the free play is adjusted correctly.
    1-1. Worn brake shoes

- 1-2. Worn brake cam
- 1-3. Worn brake pedal shaft
- 1-4. Brake shoe contaminated with oil or water
- 1-5. Stuck brake cable or rear brake link
- 1-6. Lack of grease in brake cam

(2) Brake squeaks when applied.
- 2-1. Excess worn brake shoe
- 2-2. Contaminated surface of brake shoe
- 2-3. Warped or pitted wall of brake drum
- 2-4. Excess wear of brake panel spacer

MEMO

A SAMPLE LIST OF OTHER BOOKS AVAILABLE FROM

www.VelocePress.com

PLEASE CHECK OUR WEBSITE FOR THE MOST UP-TO-DATE INFORMATION

MOTORCYCLE WORKSHOP MANUALS, MAINTENANCE & TECHNICAL TITLES

ARIEL WORKSHOP MANUAL 1933-1951
BMW FACTORY WORKSHOP MANUAL R26 R27 (1956-1967)
BMW FACTORY WSM R50 R50S R60 R69S R50US R60US R69US (1955-1969)
BSA SERVICE & REPAIR ALL PRE-WAR MODELS TO 1939, SV & OHV 150cc TO 1,000cc
DUCATI FACTORY WORKSHOP MANUAL SINGLE CYLINDER NARROW CASE OHC ENGINES 160cc, 250cc, 350cc - MONZA JUNIOR, MONZA, 250GT, MARK 3, MACH 1, MOTOCROSS & SEBRING
HONDA FACTORY WORKSHOP MANUAL 250cc TO 305cc C/CS/CB 72 & 77 SERIES 1960-1969
HONDA FACTORY WORKSHOP MANUAL 125cc TO 150cc C/CS/CB/CA 92 & 95 SERIES 1959-1966
HONDA SERVICE & REPAIR 50cc TO 305cc C100, C102, MONKEY BIKE, CE 105H TRIALS BIKE, C110, C114, C92, CB92, BENLEY, C72, CB72, C77 & CB77
NORTON FACTORY WORKSHOP MANUAL 1957-1970
NORTON WORKSHOP MANUAL 1932-1939
ROYAL ENFIELD 736cc INTERCEPTOR & ENFIELD INDIAN CHIEF
SUZUKI T10 FACTORY WORKSHOP MANUAL 250cc 1963-1967
SUZUKI T20 & T200 FACTORY WORKSHOP MANUAL 200cc X-5 INVADER & STING RAY SCRAMBLER, 250cc X-6 HUSTLER 1965-1969
TRIUMPH FACTORY WORKSHOP MANUAL NO. 11 (1945-1955)
TRIUMPH WORKSHOP MANUAL 1935-1939
TRIUMPH WORKSHOP MANUAL 1937-1951
VESPA SERVICE & REPAIR ALL MODELS 125cc & 150cc 1951-1961
VINCENT SERVICE & REPAIR 1935-1955

CLASSIC AUTO TITLES & REFERENCE BOOKS

ABARTH BUYERS GUIDE
CARRERA PANAMERICANA 1950 ~ THE STORY OF THE 1950 MEXICAN ROAD RACE
DIALED IN ~ THE JAN OPPERMAN STORY
FERRARI 308 SERIES BUYER'S AND OWNER'S GUIDE
FERRARI BERLINETTA LUSSO
FERRARI BROCHURES & SALES LITERATURE 1946-1967
FERRARI SERIAL NUMBERS PART I ~ STREET CARS TO SERIAL # 21399 (1948-1977)
FERRARI SERIAL NUMBERS PART II ~ RACE CARS TO SERIAL # 1050 (1948-1973)
FERRARI SPYDER CALIFORNIA
IF HEMINGWAY HAD WRITTEN A RACING NOVEL ~ THE BEST OF MOTOR RACING FICTION 1950-2000
LE MANS 24 ~ WHAT THE MOVIE COULD HAVE BEEN
MASERATI BROCHURES AND SALES LITERATURE ~ POSTWAR THROUGH INLINE 6 CYLINDER CARS

All VelocePress titles are available through your local independent bookseller, Amazon.com, or they may be purchased directly through our website at www.VelocePress.com. Wholesale customers may also purchase directly from us or from the Ingram Book Group.

AUTOBOOKS SERIES OF WORKSHOP MANUALS

ALFA ROMEO GIULIA 1750, 2000 1962-1978 WORKSHOP MANUAL
AUSTIN HEALEY SPRITE, MG MIDGET 1958-1980 WORKSHOP MANUAL
BMW 1600 1966-1973 WORKSHOP MANUAL
FIAT 1100, 1100D, 1100R & 1200 1957-1969 WORKSHOP MANUAL
FIAT 124 1966-1974 WORKSHOP MANUAL
FIAT 124 SPORT 1966-1975 WORKSHOP MANUAL
FIAT 125 & 125 SPECIAL 1967-1973 WORKSHOP MANUAL
FIAT 126, 126L, 126DV, 126/650 & 126/650DV 1972-1982 WORKSHOP MANUAL
FIAT 127 SALOON, SPECIAL & SPORT, 900, 1050 1971-1981 WORKSHOP MANUAL
FIAT 128 1969-1982 WORKSHOP MANUAL
FIAT 1300, 1500 1961-1967 WORKSHOP MANUAL
FIAT 131 MIRAFIORI 1975-1982 WORKSHOP MANUAL
FIAT 132 1972-1982 WORKSHOP MANUAL
FIAT 500 1957-1973 WORKSHOP MANUAL
FIAT 600, 600D & MULTIPLA 1955-1969 WORKSHOP MANUAL
FIAT 850 1964-1972 WORKSHOP MANUAL
JAGUAR E-TYPE 1961-1972 WORKSHOP MANUAL
JAGUAR MK 1, 2 1955-1969 WORKSHOP MANUAL
JAGUAR S TYPE, 420 1963-1968 WORKSHOP MANUAL
JAGUAR XK 120, 140, 150 MK 7, 8, 9 1948-1961 WORKSHOP MANUAL
LAND ROVER 1, 2 1948-1961 WORKSHOP MANUAL
MERCEDES-BENZ 190 1959-1968 WORKSHOP MANUAL
MERCDEDS-BENZ 220/8 1968-1972 WORKSHOP MANUAL
MERCEDES-BENZ 230 1963-1968 WORKSHOP MANUAL
MERCEDES-BENZ 250 1968-1972 WORKSHOP MANUAL
MG MIDGET TA-TF 1936-1955 WORKSHOP MANUAL
MINI 1959-1980 WORKSHOP MANUAL
MORRIS MINOR 1952-1971 WORKSHOP MANUAL
PEUGEOT 404 1960-1975 WORKSHOP MANUAL
PORSCHE 911 1964-1969 WORKSHOP MANUAL
PORSCHE 911 1970-1977 WORKSHOP MANUAL
RENAULT 8, 10, 1100 1962-1971 WORKSHOP MANUAL
RENAULT 16 1965-1979 WORKSHOP MANUAL
ROVER 3500, 3500S 1968-1976 WORKSHOP MANUAL
SUNBEAM RAPIER, ALPINE 1955-1965 WORKSHOP MANUAL
TRIUMPH SPITFIRE, GT6, VITESSE 1962-1968 WORKSHOP MANUAL
TRIUMPH TR2, TR3, TR3A 1952-1962 WORKSHOP MANUAL
TRIUMPH TR4, TR4A 1961-1967 WORKSHOP MANUAL
VOLKSWAGEN BEETLE 1968-1977 WORKSHOP MANUAL

All VelocePress titles are available through your local independent bookseller, Amazon.com, or they may be purchased directly through our website at www.VelocePress.com. Wholesale customers may also purchase directly from us or from the Ingram Book Group.

OTHER WORKSHOP MANUALS, MAINTENANCE & TECHNICAL TITLES

AUSTIN HEALEY SIX CYLINDER CARS 1956-1968
BMW ISETTA FACTORY REPAIR MANUAL
FERRARI 250/GT SERVICE AND MAINTENANCE
FERRARI GUIDE TO PERFORMANCE
FERRARI OPERATING, MAINTENANCE & SERVICE HANDBOOKS 1948-1963
FERRARI OWNER'S HANDBOOK
FERRARI TUNING TIPS & MAINTENANCE TECHNIQUES
MASERATI OWNER'S HANDBOOK
OBERT'S FIAT GUIDE
PERFORMANCE TUNING THE SUNBEAM TIGER
PORSCHE 356 SERVICE AND MAINTENANCE MANUAL 1948-1965
PORSCHE 912 WORKSHOP MANUAL
SOUPING THE VOLKSWAGEN IMPROVING THE PERFORMANCE OF YOUR VW
TRIUMPH TR2, TR3 & TR4 WORKSHOP MANUAL
VOLVO ALL MODELS 1944-1968 WORKSHOP MANUAL

BROOKLANDS ROAD TEST PORTFOLIOS

FIAT DINO 1968-1973
MV AGUSTA F4 750 & 1000 1997-2007
JAGUAR MK1 & MK2 1955-1969
LOTUS CORTINA 1963-1970
FIAT 500 1936-1972

All VelocePress titles are available through your local independent bookseller, Amazon.com, or they may be purchased directly through our website at www.VelocePress.com. Wholesale customers may also purchase directly from us or from the Ingram Book Group.